Arabs Without God

Brian Whitaker

Copyright © 2014 Brian Whitaker

All rights reserved.

ISBN-10: 1501064835
ISBN-13: 978-1501064838

Cover image from "Rays of the Sun" by WxMom, used under Creative Commons licence

CONTENTS

Introduction 5

PART ONE: Roads to disbelief

1: Denying God, subverting society 9
2: Atheism in Arab history 34
3: God's own book 57
4: Losing their religion 77
5: Atheism, gender and sexuality 97

PART TWO: Protecting the faith

6: The privileges of religion 121
7: Once a Muslim, always a Muslim 139
8: The right to offend, shock and disturb 155
9: A taste of freedom? 169
10: Politics of disbelief 193

Introduction

ARABS, in popular imagination, are assumed to be Muslims and potential religious fanatics. The reality is a lot more complex. Islam is far from monolithic and has many strands: Sunni, Shia, Salafi, Wahhabi, Zaidi, Sufi, Alawi, Ibadi, Isma'ili and others. Nor are Arabs necessarily Muslims. There are millions of Arab Christians, plus smaller numbers who are Druze or Jewish.

Added to this mix is a growing number of Arabs – mainly young – who openly declare themselves to be atheists, agnostics or sceptics. Non-believers have probably always existed in the Middle East, mostly out of sight, but now they have begun to find a voice. Social media have provided them with the tools to express themselves and the uprisings that toppled Arab dictators have emboldened them to speak out.

In countries where religion permeates most aspects of daily life, publicly challenging belief shocks families, society and governments. Many have been imprisoned merely for expressing their thoughts, others have been forced into exile and some threatened with execution. Many more keep their thoughts to themselves, for fear of the reaction from family, friends and employers.

For an established order that favours orthodoxy and conformity and is unaccustomed to questioning, these dissenting voices are a problem – especially for autocratic governments that base their claims to legitimacy on religious credentials. Regardless of efforts to suppress it, though, the problem (as they see it) of disbelief is unlikely to go away; more likely, it will grow.

Thanks to the internet, along with satellite television and foreign travel, young Arabs today are far more aware of the outside world than previous generations and, when they hold up their own countries to the mirror, many dislike what they see. Rejecting religion is one response to that but it is also part of broader demands for political and social change. The inclusion of religion in this wave of disaffection was almost inevitable, since religion in the Arab countries – far from being a personal, private matter – has become heavily politicised and is responsible for many of the social restrictions that cause so much frustration, especially among the youth.

It is not the purpose of this book to make a case for atheism or to single out Islam among religions for particular criticism, though Islam happens to be the dominant faith in the region. Rather, the purpose is to look at non-belief as a social phenomenon – its causes and its consequences – and to argue for the right of non-believers to be treated as normal human beings.

Public discourse in the Arab countries has opened up considerably during the last few years. Many of the old taboos have been broken and things can be said in public now that would have been unimaginable only a decade ago. Despite that, religion is still generally treated as sacrosanct: challenging it is the biggest and most untouchable of the remaining taboos.

This, in turn, raises important questions about how best to press for change. Some of the non-believers interviewed for this book could be described as activists who openly question and confront religion in all its forms (as is their right). Others simply want a quiet life; they see no need to advertise their disbelief but resent being forced to comply with rules imposed by believers. Both of these approaches are fraught with difficulties, however, and may also bring their adherents into conflict with the law.

The result is that Arab non-believers face two separate but related struggles. One is their dispute with religion itself; the other is with societies and governments that refuse to accept their disbelief. This broader struggle for personal rights – freedom of thought, freedom of expression, freedom of conscience, and so on – is one that they share with millions of religious Arabs too, especially religious minorities. Anyone who does not conform to whatever happens to be the local religious orthodoxy is liable to fall victim to blasphemy and apostasy laws or sectarian prejudices.

The irony of this is that while believers and non-believers are on opposite sides where religious ideas are concerned they may also find themselves on the same side in the struggle for freedom of belief. A substantial part of the discussion in this book is therefore concerned with broader questions of religious liberty which affect believers and non-believers alike.

Nevertheless, minority religious beliefs tend to be more accepted than atheism. There is some recognition of religious diversity, at least among the monotheistic faiths, even if prejudice and discrimination persist. Outright disbelief in God, on the other hand, tends to be greeted with general abhorrence. In lands where religion holds sway, the treatment of non-believers thus becomes the ultimate test: when an atheist can be accepted and respected as a normal human being, liberty will truly have arrived.

PART ONE:
ROADS TO DISBELIEF

1: Denying God, subverting society

IN THE PALESTINIAN town of Qalqilya, 25-year-old Waleed al-Husseini hit on an amusing if irreverent idea. He decided it was time for God to have a Facebook page – and set about creating one. He called it *Ana Allah* ("I am God") and announced jokingly that in future God would be communicating directly with people via Facebook since despite having sent prophets centuries ago His message had still not got through.

The imaginary instructions from God posted by Husseini included one written in the style of Qur'anic verses forbidding people from drinking whisky mixed with Pepsi; "God" ordered them to mix it with water instead. In another post on the divine Facebook page, "God" recommended smoking hashish.

The Palestinian authorities were far from amused, however, and few days later Husseini – an IT graduate who had been unable to find a proper job since leaving university – was sitting in a cafe playing cards when two members of the secret police came in and arrested him. He spent the next ten months in jail, some of the time in solitary confinement, and today lives in exile in France, separated from his family and friends.

Others have suffered a similar fate for their anti-religious posting on the internet. Alber Saber, an Egyptian who had abandoned Coptic Christianity in favour of atheism fled to Switzerland after being imprisoned for "defamation of Islam and Christianity, insulting the divine and satirising religious rituals and sanctities and the prophets". Kacem El Ghazzali was a Moroccan high school student who blogged anonymously about secularism. When his identity was exposed, a teacher accused him of "shaking the faith", fellow students threw stones at him and the imam in his village denounced him from the pulpit. He went into hiding and eventually, like Saber, found refuge in Switzerland.

The story of Husseini's conversion to atheism is in many ways typical. He grew up in Palestine in what he describes as a normal Muslim family but in secondary school he started asking questions – "questions like whether we are free to choose or not". Without realising it at the time, he had stumbled into a debate about free will and predestination (*al-qada' wal-qadr* in Arabic) which has exercised the minds of theologians for centuries. If God is all-knowing, He can surely foresee evil deeds; if He is all-powerful He must be capable of preventing them; if He is good, why does He allow evil deeds and then punish people for them? A verse in the Qur'an says: "Ye shall not will, except as Allah wills."[1]

Husseini put his questions to a teacher at school. "The teacher said it's *haram* [forbidden] to ask about that," he recalls. "I didn't have an answer so I went to an imam in Qalqilya and I got the same reply." This kind of response – that such questions should not be asked – is a familiar one in authoritarian societies and it is a response described by many other Arabs who have since abandoned religion. By prompting them to look further afield for answers, it has probably done more than anything else to set young Muslims on the road to disbelief.

With his curiosity aroused, Husseini embarked on his own research. "I went to the library in my school and the public library in my city. You can find many things there about religion but not about criticisms of religion," he said. "I spent around four years searching because when I started with this issue I discovered more and more. Step by step I moved away from religion until I left Islam in my first year at university."[2]

Naively, perhaps, Husseini saw nothing particularly abnormal about his decision. He knew that plenty of famous Palestinian writers had also questioned religion in the past – among them Edward Said who was an openly-declared agnostic, plus the poet Mahmoud Darwish and the novelist Ghassan Kanafani who had also been a prominent member of the Popular Front for the Liberation of Palestine. But when Husseini started telling his university friends that he was no longer a Muslim, he was taken aback by their reaction. "They said 'Oh no! It's *haram*!' They said: 'You can do anything, but don't leave Islam'." Looking for reassurance, he even approached some who claimed to be

Communists but their reaction was the same: "No," they told him, "We only take from the Communists their way of fighting."

Undeterred by that, he had started a couple of blogs – one in Arabic called *Nour al-Aql* ("The Light of Reason") and another in English called *Proud Atheist*. "I started discussions. I was just looking for the truth," he said. "It wasn't much, and in the beginning nobody was following me." In a blog post at the end of August in 2010 – two months before his arrest – Husseini wrote:

> Muslims often ask me why I left Islam. What strikes me is that Muslims can't seem to understand that renouncing Islam is a choice offered to everyone and that anyone has the right to do so. They believe anyone who leaves Islam is an agent or a spy for a western state, namely the Jewish state, and that they get paid bundles of money by the governments of these countries and their secret services. They actually don't get that people are free to think and believe in whatever suits them ...
>
> I would like to emphasise that by writing this article I did not mean to imply that Christianity or Judaism were better than Islam, and the reader should not fool himself into thinking that I only reject Islam among religions, all of which are to me a bunch of mind-blowing legends and a pile of nonsense that compete with each other in terms of stupidity.[3]

Husseini was eventually charged with insulting Muslims, defaming religions and inciting religious strife but it was four months before he appeared in court. In all, he says, he made more than ten court appearances and each time the case was adjourned without a full trial. He suspects his arrest was more connected with politics than religion itself – rivalries between the Palestinian Authority (PA) in the West Bank and the Islamist Hamas movement in Gaza. Hamas was accusing the PA of not being religious enough, and the PA wanted to display some religious credentials.

"For the first four months I slept only two or three hours a night," Husseini said. "All the time I was standing and they asked me things like 'Who paid you? Are you working with the Mossad [Israeli intelligence]? Are you working with others?' I said no, I just write my articles, my thoughts. That's all. They thought some government was paying me, so they checked my bank account. I spent the first four months like this. Alone all the time." He continued:

> They said they arrested me because they were afraid somebody would kill me – but this was just for the media. I said how are you protecting me? If I am here just for my protection, why am I not allowed to sleep, why do I have all these questions, why am I going to the court?

After ten months' detention he was released but told not to use the internet or make phone calls, and he had to report to the police station every evening. That was not the end of his problems, however. Whenever the authorities spotted something new on the internet criticising Islam, Husseini came under suspicion and he was repeatedly arrested. "They arrested me on Thursday evenings [the start of the Muslim weekend], because on Friday and Saturday there is no court. So I spent all the time there [under arrest] and on Sunday they would say: 'OK, go. It's not you.' After this kept happening I was in touch with an American journalist in Jerusalem. She knew my story and said maybe I should leave."

He then travelled overland to Jordan and sought help at the French embassy. "I knew France had been putting pressure on the Palestinian Authority and they knew my story," he said. A few days later he was granted a visa allowing him to live and work in France.

Alber Saber, an Egyptian atheist from a Coptic Christian family, was also driven into exile because of his internet postings. "I started to speak about politics and religions when I was in my first year at university," he recalls. "I had a website on Geocities and I was writing some articles ... I was trying to share my ideas." As his views became known around the university in Beni Suef, Islamists started threatening him and, he says, made three attempts to kill him. But instead of dealing with these threats, the police guarding the university advised him to give up his studies there: "They said: 'Alber, you haven't to come to this university again. We can't make you safe, we can't support you. You have to leave'." He took their advice, transferred to another college and switched his studies from philosophy to computer science.

Saber's problems resumed after the 2011 revolution in Egypt when his internet postings came to the attention of Islamists again. "Many people tried to share bad things about me," he said.

In 2012, a 14-minute video called "Innocence of Muslims", which had been produced in the United States, triggered protests by Muslims in many countries. In Cairo, the US embassy was besieged by demonstrators and riots spreading around the world left a total of 50 people dead. The viciously anti-Muslim video, which had been posted on YouTube and was supposedly the trailer for a full-length film, was described by an article in Vanity Fair as "exceptionally amateurish, with disjointed dialogue, jumpy editing, and performances that would have looked melodramatic even in a silent movie". The clip, the article added, was "clearly designed to offend Muslims, portraying Muhammad as a bloodthirsty murderer and Lothario and paedophile with omnidirectional sexual appetites".[4] News of the video caused the Egyptian rumour mill to go into overdrive. "Some Islamic websites said that it was to be a big movie, about two hours long, and it would be shown free in all cinemas in America on 11 September [the anniversary of the al-Qaeda attacks in 2001]," Saber said. "Many of my friends asked me about it."

The rumours were untrue and, according to Saber, he merely wanted to set the record straight:

> I shared this movie [on the internet] and I explained what happened – that it was a fake story and that the 'movie' was not a movie, it was a very bad video clip. I shared the film, not to insult Islam but because the movie was very bad and the story was not good and the quality of the video was not good. I explained the true story.

Before long, Saber's phone number, his photograph and his home address had been circulated through social media.

> People started calling me and sending SMS messages saying we will kill you, we will punish you, we will come to your home ... They told me you are insulting Islam, blah, blah, blah. I told them no, it is not true. I have my blog, you can read my writing and you can watch my videos. I am just comparing between religions. I studied philosophy and religions, so I am discussing these subjects.

A crowd gathered outside his home – "about 200 or 300 people, I don't know exactly," he said. "We called the police. The police didn't care at first but in the next half hour people were starting to break the door of our home and our neighbours called the police many times. Then the police came and arrested me."

Saber was charged under Article 98 of the Egyptian penal code which criminalises using religion to "promote extremist thoughts with the intention of creating dissent or insulting an Abrahamic religion" or "undermining national unity". According to the charge sheet, he had "insulted God and cast doubt on the books of the Abrahamic religions" and "denied the existence of God and His creation of mankind." He was convicted and sentenced to three years in prison. When released on bail, pending an appeal, he fled to Switzerland.

RELIGION is difficult to avoid in the Middle East, even for those who try. Loudspeakers broadcasting the call to prayer, beards and veils signalling religious allegiances and the constant use of religious expressions in everyday conversation are just a few of the more obvious signs. Look a little deeper, though, and other things become apparent. Most of the Arab countries have an "official" religion and laws shaped by religious principles. In some, religious affiliation is considered important enough to be specified on everyone's identity card and the choice may be restricted to religions that are officially recognised. Sometimes there is no choice at all: the state decides what a person's religion shall be, based on parentage. Changing to another religion can be difficult or even illegal and marrying in a non-religious ceremony can be impossible without leaving the country.

Preoccupation with religion has its roots in the region's history. The Middle East was the birthplace of three major faiths – Islam, Christianity and Judaism – all claiming a special relationship with one Supreme Being who is immortal, all-powerful, infinitely wise, and yet invisible to ordinary humans. These three monotheistic religions share much in common but they are also rivals. Not only that; sectarian rivalries exist within them too and conflicting interpretations of God's will by those claiming to know the ultimate truth have caused much bloodshed over the centuries.

In countries where multiple faiths exist, such as Lebanon, Syria and Iraq, the sectarian divide is shaped by geography and birth as much as belief. Towns, villages and districts are identified by their sect: Sunni, Shia, Maronite, Druze, Alawite, etc. The question that Lebanese constantly ask when getting to know each other – "Where are you from?" – is a polite way of enquiring about their religion, and often their politics too.

The role of religion in the Middle East, and its pervasive influence, has not gone unquestioned by Arabs themselves, including some of a religious disposition. To call for freedom of belief, a secular state and an end to sectarianism does not necessarily imply a lack of religious faith and debates about these issues have become more prevalent in the wake of the Arab uprisings.

But what of those who seek to escape from religion altogether? Arab non-believers – atheists and agnostics – are not a new phenomenon but their numbers seem to be growing. They are certainly becoming more vocal and visible, largely because of the platform afforded by the internet. For them, the demand is not merely freedom of religion but freedom *from* religion – an altogether more radical step.

To believe in God or not, to practise a religion or not, are questions that millions of people wrestle with in their minds, sometimes for years, before making a choice. In many parts of the world it is regarded as a personal decision and nobody else's business but, in the eyes of Arab society, openly declaring a disbelief in God or rejecting religion is a shocking and sometimes dangerous thing to do. Many choose to keep their disbelief private, if only to avoid upsetting their family. Those who pluck up the courage to be open about their atheism often adopt the language of gay rights activism and refer to it as "coming out". The comparison is not inappropriate. In an Arab context, both atheism and homosexuality are still largely taboo and the consequences of coming out as gay or an atheist can be very similar: it can lead to being ostracised by family, friends and the local community, not to mention conflict with the law.

While it's natural for religious families to feel some distress on learning that their loved one is destined (as they see it) for punishment in hell, in the case of an Arab who abandons Islam there are other complications. Religion in the Arab countries is not simply a matter of belief or disbelief, nor is it necessarily treated as a matter of personal choice. Islam has strong social aspects based around the concept of *ummah* – the community of believers – and expressions of individualism or nonconformity tend to be frowned upon. Members are expected to pull together and behave (at least in public) in ways that uphold its Islamic ethos. Thus, when someone breaks away from established norms – especially if they do so publicly – they are liable to be seen as damaging communal solidarity.

A further complication in the Middle East is that religion often forms a major component in people's sense of identity. One survey of six Arab countries found that in four of them – Jordan, Morocco, Saudi Arabia and the UAE – "Muslim" was the preferred identity, ahead of national identity and Arab identity. The exceptions were Egypt and Lebanon where national identity came first.[5] This brings a more political dimension to the role of religion in Arab society. The Islamic revival and the growth of Islamist movements towards the end of the twentieth century was in part a defensive mechanism – a response to perceived threats from outside, especially from the west. The retreat into what popular imagination deemed to be traditional values also held out the promise of certainty in an uncertain world.

The beginning of this trend is often traced back to the Arabs' overwhelming defeat in the 1967 war with Israel. That was a huge psychological blow which Islamists blamed on the failings of secular nationalism and a drift away from the sacred path. Several subsequent events reinforced the idea that with God on their side Muslims could become invincible: the Islamic revolution in Iran in 1979, the success of the *mujahidin* in driving out Soviet forces from Afghanistan at the end of the 1980s and Israel's unilateral withdrawal from southern Lebanon in 2000 for which the Shi'a resistance movement, Hizbullah, claimed the credit.

Treating religion as a badge of identity leads to a heightened emphasis on its outward, physical signs. For religion to be effectively linked to identity it needs to be expressed visibly, and one obvious sign of that is the increased number of women wearing the hijab compared with the 1950s and 1960s. It also tends to emphasise the minutiae of religious observance: codes of "correct" Islamic behaviour are prescribed, often down to the minutest detail, and often on the slenderest of scriptural evidence. This operates at a communal level too with efforts to create a visibly Islamic ethos in the public sphere, either through peer pressure or direct enforcement.

Alongside that is the problem of Islamophobia, particularly in the aftermath of al-Qaeda's attacks on New York and Washington on 11 September, 2001. The stereotyping of Muslims as potential terrorists, the detention of suspects in Guantanamo Bay, plus numerous cases of discrimination or abuse, has further aroused sensitivities amid claims that Muslims in general are under attack. In such a climate, questioning of the Qur'an and its teachings is liable to be interpreted as sedition.

For Arabs who decide to embrace atheism, this background presents a host of problems. At one level there is the intellectual tussle between belief and disbelief but that is not easily separated from all the other baggage that accompanies religion in the Middle East. Arabs who renounce Islam may thus be accused of betraying their identity and culture. By asserting their right to disbelieve, atheists are also asserting the right to freedom of thought and belief – a right which belongs to everyone, including the most devout.

IN SAUDI ARABIA all citizens are officially Muslims whether they like it or not and openly practising of other religions is forbidden. The image usually projected by the Saudi authorities is of a thoroughly devout country – so devout that shops have to close at prayer times and that suitably "Islamic" codes of dress and behaviour must be followed.

In 2012, however, the kingdom's claims of holiness were severely shaken when a poll by WIN/Gallup International looked at religion and atheism in fifty-seven countries – including Saudi Arabia. Of those interviewed in the kingdom, 19% said they were not religious and 5% described themselves as convinced atheists.[6] The percentage of self-declared atheists was higher in Saudi Arabia than in any other predominantly Muslim country covered by the survey. The figures, if they are anywhere close to being accurate, suggest that a quarter of the kingdom's inhabitants, at least in cities (where the survey took place) have no particular interest in religion and that one person in twenty is not only an atheist but willing to admit it to a pollster – an admission which as far as many in the kingdom are concerned is a crime punishable by death. Rather than disputing these findings, as they might have been expected to do, religious Saudis agonised over how to halt the spread of disbelief. An article in the Saudi newspaper *al-Watan* began:

> We must fight the phenomenon of atheism with initiatives that will nip it in the bud before it takes roots in the hearts of our young men and women. This is possible only by launching a massive national campaign.

Young Saudis, the article continued, are "slipping into the dark abyss of atheism" by visiting social networking websites, reading atheist authors and some of those on scholarships at western universities are "holding dialogues" with their teachers. The article ended by calling for a national strategy to combat atheism and protect religion:

> At present, efforts to contain the onslaught of atheism are limited. These are mainly concentrated on personal initiatives. There should be a participation of the entire society in dealing with this serious issue. This shall be based on a national strategy worked out by our sharia bodies to protect our religion. *Like what we did in combating terrorism, we have to root out atheism* [italics added].

The Ministry of Islamic Affairs and minister Sheikh Saleh al-Asheikh may shoulder the great responsibility of working out the strategy for an anti-atheist national campaign with the support of experts in this field. Specialised centres to hold dialogue with young men and women could be set up, in addition to launching an exclusive satellite channel to promote the cause. It is easier to treat cancer in its initial stage before it seeps deep into the body cells.[7]

The writer's call for atheism to be treated in the same way as terrorism might seem ridiculous, but the Saudi authorities were already taking the idea seriously. In January 2014, the government announced a new and extremely wide-ranging anti-terrorism law which, among many other things, outlawed "calling for atheist thought in any form, or calling into question the fundamentals of the Islamic religion on which this country is based."[8]

In Saudi terms, equating atheism with terrorism does have a certain logic since atheism presents a challenge to the most fundamental principles of the Saudi state. The Basic Law of 1992 (the Saudi equivalent of a constitution) establishes a very clear linkage between Islam and the state:

Article 1: The Kingdom of Saudi Arabia is a sovereign Arab Islamic state with Islam as its religion; God's Book and the Sunnah of His Prophet (God's prayers and peace be upon him) are its constitution ...

Article 6: Citizens are to pay allegiance to the King in accordance with the Holy Qur'an and the tradition of the Prophet, in submission and obedience ...

Article 7: Government in Saudi Arabia derives power from the Holy Qur'an and the Prophet's tradition.

Article 8: Government in the Kingdom of Saudi Arabia is based on the premise of justice, consultation, and equality in accordance with the Islamic sharia.

Article 9: The family is the kernel of Saudi society, and its members shall be brought up on the basis of the Islamic faith ...

Article 11: Saudi society will be based on the principle of adherence to God's command ...

Article 13: Education will aim at instilling the Islamic faith in the younger generation ...

Article 23: The state protects Islam; it implements its sharia; it orders people to do right and shun evil; it fulfils the duty regarding God's call.[9]

Non-believers, if they wish to adhere to their principles, cannot accept this. By the same token, the Saudi state cannot accept non-belief without changing the basis on which it has been constructed. Short of wholesale political change, it is difficult to see how this impasse can be resolved. The government, recognising perhaps that it can influence but not totally control what people think, keeps up appearances by continuing to impose "Islamic" codes of behaviour while trying to force non-believers into silence. Even some religious scholars doubt that this will work in the long run, however.

Bullying and attacking atheists is likely to be counterproductive, Ghazi al-Maghlouth, professor of Islamic culture at al-Ahsa University, told the Saudi Gazette. "Youths who follow atheism would then react vehemently and be adamant in adhering to their beliefs. Therefore, it is essential to engage them in friendly discourse," he said quoting a proverb – "Winning hearts is more significant than conquering cities." Meanwhile, Yousuf al-Ghamdi, professor of belief (*aqidah*) at Umm al-Qura University, called for "effective" and "convincing" dialogue. "Atheism is an intellectual phenomenon and not a behavioural one and hence it should be addressed in an intellectual way," he said.[10]

Saudis have also begun asking themselves why there should be so much apparent disbelief in the kingdom. Inevitably, some blame foreign influences and modern innovations such as electronic games: "The enemies of Islam use this ploy to misguide our children with games promoting atheism and polytheism, besides deviating them from the divine religion of Islam."[11]

Other (more plausible) theories suggest Saudis are being driven away from religion by the way it is taught and by the reactionary – often comically reactionary – positions of many scholars in the kingdom. A writer in *al-Madinah* newspaper pointed out that schoolchildren are made to memorise long lists of the things that are *haram* but then, when they go out of school, they see adults breaking the rules all the time:

> Our children grow up watching a great contradiction between what they are taught and what they see in real life. They observe adults indulging in many un-Islamic behaviours day in and day out.
>
> For instance, a child may see his father being lazy in going to the mosque for prayer after hearing the *adhan* (prayer call). The same child is taught by his teacher in school that not performing prayer on time is an act of atheism ...

The young boys and girls are taught that entertainment is *haram*, but they see a large number of men and women going to amusement parks or even travelling outside for entertainment.[12]

Saudi atheist Omar Hadi thinks the scale of the revolt against religion may be even larger than the WIN/Gallup International poll suggested, though some of the apparent disbelief may be "just a knee-jerk reaction" to the "extreme limits" that Saudi society places upon its citizens. "If the same individuals moved to the west they would probably become Muslims again," he said. Hadi (speaking under a pseudonym) continued:

> The doubts that I had growing up were because of the way we were taught. They did try to explain to us but the explanations did not make sense. And then they just told us to shut up and accept it. And some people did – taking it by faith, obviously, despite the evidence.
>
> If they want to combat that they need to get into a more refined way of teaching theology in this country. It works for the majority of people but you will always have people who are never going to believe.
>
> I understand their dilemma, because once they start to – I use the word lightly – "reform" religion, it becomes more man-made than God-made and loses its holiness.[13]

Saudi scholars, he said, have also done much to discredit themselves by denouncing technological innovations when they first appear and then back-tracking when they prove useful and popular:

> Many religious scholars in Saudi twenty years ago said all photography is banned – it's sinful, you will go to hell if you have your photograph taken. I know people who actually went and burned all the photographs they had of themselves. Twenty years later, the same [scholars] are all over TV and in the newsprint media and they say: "Well, maybe it wasn't so sinful to have photographs." So what about the people who burned all their photographs?
>
> With any new advancement, they are so radical and extreme in the beginning. It was the same thing with the use of camera phones, cassette tapes and video players. I have [a copy of] a fatwa that says the use of a camera phone is sinful, and now everybody has them.
>
> It's the inconsistency in how they deal with new things that adds doubt to everything else they say.

Nowadays, statements by scholars that show them to be ignorant or out of touch also tend to reach a much larger audience than previously. They are often picked up by mainstream media from religious websites where readers presumably take them seriously. The kingdom's mainstream media sometimes report them impartially and sometimes with opposing views, but they are clearly seen as having some entertainment value – as indicated by the unflattering photographs of the scholars that often accompany such reports. Once in the mainstream, the scholars' words are then at the mercy of social media.

During an outbreak of the often-lethal MERS coronavirus in Saudi Arabia, *al-Hayat* newspaper reported a claim by Abdullah al-Amrani, a preacher in Tabuk, that he had discovered a cure through his research into "prophetic medicine". Amrani refused to disclose the nature of his treatment but said he had also used it successfully to treat AIDS and leukaemia.[14] Needless to say, Twitter users immediately suggested Amrani should give up medicine and stick to religion. Meanwhile, a senior Saudi cleric pondered the question of whether people who died from MERS could be classified as martyrs. He announced that they could not, unless the World Health Organisation declared the outbreak to be an epidemic.

On another occasion, Sheikh Saleh bin Saad al-Luhaydan, an opponent of the campaign for Saudi women to be allowed to drive, claimed scientific research had shown that driving "automatically affects" women's ovaries and "rolls up" their pelvis. This, he said, is why women who continuously drive cars give birth to children "with clinical disorders of varying degrees". *Al-Arabiya*, the Saudi-owned news channel, reported his remarks along with some mocking comments posted on Twitter and a statement from the head of the religious police saying "Islamic sharia does not have a text forbidding women driving."[15] Luhaydan's claim about driving damaging the ovaries was also ridiculed in a song by Hisham Fageeh, a Saudi-born comedian, and two of his friends. Entitled "No Woman, No Drive", and sung to the tune of Bob Marley's "No Woman, No Cry", it was played more than eleven million times when posted on YouTube.[16]

Another factor leading young Saudis into "the dark abyss of atheism", according to an opinion article in *al-Watan*, is "holding dialogues, as in the case of some students on scholarship grants, with their teachers in western universities".[17] This appeared to be a veiled criticism of one of the king's pet projects – the King Abdullah Scholarship Programme – which has proved especially unpopular with Saudi clerics and ultra-conservatives. The programme, established in 2005 and costing SR9 billion ($2.4 billion) a year, provides funds for 125,000 Saudis to study at universities abroad – mostly in the United States. About 30% of the students are female. This is officially explained as an investment in the kingdom's economic future, to create a highly educated workforce and thus reduce dependence on foreign expertise, but it is also intended to promote social change by exposing young Saudis to other cultures – hence the opposition from traditionalists.

"From the vantage point of someone else's culture you can truly see your own," an article in the *Saudi Gazette* noted. Students taking part in the programme told the paper it had helped them "to accept different people and thoughts" and taught them "what critical thinking is" but it tended also to increase their frustrations on their return to the kingdom. One who had studied law abroad said: "Due to my profession, I have to deal with one of the most backward judicial systems in the world, which is improving at a very slow pace." Another said she found it "really hard to get used to the chaos here [in Saudi Arabia] after getting used to a more civilised way of living" abroad.[18]

Saud Kabli, a political scientist and columnist for *al-Watan* newspaper, likens the scholarship programme to Muhammed Ali Paça's educational missions to Europe in the 1820s "which helped the build-up of modern Egypt and triggered, later on, the Arab Renaissance". Anyone who visits Saudi Arabia today will see that Saudi youth are becoming more assertive, more open to the world and more receptive to global ideals, he said. "The youth of Saudi Arabia are a hidden force of change that will definitely change the society in the coming years, and it seems that the government realises this and even capitalises on it, probably on the hope that change will come eventually from within the society rather than forcefully from the top."[19]

The sort of exposure provided by the scholarship programme undoubtedly has an effect on the religious views of at least some students taking part. "Growing up in Saudi," Omar Hadi said, "you are indoctrinated in the idea of non-Muslims being evil and they are all going to go to hell. Every single non-Muslim is out to get you. So when you go and live with them, you eat with them, you study with them, you socialise with them in a normal innocent way, you realise that they are not evil. After a while you say: 'You know what? I've experienced so much kindness and generosity from these people that it's difficult for me to believe they are going to go to hell'."

Fears about the effects of the scholarship programme prompted one Saudi preacher to claim that "travelling to the land of infidelity for the sake of doing business or studies is forbidden except in extreme necessity" and with certain conditions, and that "whoever dies in the land of infidelity could go to hell." Sheikh Abdullah al-Suwailem, who works for a project to rehabilitate imprisoned al-Qaeda supporters, told *al-Hayat* newspaper that the first of the conditions for permitting foreign travel is that a person has to be "a strong believer" with religious "immunity" so as not to fall for "desires". "Whoever fears for himself falling for what is forbidden, such as drinking alcohol, should not travel except in the case of necessity," he added.[20]

Saudi Arabia, basically, is a victim of what Alvin Toffler described as "future shock". In the space of a few decades in the twentieth century, oil discoveries transformed it from one of the world's poorest countries into one of the wealthiest, and it is still struggling to adjust. Its society has become increasingly polarised as traditionalists fight what is probably a losing battle against the onslaught from modernity. In the absence of more rational argument for preserving the status quo, they defend it with religion and fear-mongering about immorality.

But the idea that religion is essential for a well-ordered society is demonstrably untrue. Writing in the *Cambridge Companion to Atheism,* Phil Zuckerman notes that "countries containing high percentages of nonbelievers are among the healthiest and wealthiest nations on earth".

Zuckerman looked at the worldwide ranking of countries in terms of religious belief and compared this with their ranking in the UN's Human Development Index. The results were striking. Among the 25 top-ranked countries in the Human Development Index, all but one (Ireland) had very high percentages of organic atheism.[21] At the other end of the scale, the bottom 50 countries in the index had very low levels of atheism. More specifically, and drawing on other data, Zuckerman found:

- Of the 40 poorest countries, all but one (Vietnam) are highly religious.

- Of the 35 countries with the highest youth illiteracy rates, all are highly religious.

- Non-religious countries have the lowest infant mortality rates and religious countries have the highest.

- The ten countries with the highest levels of gender equality are all strongly atheistic while the ten with the lowest levels are all highly religious.

- The countries with the highest homicide rates are all highly religious, while the lowest homicide rates tend to be in highly secular countries.

The more religious countries do appear to have lower suicide rates but this could be partly due to religious taboos against recording such deaths as suicide.

While the evidence clearly shows that widespread atheism does not lead to social breakdown, Zuckerman does not claim atheism is responsible for the benefits seen in less religious societies: "Rather, societal health seems to cause widespread atheism, and societal insecurity seems to cause widespread belief in God."

IN THE 1920s, Hassan al-Banna, founder of the Muslim Brotherhood, complained that a wave of atheism and lewdness was engulfing Egypt. Europeans, he said, had "founded schools and scientific and cultural institutes in the very heart of the Islamic domain which cast doubt and heresy into the very souls of its sons".[22] By 1994, the blame had shifted to satellite television. "These programmes, prepared by international imperialism, are part of an extensive plot to wipe out our religious and sacred values," the Iranian Ministry of Culture and Islamic Guidance warned.[23] Today, though, a more favoured culprit is the internet. Its power – supposedly – to spread atheism far and wide thus becomes an argument for controlling cyberspace and punishing those who "misuse" it against religion.

The internet is certainly a valuable tool for atheists and other kinds of dissenters in the Middle East. It provides access to ideas and information that would not otherwise be available locally, it allows people to express their own thoughts in public and it enables interaction with others, either by engaging in debates or connecting with like-minded individuals. Importantly for people in the Middle East, this also takes place – mostly – outside the usual framework of government restrictions and it levels the field, giving access to everyone regardless of location and national boundaries.

There is no doubt that the internet facilitates the spread of atheist ideas (along with many others) but the internet itself is not reason for them; it is merely a vehicle. Trying to suppress atheistic thought on the internet does nothing to address the causes of people's religious doubts and may actually increase their curiosity. People would not be seeking out this material unless they felt it had some relevance to their own situation and attempts at censorship imply a fear that religion cannot win the argument on evidence and reasoning alone. Nevertheless, it is convenient to blame the internet since there is then no need to consider whether religious doctrines and practices might play some part in driving people towards unbelief.

The main problem, according to Nasser al-Sarami, Head of Media at *al-Arabiya* TV channel, lies with "traditional attitudes" and an "inability to address the demands of modern times and younger generations and to become open to new ideas instead of resorting to repression and blaming freedom of expression for atheism":

> The internet and social networking websites have not come up with anything that was not already there. They have just unravelled what was hidden from us whether owing to the nature of our culture or the level of local and social awareness.
>
> Twitter and Facebook have turned the unknown into known and offered to people a podium through which they can express their feelings as they are, without embellishment or censorship. That is when the truth we did not want to see emerged.[24]

Another point to note is that the amount of atheistic material on the internet is minuscule compared to the vast number of Islamic websites which cover the full range from jihadism to sufism, plus others where Christians and Muslims slug it out over who has the true religion.

"The internet is a double-edged weapon because a lot of religious ideology and religious orthodoxy has also been transmitted through the internet," said Amira Nowaira, professor of English literature at Alexandria university in Egypt. "It's not one-way ... there is a great deal of movement. One needs to remember that, because Islamism has really found a voice on the net too, with so many sites advocating ultra-orthodox views."

Muslims were remarkably swift to adopt the internet, despite the wariness of conservative elements towards modern innovations and despite the technical difficulties (for the first few years) of producing web pages with Arabic text. By 2000 most of the well-known Islamist movements, including Hamas and the Taliban, had a presence on the web, along with many more obscure groups and individuals. One reason for this was that internet activity could be viewed as a form of *da'wa* – spreading the word of Islam – which many regard as a religious obligation. Some were also excited by the possibility that the internet could one day link up the billion-or-so Muslims around the world into a single religious community (or "digital *ummah*") of a kind not seen since the early days of Islam.[25]

Arab sceptics also began appearing as the social media developed. "In the decade before Twitter and Facebook, Paltalk, a video and audio group chat service founded in 1998, was all the rage in the Gulf," Sultan Sooud al-Qassemi, a prominent Emirati columnist, recalled. "Within weeks, popular Paltalk chat rooms such as 'Humanity' (run by a Kuwaiti) and 'No Religionists', dedicated to specific topics, sprang up." One pioneering blogger in the Gulf was Ahmed Ben Kerishan, an Emirati atheist who asserted that "all religions lie" and that "secularism can set people free".[26]

Today, a search of Facebook reveals about a hundred pages with "*mulhid*" (Arabic for "atheist") in their title, plus a couple of dozen using the English phrase "Arab atheist". These are a very mixed bunch: some appear inactive while others have several thousand "likes", and they include a few closed (i.e. private) groups. Outside the Middle East, ex-Muslim organisations in North America, Britain, France, Belgium, Germany, New Zealand and Scandinavia have websites, and the recently-exiled atheists, Waleed al-Husseini, Kacem el-Ghazzali and Alber Saber each have their own blog.

One effect of this online activity is that non-believers scattered around the Arab countries begin to feel less isolated and may even pluck up the courage to make contact with others – though many are still fearful of doing so.

Facebook and Twitter have "made it easy to find people who debate and are interested in secular values," a Saudi atheist told William Bauer in an interview for *Your Middle East*. "I was shocked to meet older people in their forties and fifties who been hiding their atheism for decades," he continued. "They said that only recently with the young generation in their twenties had they found other people who think like them and were able to find social group[s] that they can talk and debate about their ideas in."[27]

The Associated Press described a typical example in Egypt:

> One 40-year-old Egyptian engineer, born a Muslim, told The Associated Press he had long been an atheist but kept it a deep secret. The 2011 uprising in Egypt and its calls for radical change encouraged him to look online for others like himself. "Before the revolution, I was living a life in total solitude. I didn't know anybody who believed like me," he said. "Now we have more courage than we used to have".[28]

But the report added: "His case illustrates the limits on how far an atheist can go. Like most others interviewed by The Associated Press, he spoke on condition of anonymity for fear of reprisals, harassment or troubles with his family. His 'going public' is strictly online."

Social media, *The Economist* magazine noted, "give non-believers more clout but also make them more conspicuous, and therefore vulnerable." Most of those arrested for "defaming" religion have got into trouble as a result of their internet activity. The real blame for this, *The Economist* continued, lies with religious intolerance. "In the 1950s and 1960s secularism and tolerance prevailed in many majority-Muslim countries; today religion pervades public and political life. Sami Zubaida, a scholar at London's Birkbeck College, speaks of increasing polarisation, with 'growing religiosity at one end of the spectrum and growing atheism and secularism at the other'."[29]

Besides the threat of reprisals from the authorities, online atheists have also faced unofficial harassment, presumably from Muslim activists – sometimes by hacking and sometimes by abusing the "report abuse" systems on social networking sites:

> Bassam al-Baghdady, a Swedish atheist writer with Iraqi roots, explained that the Arab Atheists Network and other discussion groups were destroyed and deleted systematically. It is said that Islamists started campaigns through Facebook in order to "report" these pages and the profiles of its administrators. Baghdady said that his own accounts on Twitter and Facebook were blocked several times due to these reports, and many YouTube videos that he had uploaded were deleted due to their content ...

> Ever since 2010, social networks like Twitter, YouTube and Facebook have witnessed tremendous online activity of extremist Islamist groups (Salafis), and they had two ways of dealing with atheist pages: either they destroyed and hacked the websites or they organised a "report" operation where members would continually report accounts

or videos for abuse and thus automatically let the social network block the account or content.[30]

The Arab Atheists Network survived, however, and appears to be one of the most popular websites of its kind. It now has more than 18,000 members and its online discussion forum (in Arabic) has accumulated more than a million posts.[31]

Recently, activists have also been resorting to video. The grandly-named Arab Atheist Broadcasting is a YouTube channel which produces a two-hour discussion programme on alternate Fridays where various atheists hook up via Skype. The more popular videos have been viewed around 3,000 to 4,000 times.[32] In a similar vein, Black Ducks is a YouTube talk show presented and directed by Ismail Mohamed, an Egyptian atheist. The aim, it says, is to encourage Egyptian atheists and non-believers "to reveal themselves and tell the world their experience, why and how they become atheists".[33] Black Ducks derives its name from Hans Christian Andersen's story about an "ugly duckling" which is attacked and abused until it eventually grows into a beautiful white swan.

Jordan has a small atheist community linked through a Facebook group. It started in 2013 with thirty members, rising to 100 a year later. Ages range from sixteen to forty-four, and about 40% of members are female. "Some of the older ones have been atheists for years, others have just found out," organiser Mohammed al-Khadra said.

He added that he knows of a further 100 or so Jordanian atheists who are not in the group. "The reason why we don't have all 200 on the list is because we still have bigots when it comes to homosexuality, politics, etc, so I tried to collect people who are open-minded. I learned that being an atheist doesn't always change the whole mindset of the person. You can find atheists here who are homophobic or have extreme fascistic political views."

Although Khadra was willing to be identified in an interview ("I am at the point where I no longer care"), the group itself remains largely underground. Most people are afraid for their jobs or their families, he said.

At a government level, Jordan is less restrictive than Saudi Arabia though people can still be stripped of civil rights if they leave Islam or jailed for blasphemy. But the main problem in Jordan comes from the community and families. Atheism, like sexual transgression, is considered an offence against "honour" in some families and thus punishable by death at the hands of relatives, especially when the atheist is female. One man, an atheist who was also gay and a former imam, had a narrow escape after he appeared in a Black Ducks video talking about his sexuality and religion.[34] "He was few hours away from being killed," Khadra said. "I managed with the help of my members and his mother to get him out of the house. I got him to Lebanon." He continued:

> I have a friend who lost his wife because he told her he was an atheist. I myself lost my fiancée for being an atheist. I couldn't lie to her so I told her I am not a Muslim. She was fine with it at first then in a couple of months she said "You don't pray, you are not a Muslim, so you must have bad morals."
>
> The main view is that if someone is not a Muslim he or she must have bad morals. If he is an atheist then he must be living like an animal. That's how they see us. I have been asked so many times why wouldn't I sleep with my mother.

The Jordanian government, meanwhile, has to keep looking over its shoulder at the Islamist opposition – offering them a sop from time to time:

> Every once in a while when they want to appease the opposition over something, they select someone to put on trial for blasphemy.
>
> Islam Samhan, a Muslim poet, was jailed after the opposition made claims against him. Since the government doesn't give them their larger claims, such as ruling entirely by sharia law, they give them these smaller ones just to keep things rolling.

Samhan was arrested for "insulting the prophets" after publishing a book of poetry that was deemed to be blasphemous.[35]

One function of the Jordanian group is to provide mutual support for its members, along with discussing Islam and Islamist movements – especially the Islamists, Khadra said:

> Islam itself is not a threat. I don't fight Islam, I fight Islamists. I disagree with Muslims but I don't have any problem with them believing in what they wish. Islam or any religion can cause harm to any society but the main threat is Islamism since it only takes one theocrat with an atomic arsenal to prove my point.
>
> The idea that God wants a nation in his name and orders it to kill and destroy other humans is the most dangerous in the whole dogma. It's the main idea that Islamists are working on.

Nevertheless, Khadra is encouraged by the number of atheist

groups developing in other countries around the region. "Groups such as mine are everywhere now. If we can get the Muslim Brotherhood away from us and be defended by the state you will see us everywhere. Until that day we have to stay underground."[36]

The Arab Atheists Library is a Facebook page providing free downloads of books, including Arabic translations of works by Baruch Spinoza, Stephen Hawking, Hannah Arendt, Bertrand Russell, Carl Sagan and Richard Dawkins.[37] The download of Dawkins' famous book, *The God Delusion* (*Wahm Allah*, in Arabic) is an unofficial translation by the Iraqi-born atheist, Bassam al-Baghdady. Arab writers in the online library include Mohammed Arkoun, the secular Algerian scholar, Murad Wahba, the Egyptian philosopher and Farag Fouda, the scourge of Egyptian Islamists who was assassinated in 1992.

The atheists' library is one example of how the internet is giving Arabs access to books – and subversive ideas – that are hard to obtain by other means. Some are works by foreigners that might not get past the censors while others are old out-of-print works produced by Arabs in more liberal times.

Although they are often posted on the internet with scant regard for copyright, Amira Nowaira of Alexandria university is pleased to see this happening:

> Very often now you don't find books in bookshops but they are available on the net – for free. People, out of the goodness of their hearts, just scan books and put them there. Some of the books are actually out of print.
>
> I think it's a good thing, even though it may not be ethically correct. Some of the books that were produced in the 1940s were completely out of print and you would never be able to find them anywhere but they are now available on the net. It's amazing. You couldn't even buy them if you wanted.
>
> I don't know if this availability of books is going to change people's ideas – it has never happened before. When I was young we used to go to Cairo especially to buy books, or wait for the book fair. Now, you don't have to go anywhere and I wonder what the long-term impact of that will be on things like belief and disbelief.

Omar Hadi, the Saudi atheist, is confident of the answer to that. Even though Farag Fouda died more than twenty years ago, his trenchant writing is alive again on the internet. "Just go on Twitter and everything he said is being re-quoted and re-quoted and re-quoted. His influence did not go away. Everything he said ... you throw it at these religious people and they don't know how to react to it, except by quoting the Qur'an."

Fouda is not the only one. Hadi also takes encouragement by looking back even further to the tenth century and Mutanabbi, who many regard as the finest of the Arab poets:

> Mutanabbi has a wonderful statement criticising the obsession with appearances in religion and how all other nations will be laughing at us because the only things we are concerned about is that we shave our moustaches and let our beards grow.[38] He has other things, such as our biggest curse is that we have a group of people who think that God gave wisdom only to them.

Stuff like that from Islamic history shows there has always been some kind of resistance.

NOTES

1. Qur'an 81:29.
2. Author's interview, May 2014.
3. Husseini, Waleed al-: "Why I left Islam." Proud Atheist blog, 30 August 2010. http://proud-a.blogspot.com/2010/08/why-i-left-islam.html
4. Gross, Michael Joseph: "Disaster Movie." Vanity Fair, 27 December, 2012. http://www.vanityfair.com/culture/2012/12/making-of-innocence-of-muslims
5. "Arab Attitudes Towards Political and Social Issues, Foreign Policy and the Media." Poll conducted jointly by the Anwar Sadat Chair for Peace and Development at the University of Maryland and Zogby International, May 2004.
6. Global Index of Religiosity and Atheism. WIN/Gallup International, 2012. http://www.wingia.com/web/files/news/14/file/14.pdf
7. Qassem, Abdul Aziz: "Fighting atheist tendencies." English translation from al-Watan newspaper, re-published in English by the Saudi Gazette, 20 February 2014. http://www.saudigazette.com.sa/index.cfm?method=home.regcon&contentid=20140221196390
8. "Saudi Arabia: New Terrorism Regulations Assault Rights." Human Rights Watch, 20 March 2013. https://www.hrw.org/news/2014/03/20/saudi-arabia-new-terrorism-regulations-assault-rights
9. Basic Law, 1992. http://www.servat.unibe.ch/icl/sa00000_.html
10. "Containing atheism." Saudi Gazette, 12 April 2014.

http://www.saudigazette.com.sa/index.cfm?method=home.regcon&contentid=20140412201628
11. Baras, Abdurahman: "Academics warn against adverse impact of e-games on children." Okaz/Saudi Gazette, 6 December 2013. http://www.saudigazette.com.sa/index.cfm?method=home.regcon&contentid=20131206188699
12. Muayyad, Shams al-: "The absence of role models." Al-Madinah, republished in English by the Saudi Gazette, 7 May 2014. http://www.saudigazette.com.sa/index.cfm?method=home.regcon&contentid=20140507204324
13. Author's interview, May 2014. Omar Hadi is a pseudonym.
14. Al-Hayat (in Arabic), 6 May 2014. http://alhayat.com/Articles/2171453
15. "Driving affects ovaries and pelvis, Saudi sheikh warns women." Al-Arabiya, 28 September 2013. http://english.alarabiya.net/en/variety/2013/09/28/Driving-affects-ovary-and-pelvis-Saudi-sheikh-warns-women.html
16. Whitaker, Brian: "Subverting Saudi Arabia through song." Blog post, 31 October 2013. http://www.al-bab.com/blog/2013/october/subverting-saudi-arabia-through-song.htm
17. Qassem, Abdul Aziz: "Fighting atheist tendencies." Al-Watan newspaper; republished in English by the Saudi Gazette, 20 February 2014. http://www.saudigazette.com.sa/index.cfm?method=home.regcon&contentid=20140221196390
18. Bashraheel, Laura: "Scholarship students: Big dreams, slow change." Saudi Gazette, 11 March 2013. http://www.saudigazette.com.sa/index.cfm?method=home.regcon&contentid=20130311156300
19. Author's email correspondence with Kabli, October 2013.
20. "Fatwa prohibiting travelling abroad causes controversy in Saudi Arabia." Al-Arabiya, 6 May 2014. http://english.alarabiya.net/en/perspective/features/2014/05/06/Fatwa-prohibiting-traveling-abroad-causes-controversy-in-Saudi-Arabia-.html
21. Zuckerman uses the term "organic atheism" to distinguish it from "coercive atheism" in countries like North Korea, which he excluded from the comparison.
22. Banna, Hassan al-: "Between Yesterday and Today". http://m.www.islamicbulletin.org/free_downloads/resources/between_yesterday_and_today.pdf
23. Shaffer, Brenda (ed): The Limits of Culture: Islam and Foreign Policy. Cambridge, Massachusetts, MIT Press, 2006, p 63
24. Sarami, Nasser al-: "Saudi Arabia: A wave of atheism or a

misunderstanding." Al-Arabiya, 23 May 2012.
http://english.alarabiya.net/views/2012/05/23/215974.html
25. For more about Islam and the early years of the internet see: Bunt, Gary: Virtually Islamic. Cardiff: University of Wales Press, 2000.
26. Qassemi, Sultan Sooud al-: "Gulf atheism in the age of social media." Al-Monitor, 3 March 2014. http://www.al-monitor.com/pulse/originals/2014/03/gulf-atheism-uae-islam-religion.html. Ben Kerishan's Land of Sands blog is archived at http://thelandofsands.blogspot.co.uk/
27. Bauer, William: "Interview with a Saudi atheist." Your Middle East, 30 April 2013.
http://www.yourmiddleeast.com/columns/article/interview-with-a-saudi-atheist_11146
28. Jebreili, Kamran: "Arab atheists inch out of shadows despite persecution in Mideast." Associated Press, 3 August 2013.
http://www.dallasnews.com/news/local-news/20130803-arab-atheists-inch-out-of-shadows-despite-persecution-in-mideast.ece
29. "Ex-Muslim atheists are becoming more outspoken, but tolerance is still rare." The Economist, 24 November, 2012.
http://www.economist.com/news/international/21567059-ex-muslim-atheists-are-becoming-more-outspoken-tolerance-still-rare-no-god-not
30. Alyasery, Mazin and Hussein, Gehad: "Online war on Atheism in the Arab world." Your Middle East, 29 April 2013.
http://www.yourmiddleeast.com/opinion/elyasery-and-hussein-online-war-on-atheism-in-the-arab-world_13938
31. http://www.il7ad.com/
32. https://www.youtube.com/user/ArabAtheistBroadcast/
33. https://www.youtube.com/user/fiberoty
34. https://www.youtube.com/watch?v=JomoCGa36Aw&feature=youtu.be
35. "Jordanian poet prepares for jail." The National, 2 September 2009.
http://www.thenational.ae/news/world/middle-east/jordanian-poet-prepares-for-jail
36. Author's interview and email exchange with Mohammed al-Khadra, September 2014.
37. https://www.facebook.com/ArabAtheistsLibrary
38. The translated verse says: "Is it the goal of religion that you should pluck out your beards, O community whose ignorance is a laughing-stock to other nations?" See: Arberry, A J: Poems of Mutanabbi. London: Cambridge University Press, 1967. p116

2: Atheism in Arab history

THE ARABIC language has no exact equivalent of the English word "atheist". While "atheist" is derived from ancient Greek (*a-* meaning "not", *theos* meaning "god") and clearly refers to non-belief in God or gods, the Arabic terms normally used today – *mulhid* for atheist and *ilhad* for atheism – have broader connotations of deviant belief. *Mulhid* certainly includes atheists but has also been applied to other kinds of dissenters such as apostates and heretics. This causes some difficulties when considering the history of Arab atheism but it also suggests that Arab critiques of religion in the past were not simply about belief or disbelief in God.

Historically, fear of atheists seems to have far exceeded their actual numbers. Though identifiable atheists in Islamic history are rather scarce, there are lots of polemical treatises in Arabic attacking unnamed people who deny God's existence. The earliest surviving work of this kind is thought to be *Radd 'ala al-Mulhid* ("Reply to the Heretic") by al-Qasim bin Ibrahim, a Zaydi theologian of the ninth century CE. Al-Qasim was so anxious to keep Muslims on the straight path that he wrote two more books on the same subject – *The Small Book of Proof* and *The Great Book of Proof* – advising readers "what to answer the heretics and unbelievers when they ask for a proof of the existence of God".

In her book, *Freethinkers of Medieval Islam*, Sarah Stroumsa writes:

> One would naturally be inclined to infer from these facts that the

> "heretics and unbelievers" intended by al-Qasim were people who denied, or at least questioned, the existence of God, and that al-Qasim was concerned about the persuasive power of such contemporaneous atheists ...
>
> Nevertheless, in the discussions of God's existence the actual opponents are not identified as individuals. As a group, they are sometimes referred to as heretics, unbelievers, materialists, or sceptics. These designations often appear together, and they do not always seem to be clearly distinguished in the authors' mind ...
>
> And yet we can search these texts in vain for a specific contemporaneous individual accused of denying the existence of God ... The atheists themselves always remain faceless and nameless. When a name does appear, it is always that of a person accused of some specific heretical doctrine which, the theologians say, is as bad as atheism or may lead to atheism – never of somebody the core of whose heresy is actually identified as atheism.[1]

Although freethinkers certainly existed in the Islamic world in the Middle Ages, Stroumsa questions whether any of them can accurately be described as atheists. The most plausible explanation is that freethinkers of the time had different priorities. Science had not yet begun to provide alternative ideas about the origins of the universe or the development of species so there was little reason to dispute the existence of a divine Creator (and little evidence with which to do it). At the time, it was far more relevant to dispute the authenticity of prophets and divine revelation – which they certainly did.

The *shahada*, the declaration of faith which all Muslims recite, contains two essential elements: an uncompromising rejection of polytheism ("There is no god but God") and an assertion that "Muhammad is the Messenger of God". Muhammad, though not the only prophet in Islam, is regarded as the last of the prophets, delivering God's final message to humanity. Islam also recognises the prophets of Judaism and Christianity, including Jesus, and the Qur'an says repeatedly that every nation or people has had its own prophet.[2] Muhammad, on the other hand, is not recognised as a prophet by Christians and Jews.

Amid contested claims of prophethood, distinguishing between "true" and "false" prophets by examining their credentials thus became an important matter for those of a religious inclination, and no less so for others who declared that all prophets were false. Stroumsa writes:

In their effort to discredit the notion of prophecy, the freethinkers proceeded in several directions. On the theoretical front, they attempted to show the implausibility of the very notion of prophecy. On the polemical front, they endeavoured to show that throughout history, people who claimed to be prophets were in fact manipulative tricksters and impostors.

Far more than Judaism and Christianity, Islam defines itself around the concept of prophecy and, according to Stroumsa, the appearance of freethinkers who rejected prophecy demonstrates its central position in Islamic thought.

Two notable figures assigned the *mulhid* label in the ninth and tenth centuries were Ibn al-Rawandi and Abu Bakr al-Razi. Both were Persian, though Rawandi spent some time in Baghdad, and both were very different in character. Rawandi seems to have relished being scandalous while Razi was a respected scholar. The twentieth-century Egyptian existentialist philosopher Abd al-Rahman Badawi summarised their views as "anti-prophetic rationalism". Their shared premise, he said, was that reason (or intellect) is sufficient on its own for the knowledge of good and evil, so there is no need for sending divine messengers.[3]

Rawandi reportedly described the Qur'an as "the speech of an unwise being" and is said to have denounced the miracles of Abraham, Jesus and Muhammad as fraudulent tricks. Razi's critiques of prophecy and revelation have been lost but it is known from the titles of his books that he wrote about "impostors of prophecy" and "the refutation of religions". Although Razi's main focus was Islam, he also attacked Christianity, Judaism, Zoroastrianism, and Manicheanism and appears to have argued that God – if He were truly wise – would not have singled out some people as prophets, given them influence over others and then incited their followers to fight each other.

Razi does seem to have believed in a wise and compassionate God but his quarrel was with prophecy and "revealed" religions, and the bigotry and authoritarianism that can result from them. A wise God, in his view, would have gone about things in a different way. Razi is quoted as saying:

The most fitting [behaviour] for the wisdom of the Wise One and the compassion of the Compassionate One [i.e. God] is that He should inspire all His servants with the knowledge of whatever is beneficial or detrimental to them, in this world and the next. He should not set some individuals over others, and there should be between them neither rivalry nor disagreement which would bring them to perdition

> ... The followers of revealed religions have learned their religion by following the authority of their leaders. They reject rational speculation and inquiry about the fundamental doctrines [of religion]. They restrict and forbid it. They transmit traditions in the name of their leaders, which oblige them to refrain from speculation on religious matters, and declare that anyone who contradicts the traditions they transmit must be branded an infidel.[4]

One remarkable freethinker during the Abbasid caliphate was the blind poet Abu al-Ala al-Ma'arri (973-1057CE). "His poems," R A Nicholson writes, "leave no aspect of the age untouched, and present a vivid picture of degeneracy and corruption, in which tyrannous rulers, venal judges, hypocritical and unscrupulous theologians, swindling astrologers, roving swarms of dervishes and godless Carmathians occupy a prominent place."[5]

Ma'arri was a sort of monotheist though his monotheism, as Nicholson notes, seems to have been little more than "a conviction that all things are governed by inexorable Fate, whose mysteries none may fathom and from whose omnipotence there is no escape". Ma'arri was born in Syria, near Aleppo, but his ideas were strongly influenced by spending a year and a half in Baghdad which, despite being the capital of Islam at the time, "thronged with travellers and merchants from all parts of the East, harbouring followers of every creed and sect – Christians and Jews, Buddhists and Zoroastrians, Sabians and Sufis, materialists and rationalists".[6]

Returning to his home town in Syria, Ma'arri adopted an ascetic lifestyle which included vegetarianism and sexual abstinence. Rejecting the idea of resurrection, he regarded death as deliverance from the miseries of life – which led him also to reject marriage and procreation. He is said to have proposed the following epitaph for his grave:

> This wrong was by my father done
> To me, but ne'er by me to one. [7]

Ma'arri's views were clearly heretical, as a few samples of his verses illustrate:

> Hanifs are stumbling, Christians all astray,
> Jews wildered, Magians far on error's way.
> We mortals are composed of two great schools –
> Enlightened knaves or else religious fools.

Here, he mocks the pilgrimage to Mecca where the faithful are required to walk seven times around the *kaaba:*

> Praise God and pray,
> Walk seventy times, not seven, the Temple around
> And impious remain!
> Devout is he alone who, when he may
> Feast his desires, is found
> With courage to abstain.

Elsewhere, he says:

> Falsehood hath so corrupted the world
> The wrangling sects each other's gospel chide.

And ...

> Of all the godly doctrine that I from the pulpit heard
> My heart has never accepted so much as a single word

Negative as this was, Ma'arri also had a more positive side, advocating rationalism and the pursuit of truth as a moral guide:

> Take Reason for thy guide and do what she
> Approves, the best of counsellors in sooth.
> Accept no law the Pentateuch lays down:
> Not there is what thou seekest – the plain truth.

Ma'arri is perhaps fortunate to have lived when he did. Had he been writing today and posting his verses on Facebook he would surely have found himself in trouble – either from the authorities or from enraged Islamists. Besides parodying the Qur'an, he also wrote *Risalat al-Ghufran* ("Letter of Forgiveness") portraying heaven as a kind of Bohemian literary salon. This particular work also gives a clue as to how he deflected critics: it included an attack on freethinkers while expressing a hope that they were not as bad as they appeared. Nicholson comments that Ma'arri, "like so many wise men of the East", practised dissimulation as a fine art:[8]

> I lift my voice to utter lies absurd
> But when I speak the truth, my hushed tones scarce are heard.

Ma'arri ended his days as a highly respected figure, at least in his

Syrian home town. A Persian poet who visited him when he was in his seventies described him as "the chief man in the town, very rich, revered by the inhabitants and surrounded by more than two hundred students who came from all parts to attend his lectures on literature and poetry."[9]

A near-contemporary of Ma'arri was Omar Khayyam, the astronomer and mathematician, born in 1048. Khayyam was of Persian rather than Arab ethnicity but his name is as well-known in the Arab countries as it is in the west and he is often cited by Arab atheists. Though noted as a scientist during his lifetime, today he is mostly associated with the *Rubaiyat*, a collection verses that celebrate the pleasures of wine and sometimes mock religious belief:

> Look not above, there is no answer there;
> Pray not, for no one listens to your prayer;
> Near is as near to God as any Far,
> And Here is just the same deceit as There.
>
> * * *
>
> And do you think that unto such as you;
> A maggot-minded, starved, fanatic crew:
> God gave the secret, and denied it me?
> Well, well, what matters it! Believe that, too.
>
> * * *
>
> Did God set grapes a-growing, do you think,
> And at the same time make it sin to drink?
> Give thanks to Him who foreordained it thus –
> Surely He loves to hear the glasses clink![10]

Because of irreverent verses such as these, Omar Khayyam has acquired the reputation (probably wrongly) of being an atheist. He thus became one of 45 "non-believers" – ranging from the Roman poet Lucretius to the present-day activist Ayaan Hirsi Ali – featured by the late Christopher Hitchens in his book, *The Portable Atheist*. Hitchens said of him: "Khayyam clearly doubted that god had revealed himself to some men and not to others, especially in light of the very obvious fact that those who claimed to interpret the revelation were fond of using their claim in order to acquire and wield power over others in this world. He was not the first to notice this aspect of religion, but he was among the wittiest."[11]

There are several problems, however. Khayyam's actual

religious views are a matter of considerable scholarly dispute: some regard him as a mystic or a Sufi rather than an atheist. It is also unclear how many – if any – of the famous quatrains (four-line stanzas) in the *Rubaiyat* were really the work of Khayyam. In his book, *In Search of Omar Khayyam,* Ali Dashti explained:

> The inescapable facts are: that contemporary writers who knew Khayyam do not speak of him as a poet and certainly quote none of his verse; that during the two centuries following his death a small number of quatrains begin to make their appearance in a variety of biographical, theological and historical works, to a total of some sixty by the middle of the fourteenth century; and that thereafter the figures increase steadily until by the seventeenth century we find ourselves confronted with collections ranging from 500 to 1,000, many of which can be instantly dismissed on linguistic and other grounds.[12]

The celebrated nineteenth-century English "translation" of the *Rubaiyat* by Edward Fitzgerald also needs to be treated with caution. Taking the Persian verses as inspiration, Fitzgerald reorganised them to create an imaginary day in Khayyam's life in order to compose what Dashti described as "an entirely independent masterpiece". In the process, Fitzgerald employed free translation and paraphrase, to the extent that it is difficult to identify the Persian source for some of his lines.

Regardless of who wrote the original verses, though, they are still of historical interest since they undoubtedly reflect ideas that were in circulation and regarded as legitimate poetic themes at the time. That is not necessarily the case today. In 2013, Fazil Say, a renowned Turkish composer and pianist who is also an atheist, was given a suspended jail sentence after being convicted of blasphemy and "inciting hatred" in a series of tweets which included lines attributed to Omar Khayyam:[13]

> You say rivers of wine flow in heaven, is heaven a tavern to you?
> You say two *huris* [companions] await each believer there, is heaven a brothel to you?

FORMS of *ilhad* that were more clearly recognisable as atheism began to emerge in the Islamic world in the nineteenth century. Samuli Schielke writes:

> From the late nineteenth and early twentieth centuries on, a new wave of anti-religious dissent, this time explicitly including atheism, has

gained currency in different parts of the Islamic world. While early Islamic *ilhad* grew in the heartlands of a thriving empire, the second coming of *ilhad*/atheism in the Islamic world took place under the very different conditions of European imperial expansion that cast serious doubts upon established traditions of knowledge, social organisation, and religion.

First freethinking and anticlerical circles emerged in Iran, India, the Ottoman Empire, and among Muslims in Russia during the second half of the nineteenth century – notably carried by both Christian and Muslim Arabs in the Arab provinces of the Ottoman Empire. In this time, tendencies of anti-clerical and anti-religious nationalism emerged within the wider framework of secularist modernism.[14]

Although much of this can be attributed to foreign influences during the colonial period, Schielke cites evidence from nineteenth-century Iran to suggest that "contemporary Muslim atheism is not simply an adaptation of western atheism, but also draws upon indigenous heretic traditions".

The most notorious Egyptian atheist of the 1930s was Ismail Adham, a writer and literary critic from Alexandria. In 1936 he wrote a book disputing the authenticity and the historical reliability of the *hadith* (the reported sayings and deeds of the Prophet) and sent a hundred free copies to the religious scholars at al-Azhar, the ancient centre of Islamic learning in Cairo. This infuriated the Rector of al-Azhar, Muhammad Mustafa al-Maraghi, who complained to the interior ministry and within a few days Adham's book was banned. A year later Adham produced an even more contentious work, *Limadha ana Mulhid?* ("Why am I an Atheist?") which generated some heated responses from religious believers.

Quoting Adham's polemic, Schielke says it was exemplary in the way he presented science (physics, mathematics, and evolution theory in particular) as the new faith that replaces religious belief:

> I left religions, and abandoned all [religious] beliefs, and put my faith in science and scientific logic alone. To my great surprise and amazement, I found myself happier and more confident than I had been when I had struggled with myself in the attempt to maintain my religious belief.

It emerged later, though, that Adham was not only an atheist but something of a fantasist. Perhaps fearing that his work would not be taken seriously without heavyweight academic qualifications, he had assembled an impressive but fictitious list of credentials which appeared on the cover of one of his books when he was still only 25 years old:

> D.Litt. (Hon), Ph.D., Sc.D. (Moscow), Vice-President of the Russian Soviet Institute for Islamic Studies, Member of the Russian Soviet Academy for Science, formerly Professor of High Mathematics, University of St. Petersburg, Professor of Islamic History at the College of History, Stamboul.

Adham also claimed to have written a biography of the Prophet (in German), a three-volume history of Islam (in Turkish), two volumes on mathematics and physics (in German and Russian) and three volumes on the theory of relativity (also in German and Russian).[15] It was not until 1972 that the reality of these claims became clear when an article for the *Journal of Arabic Literature* revealed:

> Adham never got any doctorate, never became a member of the Academy of Sciences, never published one book or article in either Russian, French or German, never wrote his two-volume work in Turkish, entitled *Islam Tarihi*, never made friends with the Russian Orientalist Barthold, who had already died in 1930, one year before Adham claims to have gone to Russia, and never met with favourable criticism from the Russian Orientalist Kazimirsky, because there was no such person ...[16]

It has been suggested that Adham may never have travelled beyond Egypt. In 1940, at the age of 29, he was found dead in the sea off Gleem Beach in Alexandria with a suicide note pinned inside his pocket.

Abd al-Rahman Badawi (1917-2002), an Egyptian who also taught at universities in Libya and Kuwait, is regarded as the first existentialist Arab philosopher and is particularly remembered for his book, *Min Tarikh al-Ihlad fi al-Islam* ("A History of Atheism in Islam"), which was written in the 1940s and is still read today. Badawi's views were complex, however, and in his later years he defended both the Qur'an and the Prophet Muhammed against attacks by Orientalists.[17]

Abdullah al-Qasimi (1907-1996) has been described – rather inappropriately – as the "godfather" of Gulf atheism and one of his most famous statements, that "the occupation of our brains by gods is the worst form of occupation," is still quoted by Arab atheists today. Born into a conservative family in the Nejd region of what is now Saudi Arabia, Qasimi started off as a fairly typical – and by some accounts excellent – Saudi religious scholar before turning to atheism. During his religious phase he was even likened to Ibn Taymiyyah, the thirteenth-century theologian who is much admired by Islamists, and at one point he was expelled from al-Azhar University in Cairo for his Salafist views.[18]

A note posted on the Islamic Awakening website by someone who is clearly not an admirer describes Qasimi's loss of faith:

> He jumped into books of philosophy and a few years later, wrote some weird modernist books. When the Saudi shuyukh tried to shut him up, he complained to Sheikh Sayyid Qutb [a leader of the Muslim Brotherhood who was executed by Nasser in 1966]. Qutb at first defended Qasimi's right to speak, but when Qasimi sent Qutb a copy of his (Qasimi's) new books and articles, Qutb freaked and accused Qasimi – rightfully – of trying to destroy Islam.
>
> Qasimi bailed and I know at least one of his sons apostated with him, and he lived in Egypt. He tried to form an atheist political movement there, but Gamal Abdel Nasser found it to be too far and Qasimi was jailed, more than once I believe.
>
> He spent some time in Lebanon where he was involved with the Literary Society and they treated him like a VIP. Eventually, Sheikh Ibn Aqil al-Zahiri who himself is/was a man of many specialties met Qasimi in Garden City [in Cairo]. They argued back and forth into the night ...
>
> Basically, Qasimi was verbally copy-pasting from Immanuel Kant and John Stuart Mill, and when Sheikh Ibn Aqil would quote the *kuffar*'s own secular philosophers ripping those guys up, Qasimi would just change the subject. Basically he would make accusations regarding the existence of Allah based verbatim on the books of Enlightenment and post-Enlightenment philosophers, and any time Sheikh Ibn Aqil brought the hammer down on him Qasimi would just look for another topic where he could possibly make a point.

The writer adds:

> He was an arrogant beast the entire time and unrepentant to the very end. He died from cancer in Cairo in a death which one hopes was long and slow.[19]

WHILE it's worth noting the existence of atheist writers like Qasimi and Adham who were able to express their views in print, Arab debate about religion from the mid-nineteenth century onwards has generally been less concerned with the existence of God than with questions about the role of religion in society and politics. To understand the reasons for this it is necessary to look at the historical background – the decline of the Ottoman Empire, European domination, the rise of nationalism and eventual independence. Europe, in particular, became a source of both wonderment and alarm: it was seen "not only as an adversary but also as a challenge, and in some ways an attractive one," historian Albert Hourani writes.

> The power and greatness of Europe, modern science and technology, the political institutions of the European states, and the social morality of modern societies were all favourite themes [of Arab writers]. Such writing raised a fundamental problem: how could Arab Muslims, and how could the Ottoman Muslim state, acquire the strength to confront Europe and become part of the modern world?"[20]

Some of the earliest attempts to answer these questions have a familiar ring, even today. For example, the Tunisian reformist Khayr al-Din, who died in 1889, warned Muslims against rejecting "what is praiseworthy" in other religions "simply because they have the idea fixed in their minds that all the acts and institutions of those who are not Muslims should be avoided".[21] To a lesser extent, Arab Christians in Lebanon and Syria faced challenges from Europe too:

> The power of the hierarchies of the churches, recognised and supported by the state, could be an obstacle to their thinking and expressing themselves as they please. Some of them moved in the direction of secularism, or of Protestantism, which was as near as they could go to secularism in a society where identity was expressed in terms of membership of a religious community". [22]

Among Muslims, opinion was divided between those who saw Islam as part of the problem, thus seeking to diminish its role, and others who sought to rejuvenate it and make it part of the solution. In the latter camp, two prominent figures of the nineteenth century were Jamal Eddin al-Afghani (1839-97) and Muhammad Abdu (1849-1905).

Afghani, who was probably of Persian origin, tried to resolve the question of how Muslims could live in the modern world while remaining true to themselves, and did so by proposing what Halim Barakat describes as "two seemingly contradictory courses of action: a return to the original sources of Islam and the adoption of liberal European ideas and institutions, including western sciences, constitutional rule, communal unity, elections, and national representation".[23] Despite his enthusiasm for science, however, he was highly critical of Darwinism. Afghani's protégé, Muhammad Abdu, developed his ideas further, seeking to draw a distinction between the fundamental tenets of Islam, which he saw as constant and unchanging, and Muslim laws and customs which could be adapted (within limits) to changing circumstances.

The same period also brought the first murmurings of Arab nationalism, initially in response to the decline of the Ottoman Empire but later, increasingly, in opposition to western imperialism. Besides encouraging a heightened sense of Arab (as opposed to Muslim) identity, nationalism inevitably raised questions about possible forms of self-government, including the question of what part – if any – religion should play in that.

Abd al-Rahman al-Kawakibi (1849-1902) was one of the first Arabs of modern times to argue for a separation of the state from religion, advocating secular, nationalist government based on the principles of democracy, socialism, scientific thinking and tolerance. He viewed socialism as the way to overcome despotism and accused religious traditionalists of attempting "to reinforce their authority over the simple-minded believers" by using religion as "an instrument of disunity" for the purpose of spreading the "spirit of submissiveness and compliance."[24]

In 1924, Mustafa Kemal Atatürk, the fiercely secularist founder of modern Turkey formally abolished the Islamic caliphate. Established in the first few days after the death of the Prophet, the caliphate had survived in various forms and locations before being claimed in the sixteenth century by the Ottoman sultans. Its abolition by Atatürk prompted moves to revive it elsewhere, though there were some who thought Muslims were better off without it. In 1925, Ali Abd al-Raziq, an Egyptian sheikh at al-Azhar, caused controversy with his book, *Islam and the Bases of Authority,* arguing that Islam did not prescribe any particular form of government and Muslims were therefore free to create their own systems. The caliphs, he said, were wrongly assumed to have been God's representatives on Earth when in fact they were nothing more than political rulers. It was because of this mistaken belief that they had been allowed to tyrannise their subjects in the name of religion. For his efforts, Abd al-Raziq was duly expelled from al-Azhar.

Given this background, it is hardly surprising that debates about religion tended to centre on issues that were of immediate practical relevance rather than more abstract questions about the existence of God. The twentieth century produced numerous Arab thinkers who clearly leaned towards secularism, including such writers as Taha Hussein and the Nobel laureate Naguib Mahfouz. How many of them were fully-fledged atheists (in private if not in public) is a matter for conjecture.[25]

Marxism had a significant following among Arabs in the decades immediately after the Second World War and was accompanied by secularist ideas which were later overshadowed by the rise of political Islam. Even if people at the time tended to express their atheism obliquely rather than directly – in discussions of existentialism, for example – the atmosphere during the heyday of Arab leftism was certainly more conducive to religious scepticism than it has been in more recent times. Badra, a Lebanese agnostic and feminist, recalls cases in Lebanon and Syria where "atheism was lived not in isolation but in communities". She continued:

> I was not personally part of these groups but I had friends who were. When I moved to Beirut, I discovered a whole parallel world with a generation of people from this background. They grew up within leftist youth groups and were raised on these values, especially among what was called the Lebanese Nationalist Movement (Haraka Wataniyah) which gathered the Socialist Party of Kamal Jumblatt, the Syrian Social Nationalist Party and the Communists.
>
> In addition, even if atheism was not dealt with as a subject on its own, the intellectuals who were active during the civil war period were secular and provocative towards religion on many occasions. Beirut's cultural life, particularly the experimental theatre in the 1960s and then during the civil war, which had cultural influence on the other Arab countries at that time, is full of examples and references to existentialism, absurdism, etc. The Lebanese literature of the civil war portrays a lot of atheistic views. [26]

The 1950s and 1960s, Schielke writes, were a time of great optimism "vested in a progressive socialist future when religiosity was seen to be in retreat among highly-educated urban populations of the Middle East and South Asia" – though that was to change later with the growth of Islamist movements in the region and the collapse of communism in Eastern Europe. Schielke is somewhat dismissive of the Marxists' efforts to confront religion, however. Atheistic or non-religious views, if expressed at all, tended to take the form of "condescending vanguardism rather than the fierce anti-clericalism of the early twentieth century". On the whole, communists and socialists in Muslim countries rarely promoted atheism in public, he says. "On the contrary, they have usually tried to counter anti-communist propaganda by arguing that Islam, when properly understood, is perfectly in accordance with socialism." This might seem a tactical position to avoid confronting religion directly but Schielke suggests it was actually congruent with the beliefs of most communists in the Muslim world.[27]

The only historical example of Marxist-Leninist rule in the Middle East was the People's Democratic Republic of Yemen (PDRY), established in the south of the country after the British withdrew from Aden in 1967. Aspiring to build a "rational, socialist" society in the ancestral homeland of the Bin Laden family, the new government found itself grappling with the question of how to deal with Islam. An initial – sometimes violent – crackdown on the religious establishment was followed by nationalisation of the *awqaf* (religious trusts) and making the clerics employees of the state.

While maintaining control over religious institutions the regime eventually developed a more sophisticated approach, apparently acting on advice from the Soviet bloc. The Central Committee of East Germany's Socialist Unity Party reportedly told them:

> Religion is being used as a weapon against you. Why don't you use the same weapon against your enemies? Why are you relinquishing the initiative to the reactionaries and opportunists? Why shouldn't the progressives have the initiative?
> Why don't you say: "We are against exploitative capitalism" and say at the same time: "Our master Muhammad was against exploitative capitalism"? No *faqih* or *qadi* will be able at all to find any Qur'anic verse or *hadith* to prove that Muhammad was in favour of exploitative capitalism since he was, in fact, against exploitation.[28]

This led to the PDRY government promoting a socialist brand of Islam in which Lenin's birthday could be celebrated along with more traditional religious festivals. In the regime's official view, there was no real contradiction between socialism and Islam – though it seems that not everyone in South Yemen agreed. According to Salim Salih Mohammed, a senior figure in the party, there was one Islam for the rich and another for the poor. For the poor, Islam favoured social justice and an end to exploitation while the rich used it "for their own reactionary goals and to counter the benefits and striving of the people".[29] This also provided the basis for a foreign policy in which Islam was portrayed as being threatened by imperialism (despite the fact that in 1979 South Yemen was the only Arab country to support the Soviet invasion of Afghanistan and continued for some time afterwards to back the Kabul regime against the *mujahidin*).

There were some parallels between South Yemen's brand of socialist Islam and the Roman Catholic "liberation theology" movement that had emerged in Latin America focusing on poverty and social injustice – which the Vatican regarded as too political and insufficiently spiritual. In a study of the uneasy coexistence between Islam and the state in the People's Democratic Republic, Norman Cigar comments that the Yemeni socialists treated Islam "exclusively as a socio-economic phenomenon concerned only with this world" while ignoring or sidelining other aspects of the faith.[30]

Domestically, the socialists chipped away at religion's role in everyday life – if and when it seemed feasible. Sharia law was replaced by secular laws in most areas, including family law, but the regime held back from abolishing the sharia-based inheritance system. Reform of inheritance might have been considered a priority for socialists, since it contributed to inequalities in wealth, but there seem to have been fears that the public would not accept it.

South Yemen's newspapers were the only ones among the Arab countries not to publish daily prayer times or fasting times during Ramadan. Fasting during Ramadan was tolerated, but rather grudgingly. State TV pointedly broadcast cookery programmes at times when Muslims were supposed to be fasting, and there were frequent grumbles about people absenting themselves from work during Ramadan:

> The state-run media has been consistently critical of the fact that employees in the state sector come in to work late, tired from having stayed up the night before, and do little work before leaving early for home. Many, in fact, apparently feign illness to avoid coming in to work at all.[31]

Writing in 1990, shortly before the unification of north and south Yemen brought Marxist rule to an end, Cigar noted:

> Despite the state's efforts to inculcate a Marxist belief system, the bulk of the PDRY's population apparently is still deeply attached to Islam in its traditional expression ... There are strong indications, however, that the general population has not been mobilised around the regime ... Even the country's leadership has acknowledged this continuing legitimacy gap.
>
> For example, in a recent speech, Ali Salim al-Baid, the Secretary-General of the YSP [Yemen Socialist Party], complained about his countrymen's "backward mentality", and claimed that "the shaykhs have gone, the Sultans have gone, feudalism has gone, but their mentality and culture remain".

Al-Baid was not immune to the influence of that mentality himself. In 1979 and 1980 he had been suspended from all party activities for exercising his Islamic right to marry a second wife.[32]

FOLLOWING the 1967 war with Israel in which Arab forces suffered a humiliating defeat, Arab nationalism went into decline – along with the secularist ideas that had often accompanied it. Inevitably, some saw military defeat as a punishment from God, wreaked upon Muslims for deviating from the righteous path. Salah al-Din al-Munajjid, a Syrian-born scholar who eventually settled in Saudi Arabia, wrote *The Pillars of the Catastrophe or the Reasons Behind the Defeat of 1967*, arguing that Arabs had lost the war because they "gave up their faith in God, so He gave up on them".[33] The titles of Munajjid's other political writings show his general perspective: they included *The Bolshevisation of Islam* and *The Socialist Delusion*.

Meanwhile, Constantin Zurayk – also Syrian-born – offered a different explanation for the Arabs' defeat. In the 1950s Zurayk had published *The Meaning of the Catastrophe,* about the expulsion of Palestinians from their homes during the establishment of Israel. After the 1967 war he produced another volume, *The Meaning of the Catastrophe Revisited,* which mainly blamed the more recent defeat on stagnation in Arab society. Arabs, he said, needed to move "from an emotional, illusionary, mythological and poetic society into a practical achievement-oriented, rational and scientific one."[34] Zurayk, interestingly, came from an Orthodox Christian family but saw a positive role for Islam and its cultural heritage in Arab nationalism – so long as the "true nature" of Islam was understood. History, he argued, had shown that Arab civilisation flourished when Islam flourished but it waned when Arabs followed religion blindly.

Although 1967 can be regarded as the point when the tide turned against secular nationalism, it was not until the Iranian revolution of 1979 that political Islam began to emerge as a major force in the Arab countries. The 1967 war, however, had helped to prepare the way. Viewing defeat as divine punishment had a certain popular appeal, since it absolved Arabs of the need to do anything beyond clinging more firmly to religion – and in that respect its effects were debilitating rather than empowering.

The Islamic revival of the late twentieth century was a far cry from what reformers had envisaged a hundred years earlier when they advocated borrowing "praiseworthy" ideas from other faiths and cultures. What emerged instead was a backward-looking version of Islam which rejects "innovation" and "alien" ideas in the name of authenticity while constructing a supposedly Islamic identity that is based, at least in part, on an imagined past. One aspect of this is an insistence on strict interpretations of sharia law; another is a highly visible kind of religiosity where believers are expected to show "good" Muslim behaviour by observing prescribed rules. The stricter the rules become, the more likely they are to provide a distinct sense of Islamic identity and the more those who observe them are likely to feel they are behaving as good Muslims.

Rules can be found on numerous Islamic websites, including *Muttaqun Online* ("for those who fear Allah") which provides detailed guidance on "lawful" clothing for men. Men's clothes, it says, should cover the whole body but not reach below the ankles, and must not be tight-fitting. White and green are good colours for men to wear but red is bad unless mixed with another colour, and you must not tuck your shirt inside your trousers.[35] In 2006, an amusing controversy broke out in Egypt when Dr Rashad Khalil, an expert on Islamic law at al-Azhar, warned that being completely naked during sexual intercourse invalidates a marriage. His ruling was promptly dismissed by other scholars, including one who argued that "anything that can bring spouses closer to each other" should be permitted. Another religious scholar suggested it was permissible for married couples to see each other naked as long as they did not look at the genitals. To avoid problems in that area, he recommended having sex under a blanket. One of the most absurd examples of religious rule-making occurred in Iraq in 2008 when militants sought to impose "gender" segregation of vegetables. Claiming that tomatoes are feminine and cucumbers masculine, they argued that greengrocers should not place them next to each other, and that women should not buy or handle cucumbers.[36]

It's scarcely surprising if attitudes like these drive people away from Islam but some view them as a reason for staying within the faith – nominally, at least – in order to challenge them more effectively. The logic is that criticisms are more likely to be listened to if they come from Muslim "reformers", "progressive" Muslims or believing secularists than from those who reject Islam completely. This is not to suggest that reformers, secularists, etc, are necessarily insincere but there do seem to be some among them who could be described as "tactical" believers; how many is impossible to know.

In an article on "New Secularism in the Arab World", published in 1999, Ghassan Abdullah surveyed the work of a score of "secular" thinkers. Significantly, though, none of them was described in the article as an atheist. Asked about this, Abdullah replied that he thought a high proportion of them were in fact atheists, or at least did not subscribe to the idea of a God in the sky. Several of them had said so privately, he added. "Writing critically about religion in the Arab world is not easy or safe," he continued, but "as readers of rationalists in Arabic, we develop a sense of what such writers mean when they use certain ways of expressing their thoughts, and can guess their positions that they cannot declare openly".[37]

One of those mentioned in Abdullah's article was Muhammad Shahrour, a Syrian professor of engineering who in 1990 published a book analysing the text of the Qur'an. Twenty years of research had led him to conclude that traditional religious scholarship is unscientific. Essentially, Shahrour adopted an anti-Islamist position, seeking to reconcile Islam with modern philosophy as well as the rational view of the world and science. His view of the sharia was that "jurisprudence in the name of God is a farce benefiting only those wanting to maintain political power".[38] Despite his many criticisms of Islam as currently practised, he was still reluctant to dismiss religion entirely. His acceptance of it, however, looked more like a case of bowing to political reality than bowing to God:

> I consider that, since religion has an important normative role in the Middle Eastern societies, it is impossible to ignore it. Liberals tried to do so, and they failed in their attempt to transport western political formula to the Arab/Muslim states. Marxists wanted to impose a secularisation, to deconstruct religion, and also failed.[39]

The website of the Deen Research Center, which describes itself as a "modern Islamic thinktank", is another example. Rather than dismissing Islam, it says its aim is "to refresh and expand our vision of the Qur'an, to clear up misunderstandings and to understand its neglected potentials and messages".[40] While the Qur'an is quoted frequently and sympathetically, the website uses it to make a case for something very different from the way Islam is usually interpreted today:

> We believe the Qur'an rejects all forms of superstition, blind worship, discrimination, oppression, aggression, autocracy, theocracy, oppressive tradition and anti-scientism. We believe the Qur'an presents and supports a non-dogmatic, scientific, universal democratic socio-economic framework in which mankind is guided to solve their problems pertaining to war, oppression, hunger, racism, discrimination, backwardness and crime that has been present among mankind since it formed its first civilisations.

The website also stops just short of outright atheism by re-defining God:

> We do not believe in a god as seen by the mainstream within the religions. We believe in a god, or rather a force that is beyond comprehension, has no form or position, nor has any personal gains in the results of the universe but also does not play with humans as a despotic king or a dictator. We do not believe in ideas of salvational worship or the supernatural. The universe will have endless surprises for humanity, but it is part of one creation. Only God is the complete Other, the one beyond creation.[41]

Progressive versions of Islam have several typical characteristics. The most important of these is that they view the Qur'an historically, arguing that rules which applied in the time of the Prophet can (and should) be reinterpreted today in the light of changing circumstances. This is the opposite of the Islamist view that the Qur'an should be read literally and ahistorically, and that its message is unchanging and applicable to all times and places. Progressive Muslims also tend to reject the authority of the *hadith* – collections of sayings and deeds attributed to the Prophet which have formed the basis for much extra-Qur'anic rule-making over the centuries. In addition to that, they usually reject sharia in the form it is traditionally practised and favour a secular state.

Among non-believers interviewed for this book, opinions differed as to whether Islam can be reformed. A few thought, or at least hoped, it could. Gamal, an Egyptian atheist, said reform was "very possible" but he was "not convinced of this idea that there are moderate versions and radical versions within Islam". Rather, he thought it was a case of various preachers presenting religion in a variety of ways "in order to accommodate the concerns or fears of certain segments of society".[42] Badra, a feminist from Lebanon, said "I don't believe in more liberal Islam. There are new movements referring to Islamic feminism, but I don't believe in that. Maybe this goes back to my first contact with the Qur'anic text, which was not positive. I do not think that you can be both a good Muslim (or – to a lesser extent – a good Christian) and a feminist."[43] Ahmad Saeed, a Yemeni, said he had been "a very progressive Muslim" before leaving Islam but he is now more sceptical about the prospects: "I used to think Islam has faults and that we should reform the religion and update it and try to be more human and civilised, but it doesn't work on many Muslims. They have been brainwashed way too much. I think education is the solution. If we give Muslims a very strong, extensive education, in the future they are going to figure out that we have to be humans before we have to be Muslims."[44]

In a magazine interview, Moroccan atheist Kacem El Ghazzali was asked if he thought Islam could be reformed, as has happened in branches of Christianity. He replied:

> In my opinion, there can be no reform or Enlightenment in Sunni or Shia Islam because there is no Church to reform. In Islam, we are subject to the power of a sacred book and the instructions it gives. Our identity and our understanding of ourselves come from the Qur'an. If Muslims could use their reason, without instructions from a book that is recognised as the word of God, then we could talk about Enlightenment.[45]

The Qur'an is the point where atheists and Muslim reformers part company. While they share a common goal in seeking secularism, the reformers largely derive their secularist arguments from the text of the Qur'an. Much as they may try to re-interpret it for the modern world, the Qur'an is still the authority they ultimately have to rely upon to make their case. And on that, atheists beg to differ.

NOTES

1. Stroumsa, Sarah: Freethinkers of Medieval Islam. Leiden, Brill: 1999
2. See, for example, Qur'an 16:36: "We have raised in every nation a messenger" and 35:24: "There is not a nation but a warner hath passed among them."
3. Quoted by Samuli Schielke, "The Islamic World", chapter in The Oxford Handbook of Athiesm. Oxford: Oxford University Press, 2013
4. Stroumsa, op cit, pp 95-96
5. Nicholson, R A: A Literary History of the Arabs. Cambridge: Cambridge University Press, 1985. p 324.
6. Nicholson: op cit, p 314.
7. Nicholson: op cit, p 317.
8. Nicholson: op cit, p 319.
9. Nicholson: op cit, pp 323-324.
10. Richard Le Galliene's translation. https://archive.org/details/RubaiyatOfOmarKhayyam_263
11. Hitchens, Christopher: The Portable Atheist: Essential Readings for the Non-Believer. Philadelphia: Da Capo Press, 2007. p7.
12. Dashti, Ali: In Search of Omar Khayyam. Abingdon, Oxon: Routledge, 2011. p14. Dashti was an Iranian rationalist, journalist and senator who died in 1982. His book was originally published in Persian.
13. Letsch, Constanze "Turkish composer and pianist convicted of blasphemy on Twitter." The Guardian, 16 April 2013. http://www.theguardian.com/world/2013/apr/15/turkish-composer-fazil-say-convicted-blasphemhy
14. Schielke, op cit
15. Garnett, Joy: "Edham the atheist." http://newsgrist.typepad.com/joygarnett/2013/11/edham-the-atheist.html
16. Juynboll, G H A: "Ismail Ahmad Adham (1911-1940), the Atheist." Journal of Arabic Literature. 3: 1972, pp 54-71. Cited by Garnett, op. cit.
17. "Abdul-Rahman Badawi." Philosophers of the Arabs website, undated. http://www.arabphilosophers.com/English/philosophers/modern/modern-names/eAbdul_Rahman_Badawi.htm
18. Qassemi, Sultan Sooud al-: "Gulf atheism in the age of social media". Al-Monitor, 3 March 2014. http://www.al-monitor.com/pulse/originals/2014/03/gulf-atheism-uae-islam-religion.html
19. http://forums.islamicawakening.com/f17/abdullah-al-qasimi-64655/
20. Hourani, Albert: A History of the Arab Peoples. London: Faber and Faber, 1991. p 306

21. Hourani, op cit, p 306.
22. Hourani, op cit, p 307.
23. Hourani, op cit, pp 243-244.
24. Barakat, Halim: The Arab World: Society, Culture and State. Los Angeles: University of California Press, 1993, p 249
25. The Philosophers of the Arabs website describes some of them and outlines their views. http://www.arabphilosophers.com/English/philosophers/modern/modern.htm
26. Email correspondence with the author, July 2014.
27. Schielke, op cit
28. Quoted by Norman Cigar: "Islam and the state in South Yemen: the uneasy coexistence." Middle Eastern Studies, Volume 26, Issue 2, 1990
29. Quoted by Cigar, op cit
30. Somalia, on the Horn of Africa but technically an Arab country since it joined the Arab League in 1974, also had a period of Marxist rule which attempted to blend scientific socialism with Islamic tenets.
31. Cigar, op cit
32. Manea, Elham The Arab State and Women's Rights. New York: Routledge, 2011
33. Barakat, op cit, p 258
34. Barakat, op cit, p 257
35. Mutaqqun Online: 'Male hijab according to Qur'an and Sunnah'. http://www.muttaqun.com/malehijab.html.
36. "Al-Qa'eda in Iraq alienated by cucumber laws and brutality." Daily Telegraph, 11 Aug 2008. http://www.telegraph.co.uk/news/worldnews/middleeast/iraq/2538545/Al-Qaeda-in-Iraq-alienated-by-cucumber-laws-and-brutality.html. Impositions such as this were said to be a major reason for al-Qa'ida's declining support among Iraqi Sunnis.
37. Author's email correspondence with Ghassan Abdullah, April 2014.
38. Mudhoon, Loay: "In the Footsteps of Averroes." Qantara website, 2009. http://en.qantara.de/content/the-reformist-islamic-thinker-muhammad-shahrur-in-the-footsteps-of-averroes. See also Muhammad Sharour: "The Divine Text and Pluralism in Muslim Societies." Chapter in Mehran Kamrava (ed): The New Voices of Islam. University of California Press, 2007.
39. Shahrour, Muhammad: "A New Approach." Undated article on Deen Research Center website. http://www.deenresearchcenter.com/LinkClick.aspx?fileticket=ZYQFChaoOxY%3D&tabid=97&mid=706
40. Deen Research Center. http://www.deenresearchcenter.com/Home/tabid/36/Default.aspx
41. Deen Research Center. http://www.deenresearchcenter.com/DRC/AboutDRC/tabid/54/Default

.aspx
42. Author's interview, April 2014. Gamal is a pseudonym.
43. Author's interview, April 2014.
44. Author's interview, April 2014. Ahmad Saeed is a pseudonym.
45. "L'islam peut-il être réformé?" Poste de Veille website, 12 March 2013. http://www.postedeveille.ca/2013/03/l-islam-peut-il-etre-reforme-kacem-ghazzali.html. The interview was originally published in German by Die Zeit.

3: God's own book

IN ORDER to attract followers, religions need some way of demonstrating their divine credentials. Christianity has traditionally relied on the stories of miracles performed by Jesus – turning water into wine, casting out demons, healing the sick with his touch, etc – culminating in his own resurrection from the dead. Such stories are inherently implausible, leading many to conclude that they never actually happened or are not to be taken literally. But for those who can be persuaded that they *did* happen, implausibility is their strength: the fact that ordinary mortals can't perform miracles points to the conclusion that they must be the work of God.

Islam's credentials also rely on the supernatural, though not quite in the same way. Unlike Jesus, who is claimed to be the son of God, the Prophet Muhammad is regarded as an ordinary human, though one "chosen" by God. He died a normal death and did not come back to life three days later. Although he has been linked to some miraculous events these are relatively few and not particularly central to the Muslim faith. On one occasion, Muhammad is said to have travelled from Mecca to Jerusalem and back (a round trip of more than 1,500 miles), plus an excursion from Jerusalem to heaven – all in a single night.[1] There is also a story that when the Prophet was asked to provide a sign from God he pointed at the moon which was seen to be split into two parts. Both these tales have been much elaborated by Islamic tradition, though the Qur'an refers to them in just a few words and without detail:

- Glory to (Allah) Who did take His servant for a journey by night from the Sacred Mosque to the farthest mosque, whose precincts We did bless.[2]
- The hour drew nigh and the moon was rent in twain.[3]

In the eyes of Muslims, though, the most important miracle of Islam is the Qur'an itself, and in that respect Islam differs significantly from Christianity. While Christians often describe the Bible as "the word of God" and regard it as divinely inspired, they do not claim God was the author – it is a collection of writings from human sources. The Qur'an, on the other hand, is said to be the direct word of God, delivered to the Prophet Muhammad via the angel Gabriel (*Jibril* in Arabic). This claim is the essence of Islam, since without it the faith would not exist. Consequently, it is the claim that Muslims are most eager to assert and that sceptics are most eager to discredit.

In their effort to demonstrate a divine origin of the Qur'an, Muslims employ a number of arguments. These focus on Muhammad's trustworthiness, the Qur'an's uniqueness of language and literary style; the accurate preservation of its text over the centuries, and internal evidence from its content such as foreknowledge of events and scientific discoveries.

Examining these in turn, the first argument seeks to establish that Muhammad was a person of integrity and sincere in his belief that the Qur'an was a message from God. In the words of Sheikh Muhammad Salih al-Munajid (a government-employed cleric in Saudi Arabia):

> Allah chose him even though he had grown up as an orphan and was illiterate, knowing neither how to read or write. All good qualities and virtues were perfected in him, to the point of ultimate perfection. All these good qualities were combined and firmly established in him, something which no one else can attain except the Prophets whom Allah protected and guided.
>
> This combination of perfect qualities is one of the greatest proofs of the truth of his Prophethood (peace and blessings of Allah be upon him).[4]

Muhammad's apparent lack of education is also cited by the US-based Institute of Islamic Information and Education as evidence that he could not have concocted the Qur'an by himself:

The fact that Muhammad could neither read nor write is well known and uncontested by even his non-Muslim contemporaries and present day historians. He had no schooling or teacher of any kind. He had never been known to compose oral poetry or prose.
The Qur'an, with its all-embracing laws and freedom from all inconsistencies, has its greatness acknowledged even by non-Muslim scholars. Its contents treat social, economic, political and religious legislation, history, views of the universe, living things, thought, human transactions, war, peace, marriage, worship, business, and everything relating to life – with no contradicting principles.[5]

Having thus ruled out Muhammad himself as the author of the Qur'an, the institute then goes on to consider other possible authors – Arabs, non-Arabs, even Satan – and by a process of elimination concludes that the real author must have been God.

Claiming divine authorship of a book is not without its hazards, however, since a literary work produced by God cannot afford to be anything less than perfect. Describing the Qur'an as "the greatest sign" from God, Sheikh Munajid says it "contains in its pages miracles of both style and content, which all of mankind cannot match or imitate". The Qur'an's literary style – delivered in the local Quraishi dialect of Arabic – lies somewhere between prose and poetry, constructed in a way that makes it easy to memorise, and few would dispute its eloquence. Muhammad Marmaduke Pickthall, a British convert to Islam who in 1930 published one of the best-known translations of the Qur'an, described its language as an "inimitable symphony, the very sounds of which move men to tears and ecstasy".[6]

The Qur'an itself not only claims there can be no imitation but challenges others to try, on pain of hellfire:

> And if you are in doubt as to which We have revealed to Our servant, then produce a *sura* [chapter] like it ...
>
> But if ye cannot – and of a surety ye cannot – then fear the fire whose fuel is men and stones, which is prepared for those who reject faith.[7]

Despite the threat of eternal punishment, there have been plenty of attempts to mimic it. Abu al-'Ala al-Ma'arri, the Syrian philosopher-poet who died in 1057CE, produced a parody of the Qur'an and after being informed that his own work did not have the resonance of the holy book he is said to have replied: "When you read it days and nights for years, it will" – implying that readers' familiarity with the Qur'an, more than the language, was what gave it resonance.[8]

A more recent parody was *al-Furqan al-Haqq* ("The True Criterion") a book published in the United States in 1999 and written in the style of the Qur'an but with a Christian message.[9] It appears to have been designed so that the unwary might mistake it for a copy of the Qur'an.

Around the same time there was a campaign against SuraLikeIt, a website which had published four *suras* written in the style of the Qur'an, with English translations. One of them began:

(1) Alef Lam Saad Meem

(2) Say: O Muslims, You are far astray.

(3) Those who disbelieved in God and his Christ shall have in the lifeafter the fire of hell and a severe torture.

(4) Some faces that day will be subdued and darkened seeking forgiveness from God and God shall do whatever He wants ...

The *sura* went on to suggest that Muslims had been led astray by Muhammad and that Muhammad had in turn been led astray by Satan. SuraLikeIt became front-page news in Egypt, where scholars at al-Azhar denounced the website as "aggression on the human heritage and sacred values not only of Muslims, but of all humanity". Eventually, America On Line, which hosted the website, was persuaded to delete it. AOL, apparently unaware that people have been parodying the Qur'an for centuries, explained its decision by saying: "Our terms of service are very clear on what we call appropriate content, such as content which is defamatory in nature. This page had that. It was particularly targeting Islam." SuraLikeIt did not disappear, however. It found a host for its web pages elsewhere and the number of imitation *suras* has since grown from four to twelve.[10]

If the Qur'an is to be accepted today as the word of God it is necessary to show that the text currently in use has been preserved unchanged since the time when it was delivered to the Prophet. Its 144 *suras* were revealed piecemeal over a period of twenty-three years, with the Prophet reciting each part to his followers and encouraging them to commit it to memory. It was also recorded in writing, in an ad hoc fashion on whatever materials were available – leather, bone, palm fronds, etc. By the time of Muhammad's death in 622, however, it had not yet been compiled into book form. During the Battle of Yamama in 633, many of the Prophet's companions were killed, raising fears that large parts of the Qur'an could be lost unless something were done to preserve it:

> Zaid ibn Thabit [who had been Muhammad's personal; scribe] was requested by Abu Bakr [the first Muslim caliph] to head a committee which would gather together the scattered recordings of the Qur'an and prepare a *suhuf* – loose sheets which bore the entire revelation on them.
>
> To safeguard the compilation from errors, the committee accepted only material which had been written down in the presence of the Prophet himself, and which could be verified by at least two reliable witnesses who had actually heard the Prophet recite the passage in question.
>
> Once completed and unanimously approved of by the Prophet's Companions, these sheets were kept with the Caliph Abu Bakr, then passed on to the Caliph Umar, and then Umar's daughter and the Prophet's widow, Hafsa.[11]

As Islam spread further afield, however, differences were found in versions of the text being used. The differences are said to have been adaptations to suit local dialects, but in order to preserve the integrity of the text 'Uthman (who ruled as caliph from 644 to 656 CE) declared the version handed down from Abu Bakr to be the official one and ordered other versions to be destroyed.

These efforts to prevent the original text from becoming lost or corrupted form an important part of claims to its authenticity. But the fact that such efforts were necessary is seen by some as evidence that the Qur'an did not come from God: surely God, in his perfection, would have chosen a more reliable delivery method. "It's ridiculous trying to convince me that this would be the only way that God could have transmitted His most important knowledge to humanity, and that it has to be in Arabic," Mohammed Ramadan, an Egyptian atheist commented.

IN RECENT years traditional arguments for a divine origin of the Qur'an have increasingly been overshadowed by claims that the Qur'an is a "scientific miracle". The basic idea is that its verses contain information, usually of a scientific nature, that could not have been known to humans in the time of the Prophet – in which case the information must surely have come from God.

Expounding further on this idea, the Institute of Islamic Information and Education says:

> Within the Qur'an are recorded facts about ancient times that were unknown to Muhammad's contemporaries and even to historians in the first half of the 20th century. In scores of verses, we also find references to scientific wonders, some only recently discovered or confirmed, regarding the universe, biology, embryology, astronomy, physics, geography, meteorology, medicine, history, oceanography, etc.[12]

Since the 1980s, the "scientific miracle" has become a major tool for Islamic proselytising and appears to have met with considerable success. It has also given many Muslims a renewed sense of pride in their religion. In the eyes of others, though, it has done much to discredit Islam.

The origins of "Qur'anic science" can be traced back to a French doctor, Maurice Bucaille, who served as family physician to King Faisal of Saudi Arabia in the early 1970s. Bucaille wrote a book, *The Bible, The Qur'an and Science,* which was published in 1976. In it, he argued that while the Bible contains many scientific errors, the Qur'an was remarkably prescient: references to the Big Bang, black holes and space travel can all be found in its verses. Bucaille died in 1988 but his name lives on: the practice of searching the Qur'an for advance knowledge of scientific discoveries became known as "Bucailleism". Pervez Hoodbhoy, a Pakistani physicist, comments:

> Bucaille's method is simple. He asks his readers to ponder on some Qur'anic verse and then, from a variety of meanings that could be assigned to the verse, he pulls out one which is consistent with some scientific fact ... To this end, he marshals an impressive number of Qur'anic references to bees, spiders, birds, plants and vegetables of different kinds, animal milk, embryos, and human reproduction.[13]

One obvious weakness of this approach is that it only operates retrospectively: the scientific "knowledge" in the Qur'an does not become apparent until *after* it has been established by science. Hoodbhoy adds: "In Bucaille's book there is not a single *prediction* of any physical fact which is unknown up to now, but which could be tested against observation and experiment in the future."[14]

One of the key Bucailleist figures of the 1980s was a Yemeni sheikh, Abdul Majeed al-Zindani, who worked at King Abdulaziz

University in Saudi Arabia and began seeking out western scientists who were visiting the kingdom, with the aim of getting them to say positive things about scientific "knowledge" in the Qur'an. Zindani's technique was described by Daniel Golden in an article for the *Wall Street Journal:*

> His breakthrough came when one of his assistants, Mustafa Abdul Basit Ahmed, presented a leech to Keith Moore, a University of Toronto professor and author of a widely used embryology textbook.
>
> Mr Ahmed wanted to show that a verse from the Qur'an, which states that God made man as a leech, was an apt simile to describe early human gestation as seen under a microscope. Mr Ahmed says Prof Moore was bowled over by the resemblance between the leech and the early embryo. Since the Qur'an predated microscopes, Prof Moore, son of a Protestant clergyman, concluded that God had revealed the Qur'an to Muhammad.[15]

Moore was so impressed that in 1983 he produced an "Islamic edition" of his embryology textbook, *The Developing Human*, which he described as containing the same material as the original version but with the addition of "numerous references to statements in the Qur'an and Sunnah about human embryology". In a foreword to the book, Moore wrote:

> For the past three years, I have worked with the Embryology Committee of King Abdulaziz University in Jeddah, Saudi Arabia, helping them interpret the many statements in the Qur'an and Sunnah referring to human reproduction and prenatal development.
>
> At first I was astonished by the accuracy of the statements that were recorded in the 7th century AD, before the science of embryology was established. Although I was aware of the glorious history of Muslim scientists in the 10th century AD, and some of their contributions to medicine, I knew nothing about the religious facts and beliefs contained in the Qur'an and Sunnah.
>
> It is important for Islamic and other students to understand the meaning of these Qur'anic statements about human development, based on current scientific knowledge.[16]

Sheikh Zindani left King Abdulaziz University but in 1984 secured Saudi funding to establish the "Commission on Scientific Signs in the Qur'an and Sunnah". Mustafa Abdul Basit Ahmed – the man who had presented the leech to Professor Moore – was then employed by the commission at $3,000 a month to travel around North America cultivating scientists, according to Golden.

> The commission drew the scientists to its conferences with first-class plane tickets for them and their wives, rooms at the best hotels, $1,000 honoraria, and banquets with Muslim leaders – such as a palace dinner in Islamabad with Pakistani President Mohammed Zia ul-Haq ...

During the course of their trips, scientists were presented with verses from the Qur'an to consider in the light of their expertise. Zindani then interviewed them about the verses in front of a video camera, pushing them to acknowledge signs of divine inspiration. Golden spoke to several who felt they had been tricked or manipulated. Here is one account:

> Marine scientist William Hay, then at the University of Colorado, was assigned a passage likening the minds of unbelievers to 'the darkness in a deep sea ... covered by waves, above which are waves.' As the videotape rolled, Mr Zindani pressed Prof Hay to admit that Muhammad couldn't have known about internal waves caused by varying densities in ocean depths.
>
> When Prof Hay suggested Muhammad could have learned about the phenomenon from sailors, Mr Zindani insisted that the prophet never visited a seaport.
>
> Prof Hay, a Methodist, says he then raised other hypotheses that Mr Zindani also dismissed. Finally, Prof Hay conceded that the inspiration for the reference to internal waves 'must be the divine being', a statement now trumpeted on Islamic websites.
>
> "I fell into that trap and then warned other people to watch out for it," says Prof Hay, now at a German marine institute.

Years later, many of the comments from scientists targeted by Zindani are still circulated on the internet.[17] Zindani, who had ties to Osama bin Laden long before he became notorious, eventually returned to Yemen where he became a prominent figure in the conservative/Islamist Islah party and founded Iman University, a Yemeni religious institution with about 6,000 students. Thanks to the university's research efforts, Zindani claims to have developed a herbal cure for HIV/AIDS. Since 2004, he has been listed by the US as a Specially Designated Global Terrorist, mainly because of his connections with Bin Laden and al-Qaeda.[18]

HUNTING for scientific foreknowledge in the Qur'an is an activity that almost anyone can take part in. It doesn't require any theological expertise, and digital versions of the text have made searching easier than it used to be. There's also a fair chance that somewhere among the Qur'an's 6,000-plus verses something can be found that could, conceivably, with some stretching of the imagination, be interpreted as referring to a recent scientific discovery. Consequently, the internet is full of examples that people have supposedly found.

These searches often appear to bear fruit because of ambiguities or obscurities in the language of the Qur'an. The vocabulary of seventh-century Arabic had developed to suit the needs of the time but in the absence of precise scientific terminology figurative expressions or approximations often had to be used. The planets, for instance, are described in the Qur'an as "swimming" in space.[19] This imprecision creates ambiguities which allow people to read things into the text that may or may not have been intended. The ambiguities also allow sceptics to argue that if God had wanted to impart scientific knowledge through the Qur'an He might have spelled it out more clearly.

Similar claims of foreknowledge are made for other religions. For example, a verse from Hindu scripture – "What does not exist cannot come into existence, and what exists cannot be destroyed"[20] – has been interpreted as referring to the law of conservation of matter and energy in physics. But this can be a risky business, as Hoodbhoy points out: "Science is quite shameless in its abandonment of old theories and espousal of new ones." Hindus used to claim their scripture was full of evidence supporting the Steady State theory of cosmology – until scientists abandoned the Steady State theory in favour of the Big Bank theory. Needless to say, Hindus soon found other scriptural passages "which were in perfect accord with the newer theory and again proudly acclaimed as a triumph of ancient wisdom".[21]

A few examples illustrate how the search-and-ye-shall-find technique works in the Qur'an. An article on the True Islam website talks about the ozone layer and begins by explaining its importance in shielding the Earth from harmful rays. "The discovery of the ozone layer," it continues, "took place many centuries after the Qur'an was revealed, nevertheless, there is mention in the Qur'an about this protective layer that shields us against the sun's harmful rays." Then comes the all-important verse:

Until he reached the rising of the sun, he found it rising on a people for whom We had provided no shield against it [i.e. the sun].[22]

For those who don't immediately see that this refers to a hole in the ozone layer, the writer explains:

> Five implications are drawn from this verse:
>
> 1. The word "shield" implies that there is something harmful from the sun, because if there was no harm to come from the sun, there would be no need for a shield.
>
> 2. In earlier interpretations of the Quarn [sic] the word "shield" was taken to mean mountains or hills, but mountains and hills do not shield us from the sun's rays ultra violet rays unless we live all our lives inside one!
>
> 3. The phrasing of the verse indicates that the people mentioned as having no shield are in fact the exception and that for the rest of mankind there exists a shield.
>
> 4. The words "We had provided no shield" indicate that the shield is a natural one (of God's making) and not a man-made one. This automatically eliminates the suggestion of houses and other man-made shelters.
>
> 5. The verse indicates the presence of a people, and thus areas, that are not shielded. This is in line with the current knowledge concerning the existence of holes in the ozone layer. It is generally thought that these holes have always existed. The matter has suddenly acquired an alarming nature because the size of these holes are greatly being enlarged as a result of man's pollution of the planet.
>
> The only phenomenon that is able to accommodate all these five implications is the ozone layer.[23]

A possibly more significant observation about the quoted verse is that it seems to assume there is an actual spot, somewhere on Earth and yet to be discovered by science, where the sun rises. A few verses earlier, the Qur'an also talks of the place where the sun sets. It is described as having "a spring of murky water" with people nearby.[24]

Meanwhile, an item on the Islam Guide website looks at the Qur'an's knowledge of geology:

> A book entitled *Earth* is a basic reference textbook in many

universities around the world. One of its two authors is Professor Emeritus Frank Press. He was the Science Adviser to former US President Jimmy Carter, and for 12 years was the President of the National Academy of Sciences, Washington, DC. His book says that mountains have underlying roots. These roots are deeply embedded in the ground, thus, mountains have a shape like a peg.[25]

The swift transition here from "root" to "peg" provides the cue for a Qur'anic verse:

Have We not made the earth as a bed, and the mountains as pegs?[26]

Islam Guide adds: "The history of science tells us that the theory of mountains having deep roots was introduced only in the latter half of the nineteenth century." So, is this an example of the Qur'an revealing information that could not have been known in the Prophet's lifetime or a case of wishful thinking? Some mountains do have roots and some of those roots can be considered as peg-shaped, but there is no strong reason for supposing this is what the verse alludes to.

We also now know that the Earth's abundant supplies of iron originated in outer space – created by fusion in extremely hot stars. Numerous Islamic websites claim to have found prior knowledge of this in the Qur'an, citing a phrase which can be translated as saying "We [i.e. God] sent down iron".[27] An article on the Religion of Islam website comments:

> This shows that iron did not form on the Earth, but was carried from Supernovas, and was 'sent down', as stated in the verse. It is clear that this fact could not have been known in the 7th century, when the Quran was revealed.
>
> Nevertheless, this fact is related in the Quran, the Word of God, Who encompasses all things in His infinite knowledge. The fact that the verse specifically mentions iron is quite astounding, considering that these discoveries were made at the end of the 20th century.[28]

However, that is not the only possible interpretation of the Qur'anic verse. It could also mean that God "revealed" iron and its many uses to mankind, or simply that He "provided" it for mankind.[29] The website does acknowledge these other possibilities but dismisses them by saying that the relevant verb (*anzalna* in Arabic) occurs in the Qur'an only when used in its literal "sending down" sense. This is incorrect. Other verses in the Qur'an state that God "sent down" clothing, food and eight kinds of cattle – and nobody has suggested that any of them originated in a supernova.[30]

Needless to say, when articles of this sort appear on the internet other articles appear, pulling them apart. There are also anti-Islam websites that highlight what they claim to be scientific errors in the Qur'an. Others point out that the Qur'an is not alone in its apparent foresight. Yemeni atheist Ahmad Saeed said: "Whenever I have discussions about the Qur'an [people] say: 'But how can an illiterate person find out about all these scientific discoveries and miracles 1,400 years ago?' I tell them that Star Trek also foresaw how the future is going to look, so why don't you believe in Star Trek instead?"

Hamza Andreas Tzortzis, a convert to Islam who has engaged in public debates with several high-profile atheists, describes the "scientific miracles" narrative as an intellectual embarrassment and suggests that while it does attract many to Islam it also drives others away:

> Millions of booklets and pamphlets have been printed that make the claim that there are scientific miracles in the Qur'an, and countless non-Muslims have converted to Islam as a result ... Famous popularisers such as Dr Zakir Naik and Yusuf Estes have also used the scientific miracles narrative to verify the Divine nature of the Qur'an.
>
> Due to this intense popularisation over the past few decades, there is now a growing counter movement that attempts to demystify the so-called scientific statements, and they seem to be more nuanced, with a growing popularity. A significant number of apostates from Islam (many of whom I have had private conversations with) cite the counter movement's work as a causal factor in deciding to leave the religion.[31]

ALTHOUGH there is a long history of conflicts between science and Christianity, Muslims have not generally regarded scientific discoveries as a threat to their belief system. The famous occasion in 1633 when the Italian scientist, Galileo Galilei, was forced by the Roman Catholic Church to recant his "heretical" belief that the earth revolves around the sun has no Islamic equivalent. Muslims' historical eagerness to engage with science – and to explore it – was at least partly connected to their faith. Astronomy was of particular interest since they used a lunar calendar, and they also needed to ascertain the direction of Mecca when praying.

Borrowing Ptolemaic and Aristotelian ideas, Muslim astronomers readily accepted that the Earth is spherical. Around

830CE, under the Caliph al-Ma'mun, they measured the distance between two cities in what is now Syria, which were known to be separated by one degree of latitude. From that, they calculated the Earth's circumference at 24,000 miles – a remarkably accurate result.[32] Later, Abu Rayhan al-Biruni (973-1048) devised a new way to calculate the radius of the Earth using trigonometry and a mountain, and the figure he came up with was little more than ten miles out.[33] Biruni also speculated that the Earth rotates on its axis, though he was unable to find proof. At the Maragha observatory in what is now Iran, thirteenth-century Muslim astronomers discussed whether the Earth revolves around the sun but eventually abandoned the idea. Some of their arguments bore a resemblance to those later put forward by Copernicus, though they do not seem to have caused theological problems.

Publication of Charles Darwin's book, *On the Origin of Species*, in 1859, drew a variety of responses from Muslims – some predictable, some less so. One early Muslim critique – from Jamal al-Din Afghani in 1881 – cited the continued existence of male foreskins as evidence that Darwin's ideas on natural selection must be wrong: "Is this wretch [Darwin] deaf to the fact that the Arabs and Jews for several thousand years have practised circumcision, and despite this until now not a single one of them has been born circumcised?"[34] On the other hand, Hussein al-Jisr, a nineteenth-century Lebanese Shia scholar who advocated combining religious education with modern science, saw room for an accommodation between evolution and scripture. "There is no evidence in the Qur'an," he wrote, "to suggest whether all species, each of which exists by the grace of God, were created all at once or gradually."[35]

Significantly, one of the first conflicts about Darwinism in an Arab country involved American Christians. It occurred in 1882 at what is now the American University of Beirut. In a speech at a graduation ceremony, Edwin Lewis, a popular professor of chemistry, referred to four "ideal men of science" – one of whom was Darwin. Lewis went on to describe Darwin's work as "an example of the transformation of knowledge into science by long and careful examination and accurate thinking". This proved too much for the Board of Trustees since the institution – known at the time as the Syrian Protestant College – had been founded by American missionaries, and Lewis was forced to resign. In the ensuing furore, several senior faculty members also resigned and students declared a strike in support of Lewis; seventeen of them were suspended. To prevent a recurrence, staff were then forced to sign a declaration promising to uphold "Christian values". The declaration was not repealed until 1902.[36]

Noting the theological problems that Christians faced in connection with evolution, some Muslims spotted an opportunity to further their own cause. Marwa Elshakry writes:

> The theological controversy over evolution in Europe ... could actually be used against European claims of superiority. With the well-publicised opposition to Darwin often regarded from outside Europe as symptomatic of Christianity's peculiar difficulty with science, many felt motivated to show just how easily Darwin's ideas could be embraced within their own tradition ...
>
> Just as missionaries, Orientalists and diplomats were claiming that it was Islam that hindered social and intellectual development, Abduh [Muhammad Abduh, the grand mufti of Egypt] made the reverse case: it was Christianity rather than Islam that was the real obstacle.[37]

Far from dismissing Darwin, some Muslims went so far as to claim part-ownership on the grounds that precursors for parts of his theory could be found in Islamic culture. Elshakry continues:

> Supporters and critics alike pointed out that Muslim philosophers had long referred to the idea that species or "kinds" (as the Arabic term *anwa'* suggests) could change over time. The notion of transmutation was also recalled in these discussions, and early Muslim philosophical and cosmological texts were cited whenever Darwin was discussed ...
>
> Analogies were drawn with earlier notions of a hierarchy of beings, from matter and minerals to flora and fauna, and finally to humanity itself. That some mediaeval works also argued that apes were lower forms of humans provided more evidence for nineteenth-century Muslims that Darwin's theory was "nothing new".

Even today, some suggest that evolutionary theory had Islamic origins. A book published in 2005, *Evolution and/or Creation: An Islamic Perspective,* claims that Darwin's ideas about evolution and natural selection were partly derived from Muslim philosophers and scientists, including Ibn Sina (also known as Avicenna) who died in 1037.[38]

Fortunately for Islam, the Qur'an is a lot more vague than the Bible about the process of creation. It says God made "every living thing" from water;[39] that God created humans from clay[40] and that He created them "in stages"[41] – which leaves some scope for interpreting it within an evolutionary framework. Today, however, Muslim opposition to Darwinism appears to be growing, under pressure from religious conservatives and the influence of American Christian creationists. It's an area where Arab schools, universities and media nowadays tread warily and often timidly for fear of provoking complaints.

One well-funded organisation promoting an Islamic version of creationism internationally is the Foundation for Scientific Research (BAV), based in Turkey and headed by Adnan Oktar, who has written dozens of books under the pen-name Harun Yahya. Although superficially Islamic in content, BAV's publications have been shown to rely heavily on Christian material produced by the Institute for Creation Research in California.[42] The books are freely available on the internet[43] – which means they can be easily regurgitated in student essays anywhere in the world.[44]

Teaching about evolution in Arab schools ranges from cautious to non-existent. Ahmad Saeed, a Yemeni, described what happened in his biology class:

> My school used to take the science books from Oxford University and there were a lot of chapters that our teacher told us to cancel. Whenever a teacher cancelled a chapter students would say "Thank God!" because they didn't want to learn more, but I used to read these cancelled chapters and one of them in our biology class was about evolution theory – though the chapter wasn't called "evolution" it was called "natural selection", which is one part of evolution theory.
>
> I remember going through this natural selection chapter [by myself] and at the time I thought it was just ridiculous – I was fine with the teacher for deleting it.

According to Saeed, the teacher said the chapter was excluded on instructions from the education ministry. "Now that I look back at it," Saeed continued, "I realise the brainwashing that they perform on these children." Today, he argues with friends on Facebook in support of evolution:

> Ninety-nine per cent of the people on my Facebook account say things like "You seriously think we came from monkeys?" I try to explain that that's not the theory. The theory says we share ancestors with monkeys, and it just goes to show how really ignorant we have been.

Mohammed Ramadan noticed a similar approach when studying at a state school in Egypt:

They have a chapter [in the textbook] – the final chapter – and it's all done in a kind of comic way. Most of it doesn't come in the exams, but if it does it's mostly about the birds that migrated from certain places and how they changed their colours – a very, very superficial concept of evolution. Some of the teachers accept that evolution may happen through adaptation but they say even if it's likely to happen in animals it won't happen in humans, because humans are special.[45]

Ramast, an Egyptian ex-Christian, studied evolution at school but found it presented in an equivocal way: "We studied it as a theory that might be right or wrong. But later I started to learn on my own, for example from the Discovery Channel, HowStuffWorks, Digg, and other websites. I learned out of curiosity. I wanted to understand how dinosaurs become birds or a monkey can evolve into a human. I know now that it didn't happen exactly like that but I had to learn about evolution to find out." He added that ideas about evolution eventually became "the last thing" in his journey to atheism: "My decision when I grew up was whether I wanted to believe in Adam and Eve or evolution." Egyptian universities are "not exactly crawling" with evolutionists either, according to Nour Youssef in a post on the Arabist blog: "Professors almost always introduce the subject as an obsolete, wrong theory, misrepresent it and then conclude with things like: Why are monkeys still around if we came from them?"[46]

Although some flatly reject evolution theory – the On Islam website says it is "incompatible with the Qur'anic account of creation" and "all the teachings of all heavenly revealed religion"[47] – others seek a half-way house. A study of attitudes towards evolution among Muslim students (Turkish and Moroccan) in the Netherlands found that while a few rejected the whole of evolution theory on the grounds of incompatibility with the Qur'an, "the vast majority constructed types of bridge models in which some aspects of evolution were accepted and others rejected":

> Microevolution [small changes over a relatively short period] and the concept of "the survival of the fittest" appeared on the accepted side of the equation. Students reasoned that it is impossible to deny the logic and empirical backing of these concepts. They also connected microevolution to theistic evolution, the idea that God has guided the adjustments in his creatures. Several students accepted the Big Bang and believed that the Qur'an contains references to both the Big Bang and evolution theory.

On the other hand ...

> For almost every student ... macroevolution [the development of new species, etc] was on the negated side in the bridge models. In contrast to microevolution, macroevolution was connected to atheist aspirations ... Likewise, no student accepted the idea that human beings have sprung from apes.[48]

According to the study, these students also "hardly recognised" the evolutionary assumptions that are nowadays implicit in subjects such as medicine, chemistry, and the bio-medical sciences. "Students in these disciplines were of course aware that they were required to take some courses and exams related to evolution theory, but they considered this quite unproblematic as they felt that external reproduction [of Darwin's ideas in an exam] does not require internal acceptance."

Given the lack of proper teaching about evolution in schools, it's scarcely surprising that Arab journalists mislead the public when the subject crops up in the news. In 2009 al-Jazeera, the Middle East's most widely-viewed news channel, announced that American scientists had found "new evidence that Darwin's theory of evolution was a mistake". The report was referring to a discovery of the fossilised remains of an *Ardipithecus ramidus,* an early human-like species 4.4 million years old. Although this raised new questions about humans' distant ancestors it did nothing to undermine evolutionary theory. Regardless of that, al-Jazeera turned for a comment to Dr Zhaghloul el-Naggar, who it described as a famous Arab geologist. Naggar told the channel that the discovery "dealt a heavy blow to Darwin's theory" and showed that westerners were beginning to "return to their senses" after "dealing with the origin of Man in terms of materialism and the denial of religions".[49] Naggar is an Egyptian Fellow of the Islamic Academy of Sciences who also has a website promoting stories of "scientific miracles" in the Qur'an.[50]

In 2014, National Geographic's Arabic channel, based in Abu Dhabi, broadcast "Cosmos: A Spacetime Odyssey" – a follow-up to the famous science documentary series originally presented by Carl Sagan in the 1980s. Watching the first episode, Palestinian atheist Waleed al-Husseini noticed some odd changes and omissions to "certain parts that did not conform to the Islamic faith, or might have caused controversy in the Arabic speaking world". A sentence in English saying "We humans only evolved within the last hour" was translated into Arabic as "We humans only *existed* within the last hour." In another sentence which said

"For more than 100 million years, the dinosaurs were lords of the Earth, while our ancestors, small mammals, scurried fearfully underfoot", the words "our ancestors" were removed from the Arabic version. Writing on his blog, Husseini said:

> For a channel supposed to represent science in the eyes of Arabic speakers, especially with the already poor scientific content in the Arab media, most of which is tainted by pseudoscience (scientific miracles in the Koran and such), it was quite dishonest to censor what little information the Arab viewer might get about our own history and evolution, as revealed by modern science.[51]

NOTES

1. "Isra and Miraj: The Miraculous Night Journey." https://www.islamicity.com/articles/Articles.asp?ref=IC0608-3086
2. Qur'an 17:1
3. Qur'an 54: 1
4. Munajid, Muhammad Salih al-: "Evidence for the truth of the Prophethood of Muhammad" http://islamqa.info/en/2114
5. Institute of Islamic Information and Education: "The Authenticity of the Quran" http://www.iiie.net/index.php?q=node/46
6. Pickthall, Marmaduke: The Meaning of the Glorious Qur'an. http://web.archive.org/web/20071114044153/http://www.al-sunnah.com/call_to_islam/quran/pickthall/
7. Qur'an 2:23-24
8. "Arabs Hated The Quran." Australian Islamist Monitor, 28 October 2008. http://www.islammonitor.org/index.php?option=com_content&view=article&id=1680:arabs-hated-the-quran&catid=183&Itemid=20
9. The True Furqan. http://en.wikipedia.org/wiki/The_True_Furqan
10. For details of the SuraLikeIt affair, see: Bunt, Gary: Virtually Islamic. Cardiff: University of Wales Press, 2000, pp 125-130.
11. Institute of Islamic Information and Education: "The Authenticity of the Quran" http://www.iiie.net/index.php?q=node/46
12. ibid.
13. Hoodbhoy, Pervez: Islam and Science: Religious Orthodoxy and the Battle for Rationality. London and New Jersey: Zed Books, 1991. p67.
14. Hoodbhoy, op cit. p 68.
15. Golden, Daniel: "Western Scholars Play Key Role In Touting 'Science' of the Quran." Wall Street Journal, 23 January 2002. http://online.wsj.com/news/articles/SB1011738146332966760
16. Dr Moore's "The Developing Human with Islamic Additions"

textbook. The Islam Papers, 1 November 2013. http://islampapers.com/2013/11/01/the-developing-human-with-islamic-additions/
17. See, for example, Zindani's video, "This is Truth" https://www.youtube.com/watch?v=YJCchGjTzGQ
18. "United States Designates bin Laden Loyalist." US Treasury Department, 24 February 2004. http://www.treasury.gov/press-center/press-releases/Pages/js1190.aspx
19. Qur'an 21:33
20. Bhagavad Gita, 2:16.
21. Hoodbhoy, op cit. pp 66-67.
22. Qur'an 18:90
23. "Life on Earth." http://www.quran-islam.org/main_topics/quran/science_in_quran/life_on_earth_(P1213).html
24. Qur'an 18:86
25. "The Quran on Mountains" http://www.islam-guide.com/ch1-1-b.htm
26. Quran, 78:6-7
27. Quran 57:25
28. "The Miracle of Iron" http://www.islamreligion.com/articles/562/
29. For a variety of translations of this verse, see http://www.multimediaquran.com/quran/057/057-025.htm
30. Clothing: Qur'an 7:26; food: 10:59, 45:05, 2:57, 7:160; cattle: 39:06
31. "Does the Qur'an contain scientific miracles?" Blog post by Hamza Andreas Tzortzis, 21 August 2013. http://www.hamzatzortzis.com/essays-articles/exploring-the-quran/does-the-quran-contain-scientific-miracles-a-new-approach/
32. The Book of Curiosities. Chapter 1: On the mensuration of the Earth and its division into seven climes, as related by Ptolemy and others. http://cosmos.bodley.ox.ac.uk/hms/home.php
33. "Abu Arrayhan Muhammad ibn Ahmad al-Biruni." http://www-groups.dcs.st-and.ac.uk/~history/Biographies/Al-Biruni.html
34. Quoted by Iqbal, Muzaffar: Science and Islam. Westport, CT: Greenwood Publishing, 2007. p. 157.
35. Ziadat, Adel: Western Science in the Arab World: The Impact of Darwinism, 1860–1930, London: Macmillan, 1986, p. 94 Quoted in 'Muslim Responses to Darwinism.' Islam Herald website. Retrieved 27 November 2008. http://www.islamherald.com/asp/curious/evolution/muz/muz-part3.asp.
36. "Academic Year Launched." http://staff.aub.edu.lb/~webbultn/v1n1/
37. Elshakry, Marwa: Reading Darwin in Arabic, 1860-1950. Chicago: University of Chicago Press, 2014. pp 8-9
38. Shanavas, T O: Evolution and/or Creation: An Islamic Perspective.

Philadelphia: Xlibris Corporation, 2005.
39. Qur'an 21:30, Al-Anbiya (Pickthall's translation): "Have not those who disbelieve known that the heavens and the earth were of one piece, then We parted them, and we made every living thing of water? Will they not then believe?"
40. Qur'an 6:2, Al-Anaam (Pickthall's translation): "He it is Who hath created you from clay, and hath decreed a term for you. A term is fixed with Him. Yet still ye doubt!"
41. Qur'an 71:14, Nuh (Pickthall's translation): "When He created you by (divers) stages?"
42. Edis, Taner: 'Cloning Creationism in Turkey.' Reports of the National Center for Science Education, vol. 19 no. 6, pp. 30–35, Nov–Dec 1999.
43. Atlas of Creation. Available online at: http://www.harunyahya.com/books/darwinism/atlas_creation/atlas_creation_01.php.
44. For example, in 2004 a group of Muslim students in biomedical sciences at the Vrije Universiteit in Amsterdam were reported to have uncritically copied text from "Islamic creationist" websites for an essay assignment on "Man and evolution". See: Koning, Danielle: "Anti-evolutionism among Muslim students." ISIM Review, Autumn 2006. http://www.isim.nl/files/Review_18/Review_18-48.pdf.
45. Author's interview, February 2012. Mohammed Ramadan is a pseudonym.
46. Youssef, Nour: "Last week in Egypt in TV." Arabist blog, 17 November 2013. http://arabist.net/blog/2013/11/17/last-week-in-egypt-in-tv
47. "Darwinism from an Islamic Perspective." On Islam, 24 July 2012. http://www.onislam.net/english/ask-the-scholar/muslim-creed/muslim-belief/174719-darwinism-from-an-islamic-perspective.html
48. Koning, Danielle: "Anti-evolutionism among Muslim students." ISIM Review, Autumn 2006. http://www.isim.nl/files/Review_18/Review_18-48.pdf
49. A video of the news report with commentary from the Arab Atheists Network can be found at https://www.youtube.com/watch?v=7SRE1kz3HG4. A text version of the news report, in Arabic, is here: http://www.aljazeera.net/news/pages/bda5151b-42f2-4aeb-aff3-ea0efe321b1e
50. Zhaghloul el-Naggar's website: http://www.elnaggarzr.com/en/
51. Husseini, Waleed al-: "Cosmos and Islamic censorship." Blog post, 16 March 2014. http://proud-a.blogspot.com/2014/03/Cosmos.html

4: Losing their religion

FOREIGNERS who embrace Islam often make news in the Gulf media, especially if their line of work makes them seem unlikely candidates for conversion. Thus when the French female rapper known (with an apostrophe) as Diam's converted to Islam it was an event to be celebrated in the Saudi press.[1] In the Emirates each year, the government publishes a list of foreign residents who have converted, and reports such as these no doubt give believers a feeling that their faith has been validated. But there are other kinds of conversion stories that receive less attention.

"I went for a job to Saudi Arabia as a pious Muslim and returned to my beloved country as an atheist," Mirza Ghalib, an Indian, wrote in an article posted on the internet. His journey to atheism began, he said, when Arab colleagues began teasing him "for not being a perfect Muslim". This surprised him because in India he had been taught to pray five times a day and to read the Quran daily in Arabic. As far as he was concerned, he was a good Muslim "according to the Indian standard of Islam".

Up to that point Ghalib had only read the Qur'an in Arabic, which he had been told was "the language of Paradise" and would bring him more virtue, even though he did not understand Arabic. But as a result of the taunts from colleagues he decided to read it in his mother tongue, Urdu, "so that I could understand its meaning and could become a more pious, a better, Muslim". Instead, he was shocked by what he found: "Many of the verses seemed barbaric."

He was also appalled by some of the cultural practices he found in Saudi Arabia – practices which are often legitimised on religious grounds:

> I witnessed an old man, aged over 75 years, with his two wives alive, [who] took a third [wife] – a 17-year-old Jordanian girl (because the "cost" [dowry] of the girl is comparatively cheaper in Jordan). As he returned with the young bride, he was given a very warm welcome by his well-educated sons, aged between 40 and 50. They took him on their shoulders, clapping and singing. They [didn't] even bother about the fate of their own mothers. They shared the joyful moments by praising their father's "manliness" with their neighbours and friends. The language they used to glorify their father's "manliness" can't be explained here, as it is too crude, pornographic. Given the sons were well-educated, we can't blame their lack of education for such behaviour.

Returning to India after a decade in Saudi Arabia, Ghalib said he then set about trying to convince his aged parents that they had been misled about Islam – and eventually succeeded.

> [My father] repeatedly asked me, like an innocent child, about the outcome of his 80 years of worship of Islam, and the valuable time he had spent in five-time daily prayers, midnight prayers and other Islamic deeds. I consoled him by saying not to worry about the past; instead, I encouraged him to feel happier, as he [had] been freed of the fear of all alleged punishments and tortures during death, in the grave and in the hereafter. He was convinced, but still he couldn't tolerate the way he had been cheated by the mullahs all his life. He thanked me for rescuing him from the fear of the horror of the Islamic grave and the hell.
>
> Sadly, I ... lost my beloved father within a few months of his enlightenment about Islam, as he was unable to come to terms with the shock, which not only perished his faith but also deteriorated his health. I felt a sense of guilt ... but when I recall his last days, I also feel satisfied that he faced his bodily end on earth with confidence, without the fear of tortures and hellfire as taught in Islam ... For a Muslim, getting to the truth about Islam is the toughest battle in life. And the shock they get when they find out the truth can be tough to come to terms with.[2]

Atheism is a response to religion, and without religion no one would bother to become an atheist. Without religion, God would be an unknown concept and there would be no particular reason for anyone to question His existence; belief and disbelief would both turn into non-belief. This has been the fate of earlier religions, now abandoned. Today, nobody spends time arguing about the gods of ancient Greece and Rome, because they faded into irrelevance long ago.

The role of religion in the development – even the unintentional promotion – of atheism is perhaps so obvious as to be easily overlooked. But it is important to keep this in mind when considering why and how Arabs become atheists. *Being* an atheist means having no belief in God but *becoming* an atheist involves a conscious rejection of God. Some non-believers might thus be described as atheists merely by default, since they have never faced a conscious choice; religion has made little or no impact on their lives and, for them, God is scarcely any different from Zeus or Apollo.[3]

In the Arab countries, however, atheism is almost always a deliberate choice – often with a price attached. Belief is the norm and in many cases it is belief by default: society not only expects people to believe but also tries to shield them from ideas that might lead them to doubt. Despite these pressures, though, some do slip through the net – and apparently in increasing numbers. So how does it happen?

"It's generally assumed that there's one sole trigger that destroys all belief in God or gods," said Saeed Kayyani, an Emirati atheist. "I disagree. From my own and others' experiences, I find it to be more of a complex process that involves several factors within yourself and your environment."[4] He added: "It's an internal journey of how ideas and events are processed and what a person's feelings are about the conclusions. It's like two piles of straw being weighed on a scale. The quality, structure, and material of the scale is what decides a person's religiosity."[5]

Research in the United States suggests a religious environment "plays a fundamental role in the construction of an atheist identity". Among forty American atheists who were interviewed, thirty-five had an upbringing that lay between "somewhat religious" and "extremely religious". The study, by Jesse Smith of Colorado University, noted: "Even those few who were raised in families without much religion (or no religion at all) nevertheless encountered, and were influenced by, the high levels of religiosity and belief present in the general milieu of American culture."[6]

Other evidence that religion can be a trigger on the road to atheism came from a Pew survey in 2010 which found that in a test of religious knowledge American atheists and agnostics performed better than Protestants and Catholics. This was only partly explained by differences in their general levels of education.[7] According to one of the authors of the Pew survey, about three-quarters of the atheists and agnostics had been raised as Christians. Their knowledge of religion suggested they had thought about it in some depth before deciding to abandon it. This prompted Dave Silverman of the American Atheists organisation to comment:

> I have heard many times that atheists know more about religion than religious people. Atheism is an effect of that knowledge, not a lack of knowledge. I gave a Bible to my daughter. That's how you make atheists.[8]

Based on the interviews with American atheists about their journey into disbelief, Smith proposed a four-stage process ...

(1) the starting point: the ubiquity of theism
(2) questioning theism
(3) rejecting theism
(4) "coming out" as an atheist

In interviews for this book, Arab non-believers broadly confirmed that pattern, though with some differences. They described a similar story of gradual progression away from religion, sometimes spread over a period of years; there was no sudden "road to Damascus" moment of conversion to atheism. Almost all cited some aspect of their own encounter with religion as the initial trigger for doubt – a feeling that something about religion, as it had been taught to them, was not quite right.

Typically, it began with a niggling question about an aspect of religious teaching that struck them as illogical or self-contradictory. They would then explore the question further, often in the sincere hope of finding an answer. Instead of providing an answer, however, the exploration process merely raised more questions – and new doubts.

Although questions about doctrine were the usual starting point, a few said they had also been influenced by the way religion is practised: some cited the treatment of women and an Egyptian activist saw religion as an impediment to revolution, but this was not the most usual starting point. The science-versus-religion debates that have become so familiar in the west played little or no part in the initial stages of religious doubt among Arab interviewees unless they had a particular interest in science. Some later turned to books by Richard Dawkins, Christopher Hitchens and other prominent atheists but by that stage the effect was mainly to reinforce existing doubts and provide a more coherent framework for their growing disbelief. Gamal, an Egyptian atheist, said: "I have seen a number of people, students of biology and medicine, who appear to be very well read and up to date on books that are questioning the existence of God based on science, but the majority of the crowd that I know who subscribe to atheism, particularly here [in Egypt] have gone this way as a result of intellectual, logical or societal reasons – much more philosophical."[9]

Smith's study speaks of Americans questioning and then rejecting "theism" as they progress towards atheism but this is not strictly accurate in the case of Arab interviewees. Initially, their questions were not so much about the possibility of God's existence as about whether God could exist in the form described by organised religions. A few, while rejecting organised religion, still maintained a vague belief in some kind of deity or expressed a yearning for "spirituality".

IN INTERVIEWS, the issue most often cited by Arabs as their first step on the road to disbelief was the apparent unfairness of divine justice. The picture they had acquired was of an irascible and sometimes irrational Deity who behaves in much the same way as an Arab dictator or an old-fashioned family patriarch – an anthropomorphic figure who makes arbitrary decisions and seems eager to punish people at the slightest opportunity. Dire warnings – constantly repeated in the Qur'an – of what would happen to non-believers had clearly made a strong impression on them in childhood.

"The idea of eternal hell was very disturbing to me," said Mohammed Ramadan, an Egyptian. "I was nine when I asked my parents why would God punish us for ever when we live for an average of only 70 years."

At school, Ahmad Saeed, a Yemeni, asked his teachers why God would punish people simply for not believing in Him – and found the answers far from satisfactory: "They would just reply to me that this is what God says, so we are not supposed to question." He continued: "I always used to argue that if I were born in a secular country, if I were not born in Yemen or a Middle Eastern country, I would not have been a Muslim. If I had been born in India there is a good chance that I would have worshipped a cow. [Being raised as] a Muslim is not something I chose, it's a matter of demographic placing."

A Saudi who is known on Twitter as "Arab Atheist" was troubled by the question of why seemingly decent non-Muslims should be punished by God. Arriving in the US to study at a Jesuit college, he began to realise "how similar all religions are" in their basic teachings. "In Islam," he said, "we are taught that all non-Muslims are going to hell. I had Jewish neighbours who were the kindest and sweetest couple and it made me wonder why should they go to hell? And suddenly Islam started to crumble in my eyes."

Ramast, an Egyptian raised in the Coptic church who objects to being described as Arab ("People call Egypt an Arab country for religious reasons, which I don't have"), grappled with a similar problem:

> It started with one question. It was very simple: if good people go to heaven and bad people go to hell, then what makes a person good and what makes a person bad? Could it be the environment? But God created that environment. Could it be the way he was raised? But God chose his parents and the way he would be raised. Whatever the reason you come up with, you will eventually say "But God created that" and so logically it is not the person's fault if he is bad or good.

> I couldn't find an answer to this question but it didn't make me immediately change, it just made me doubt and open my mind a little bit. I was thirteen, fourteen, something like that. At that time I was very religious and thinking a lot about these things.

Such questions are probably as old as monotheism itself, and a thousand-year-old story illustrates the conundrum. It concerns a dispute between Abu Ali Muhammad al-Jubba'i, a Muslim theologian of the Mu'tazilite school who died around 915CE, and his pupil, Abu al-Hasan al-Ash'ari:

> Ash'ari proposed to Jubba'i the case of three brothers, one of whom was a true believer, virtuous and pious; the second an infidel, a debauchee and a reprobate; and the third an infant; they all died, and Ash'ari wished to know what had become of them.

> To this Jubba'i answered: "The virtuous brother holds a high station in Paradise; the infidel is in the depths of Hell, and the child is among those who have obtained salvation [i.e. spared from Hell but excluded from Paradise]."

> "Suppose, now," said Ash'ari, "that the child should wish to ascend to

the place occupied by his virtuous brother, would he be allowed to do so?"

"No," replied Jubba'i, "it would be said to him: 'Thy brother arrived at this place through his numerous works of obedience towards God, and thou hast no such works to set forward'."

"Suppose, then," said Ash'ari, "that the child say: 'That is not my fault; you did not let me live long enough, neither did you give me the means of proving my obedience'."

"In that case," answered Jubba'i, "the Almighty would say: 'I knew that if I had allowed thee to live, thou wouldst have been disobedient and incurred the severe punishment [of Hell]; I therefore acted for thy advantage'."

"Well," said Ash'ari, "and suppose the infidel brother were to say: 'O God of the universe, since you know what awaited him, you must have known what awaited me; why then did you act for his advantage and not for mine?'" Jubba'i had not a word to offer in reply. [10]

Reem Abdel-Razek, another Egyptian, was curious to know where animals fitted into the system of reward and punishment. "In Islam we are taught that humans are being put through a sort of test to see if they will go to hell or heaven," she said. "There is a lot of suffering in the world and whenever I talk about human suffering it's always attributed to that test. But when I talk about animals I don't understand how God would create such a huge amount of suffering without any reason." As a child, when she asked about animals eating other animals, she was told that in the afterlife the animals that had been eaten would get their revenge, but then turn to dust. "It didn't make sense to me."

Abdullah, a Kuwaiti, said:

> The first thing I started questioning was what is God, specifically. What is God as an entity? That was when I was about 12 and things didn't add up, because I always got "You'll figure that out by the time you are dead." I'm talking about mum, who was supposed to be an expert on the faith itself, and it seemed such bullshit. It kind of progressed from there and slowly slid downhill until I was sixteen when I had one of my friends pass away because of a car accident and that's where I started questioning even more and more. It started to kind of dominate my life – "I want to know, I want to know."

The reactions from other people when they asked questions such as these often pushed them further along the road to disbelief. "They always have this perspective that 'We don't know but God knows'," Ahmad Saeed said.

In Egypt, Reem Abdel-Razek found it wasn't just a matter of being told "Don't ask questions like that." She said the reaction from people around her was more a kind of aggression. "That made me more curious, because it was rather defensive. It was as if I was attacking them – which I wasn't. I think deep down they felt I was right, and this hit a nerve with them because they didn't want to think about these things." But defensiveness is not the only response. An article in the Saudi newspaper, *al-Watan,* told of a woman teacher in her twenties who tried to discuss her doubts with a scholar. He replied that she was mentally sick and should seek treatment.[11]

In Bahrain, Nabila had the unusual experience of being raised by parents who were "basically atheists". Her father belonged to an underground Marxist-Leninist group and her mother was an active feminist but for safety reasons they concealed this from the children. "They were wired to keep everything secret." Thus, for the first few years of her life, Nabila assumed she was a Muslim like other children at her school. Even so, there were things about her home life that puzzled her.

> I used to ask my parents all the time: "Why don't you pray?" "Why aren't you fasting?" and my mum would give me these excuses. She would say: "We do pray, inside our rooms." OK, why aren't you fasting? My mum would say: "I have an ulcer and your father can't quit smoking" – these very silly excuses, but for a while I bought them.
>
> Of course, we heard stories here and there about my dad's friends. For instance, we grew up with two kids who were like brothers to us, who had lost their father in 1986 in prison. We always wondered why they didn't have a father and what we were told as kids was that he was a martyr who had fought in Palestine. I think my father told me when I was twelve or thirteen that he had actually died in prison in Bahrain but even then he did not give me details about how or why, and I had no idea there were actual parties working underground.

Meanwhile, Nabila's grandmother took upon herself the task of trying to turn her into a good Muslim, encouraging her to learn the Qur'an by heart.

> She told me to memorise it. I tried to memorise it but I couldn't. She said: "How do you memorise your schoolwork?" I said "Because I understand it. I don't understand this."
>
> So she tried to explain it to me and after she was explaining it I

started to have these questions. She told me God has created everything, God knows everything, he knows whatever is unknown to us, and things like that.

I said: "Wait. You're saying God knows everything. He knows that I am going to be born, he knows every single action I'll do, everything I'll say. So if he knows everything, he knows I'm going to make a mistake. Why punish me for it?"

She said: "No, it's not like that. He puts paths in front of you and you get to choose."

I said: "So He doesn't know my choice and He doesn't know everything."

That's how I started to have my doubts. How can you say He's forgiving and merciful and everything when He's a strict punisher? There was no logic for me.

Sarah Way, from a Syrian Alawite family living in Kuwait, also had problems with the Qur'an – especially what she saw as its lack of clarity when she began reading it on her own. "The problems for me were more than just God," she said. "There was stuff in the Qur'an that made me think 'Why can't it just be clear?' There were contradictions in it and the whole idea of God is that it's supposed to be someone or something divine. But errors don't happen in something divine. Even the tiniest error makes it invalid."

She continued: "Before I read it I had no idea there was such a thing as an ex-Muslim. I thought that I was just a bad Muslim. Then I thought, 'Oh! Wait! It doesn't have to be this way'." Today, though, she prefers to be called an atheist rather than an ex-Muslim. "The more I think about it, the more I think why should I be an 'ex' of something I didn't even choose? Even though I've shown interest in religion at a lot of points in my life, when I look back I feel I wasn't showing interest because I had faith, I was showing interest because it was peer pressure."[12]

Among the Arabs interviewed for this book, abandoning religion was mostly a private, thoughtful and sometimes lonely journey. This was largely an intellectual process but also one that was shaped, to varying extent, by their personal experiences of religion. Contrary to popular notions in the Middle East, none viewed atheism as an excuse for a dissolute lifestyle. Another popular idea – usually expressed in terms of conspiracy theory – is that Arab atheists have succumbed to "westernisation" or "foreign influences". There does seem to be a degree of truth in this if the conspiracy element is removed, though it certainly does not apply in all cases and, where it does apply, it is usually more a matter of Arabs having their eyes opened through contact with non-Muslims or new ways of thinking than direct attempts by foreigners to lure them away from Islam.

Yemeni Ahmad Saeed, for example, said the change in his beliefs came when he started reading "from outside the perspective of Islam" and began debating on the internet "with people who are atheists and deists and agnostics". The debates were in English, he said, "because most of the people who speak Arabic are Muslims and at that point I didn't want to argue with Muslims because it would be pointless. I wanted to look at it from a different perspective, from a different point of view." He joined an online discussion forum called "Atheist vs Theist" which had 30,000 members. "I spent a lot of hours on this group, and when I joined I was 100% theist – I believed in God – but I found I have zero evidence to prove that God exists. Then I realised that all religions are organised by men and the idea of a God is man-made."

Mohammed Ramadan said his eyes were opened mainly after he moved from a state school to a private university in Egypt and "started to see a whole different kind people, richer people who travelled a lot to places like Canada – Egyptians who had mixed origins, with totally different ideas". The biggest influence on his views at that time was a friend with whom he shared a dormitory. "He was an atheist, although at the time he didn't know it. We argued a lot and I was on the other side of the argument, but also at the same time I realised I was talking to someone who confirmed some of my inner doubts." He continued:

> The very first discussion was about certain things that are morally accepted only being accepted by the social circle you are surrounded with. Then I came up with a stupid thing like "Would you allow your sister to be in a bikini somewhere in Europe?" and he said: "Of course, yes."
>
> And when he said that, I said: "What do you mean? How could you allow your sister to expose herself like that?" We had a long argument about ethics and morals. That was basically one of the first triggers.

Interestingly, though, one of Mohammed's cousins arrived at atheism by a very different route – from hardcore Salafism. "That was a very powerful story for me because he didn't travel and he never met anyone who was an atheist," Mohammed said. "He was always in the village until he finished his studies. He kind of went on his own to discover this." Mohammed also has a theory about what happened to his cousin. While some Muslims retain their belief by interpreting scripture flexibly, Salafis do not have that option. "Salafis can't use the argument of not reading the Qur'an in a literal sense. They tell you it is the direct word of God – it has to be taken literally and we have to follow it word by word," he said. This all-or-nothing approach means that if they find one thing in scripture that is difficult to accept, the whole ideological structure is liable to fall apart. Mohammed said his cousin seems happier now but "being where he is in Egypt, surrounded by family and all that, he can't do everything he would like. One of the things he did was to shave his beard. That was quite shocking for his family. He stopped praying, and it has become obvious that he doesn't pray. Last time we spoke, he told me: 'Remember to bring some ham'."

In Syria, Hashem al-Shamy came from a Sunni Muslim family, though not a particularly devout one: they viewed religion as "a cultural and traditional norm", he said. His father, who had no qualms about drinking alcohol, attended Friday prayers – but basically as a social event.

Nevertheless, Hashem was sent to one of the many primary schools in Damascus organised by the Qubaysiyat, a religious movement run by women which has been supportive of the Assad regime. "Their version of Islam is very much mainstream, the one that is accepted by the government generally speaking, which is not contentious," he explained.

Being uncontentious included not mentioning that the Qur'an had been revealed to the Prophet bit by bit over a long period rather than as a finished book and that there were multiple versions for a while, or talking about the differences within Islam – Sunni, Shia, Alawi, etc. It was only after he entered secondary school that Hashem became aware of what he regards as some inconvenient facts about the faith and its diversity.

Presenting Islam in this way, as a solid monolith, was a deliberate policy of the Assad regime, and there were political reasons behind it (discussed in Chapter Six). Reflecting on it now, Hashem feels he and his classmates were lied to. "As Muslims from Syria's Sunni society we were patronised, we weren't told the truth because there is this presumption by the scholars that it's too much to handle – the fact that there were disagreements between the Companions [of the Prophet] and Ali [his son-in-law] that drove the Shia from the Sunnis, how the Qur'an was transmitted, how we were presented with one version of Islam and weren't told about Druzes and Shias and Isma'ilis and others."

He continued: "The government didn't want to have this discussion and on the family or social level there was no discussion either. I felt there must be something substantially wrong if you are not told about these things from the beginning. There are a lot of shortcomings in religion and they would like to hide them away as long as they can, so that you to embrace religion as it's presented to you, and by the time you discover there are lots of issues the dogma will be already in place."

As he grew up, though, Hashem did go through phases of getting closer to religion but was eventually put off by the people involved. At the age of sixteen, during the summer holidays, he was briefly drawn into what were officially known as the Hafez al-Assad Circles of Religion:

> They taught you how to read the Qur'an properly and how to memorise it. They taught you about the hadith and being a good Muslim in a general sense. There were also social activities and sports and picnics. Some of my friends started going and they asked me if I wanted to come along. My parents were OK with that ... initially.

The programme was approved by the Syrian government, with preachers appointed by the Ministry of Endowments, but most of those involved in the teaching were young men in their early twenties.

> They started trying to get me to go more regularly and soon I was going there twice a day, then three times. Then I started going at the weekend, and eventually going for the dawn prayers, around five in the morning. At that point my dad got really anxious. If I wanted to pray, he said, I could pray at home. He was asking me about the people I was meeting with, and all that.

> I started realising that the job of these circles was only to recruit us. They didn't have any real interest in caring for our affairs or teaching us. They just needed to meet a target of having enough young men coming to the mosque, and then when that was reached they moved on to the next group.

For Hashem, the top-down approach that he found in the Hafez al-Assad Circles of Religion echoed that of Assad's Baath party. Both were focused on the number of people they could recruit. It was basically a one-way relationship, he said, with no real interest in getting a view from the bottom.

> I started seeing the interaction between the older ones and how they kind of looked down on the people beneath them, and how this whole thing was not organic – it didn't feel right to me.
>
> I kept doing it for about a month-and-a-half on a daily basis, so I dedicated a lot of time praying and memorising. They even wanted me to start teaching ten-year-olds. But didn't feel I wanted to do it, so I stopped going. Then they started sending friends, saying "Why did you stop coming?"
>
> I kept going to the Friday prayers. I would run into the same people and I saw the relationship changing, how I was now seen as an outsider – even worse, because I was someone who had been inside and now betrayed them.

Hashem's first glimpse of a different world came when he spent a year studying in Latvia. "The former Soviet Union states are very atheist, so people drink, they eat pork, they sleep around," he said – adding that he chose not to join in any of those activities, at first because of religious inhibitions though later for more cultural reasons. "I was always thinking my family in Syria would be disappointed, how would I explain it to them? So for a whole year I didn't drink or do anything like that."

His first experience of alcohol came in Lebanon in 2004. "I used to visit friends at the American University of Beirut and every time they tried to persuade me to drink I would say "No, no, I don't want to do it." And then all of a sudden I just told them, OK. The first night that I drank I didn't stop speaking for about six hours and I think they regretted encouraging me after that." But he did not regret his decision. "I felt that I had missed out on some good times, that I should have done it earlier. It didn't change anything about my life – I don't feel less about myself as a person now that I'm drinking."

Later, in Madrid, he started meeting girls but, perhaps surprisingly, still refused to eat pork.

> I just felt that pork was a red line for me. My friends would try to understand where I was coming from, they would tell me: "You don't have a problem drinking or sleeping with girls, so what's the issue with pork?" I think pork or pigs in the Arab world are just associated with everything that's bad or nasty or dirty. It's not like drinking, where you either drink or don't drink. With meat, you can eat lamb, or beef or chicken. I started eating pork, I think, in 2008 and it was the same realisation as with drinking.

As Hashem's drift away from religion continued, he eventually declared himself an atheist, though his family still do not know. "I don't think I will tell them," he said. "I don't need to open a can of worms about this." The problem, he believes, is not because of religion itself but because "on a social level there is a difference between being a passive Muslim and an active atheist":

> Sometimes I get into a discussion with my mother and I once told her: "If you believe God exists and He cares about us what the hell is going on in Syria and other countries?" It's a useless discussion but I put these rhetorical questions every now and then.
>
> At the end of the day, though, to her I'm still a Muslim even if I have issues with some aspects of Islam. I can say I don't pray, I don't fast but if I tell her I am an atheist there's going to be a total collapse. They are still in a state of denial and that, I think, applies to society as a whole, not just our family.[13]

FOR MUSLIM ex-believers, one especially problematic aspect of divine punishment is the doctrine that atheists and people from other faiths will suffer in hell. Thus, people who have never had an opportunity even to consider becoming Muslims, plus others who have considered it honestly but not been convinced by the evidence, all face eternal damnation – simply for not believing. Furthermore, many of the damned appear, by any normal standards, to lead civilised and largely blameless lives. "I came to the conclusion," Ahmad Saeed said, "that religion is just a matter of where you are born and what [religion] your parents tell you that you are supposed to be".

A common reply to this is that people who don't believe in God have no "moral compass" (or, in the case of other faiths, the wrong moral compass) and consequently drift into sin. However, according to Sheikh Muhammad al-Munajjid, a prominent Saudi scholar who claimed that the 2004 Indian Ocean tsunami was God's vengeance for "immorality", atheism is a sin in itself – and a particularly heinous sin, worse even than idolatry or polytheism. In his view, idolators and polytheists are less bad than atheists because they recognise God up to a point, even if their worship is mis-directed:

> The atheist who denies the existence of Allah and rejects His Messengers and disbelieves in the Last Day is in a greater state of *kufr* [disbelief] and his beliefs are more reprehensible ... [The atheist] is stubborn and arrogant to an extent that cannot be imagined or

accepted by sound human nature. Such a person would transgress every sacred limit and fall into every sin; his worldview would be distorted to an inconceivable level.[14]

Munajjid goes on to quote a fatwa from Abd al-Aziz Bin Baz, the late Grand Mufti of Saudi Arabia, that Muslims should take particular care not to eat meat from animals slaughtered by Communists: "Meat slaughtered by Communists is *haraam* and is like the meat of the Magians and idol worshippers; in fact their meat is even more *haraam*, because their degree of *kufr* is greater due to their atheism and denial of the Creator."

In the words of another scholar quoted by a Saudi newspaper, "Upholding religious values is the only solution for the growing moral degradation and cultural anarchy in the modern society."[15]

Despite many frequent assertions of this kind, there is no real evidence that atheists in general behave any worse (or better) than believers, though both tend to claim moral superiority. Ideas about morality – such as fairness and justice – were of central importance to the Arab interviewees in their questioning of religion. This tallies closely with the findings of Smith's study of American atheists where participants "saw themselves as good and moral individuals" but doubted that this had been inherited from religious rules and practices: "They each in some way observed – and criticised – the idea that people need religion to be moral and good." The atheists in the American study also held broadly conventional views about right and wrong – "They all considered actions such as lying, cheating, stealing, murder, and basically anything else that harms other human beings to be immoral."

The key difference here is in the way atheists approach questions of morality. By rejecting belief in God, they set aside pre-ordained rules and instead make ethical judgements based on their own reasoning. Many argue that this is a better method because choices are based on what they consider to be right rather than what they have been told to do under the threat of punishment. One of the participants in Smith's study commented:

> Many religious people ... don't realise that you can simply choose to act moral, and define an ethical framework on a rational basis. They think it has to be something that God told you to do, and that you'll be punished for not doing it. You know, a very simple reward/response kind of scenario...if you're doing something because of fear of being punished, that completely removes what I consider a moral dimension.

THE PROGRESSION outlined in Smith's study of American atheists culminated in a "coming out" phase. From the initial stages of questioning God and religion, they moved to "a more deliberate and active stage of rejection" and finally started openly describing themselves as atheists in the presence of others.

In societies where religion predominates, "coming out" as an atheist can be a difficult step, even in America. "Because of the stigmatised and deviant status of atheism, it can initially be difficult to claim the identity in a social setting," Smith writes. Although the American constitution separates religion from the state, the US is nevertheless one of the world's most religious countries. The phrase "In God we trust" appears on its banknotes and religion often influences politics. It was not until 2007 that Pete Stark became the first openly atheist member of Congress and there are many who still doubt that an openly-declared atheist could ever be elected as president. Sixty per cent of Americans describe themselves as religious and only 5% as atheists. This helps to explain why, even though freedom of speech and religious liberty are fundamental principles of the American constitution, some atheists still hesitate to come out in the United States. Ultimately, though, coming out proved a positive experience for those who decided to make the leap, Smith says. "Finally, despite any initial reticence, as interviewees began to claim atheism overtly in social interactions, a concomitant sense of empowerment, confidence, and new sense of self emerged."

This, of course, is something that few Arabs can currently aspire to. The hazards of coming out are far greater, and for those who do the result can be disastrous. Nevertheless, individuals' circumstances vary, largely dependent on the attitudes of family, friends and the local community. Most interviewees for this book asked not to be identified by their real name – often to avoid upsetting their families. "I've lost some friends because of my views and I am still resisting the urge to tell my parents," Mohammed Ramadan said. "I can imagine my father having a heart attack or something. I do care about my parents and I don't want to hurt them. They wouldn't do anything to me but I would live the rest of my life with regret, having hurt them so much. At least, I'm happy with the fact that they know I don't pray. And I sometimes tell white lies to please them."

Since many families would be distressed by the thought of having a non-believer in their midst, relatives do not usually seek to have their worst fears confirmed, and so a "don't ask, don't tell" approach tends to suit both sides." We don't talk much," Badra, a Lebanese agnostic, said:

> My policy was not to let them get involved in my private life. At the age of eighteen I left the house and went to university in Beirut, so it was easier for me to distance myself and I stopped fasting [during Ramadan]. They know that I think differently but I don't shout my beliefs – I don't want to hurt them. They know that I question the existence of God but they prefer to ignore this. They avoid admitting it, because it would hurt. Even if I told my mother something really definitive – that I don't want to be buried in the family cemetery, that I want to be cremated, or something like that – she might simply ignore it or still think I have a chance to be a believer like her.

Worried families sometimes console themselves with the hope that their wayward relative will eventually repent and return to the fold. "Many of my friends and family members think it is a phase that I'll grow out of," Arab Atheist said. "But I am almost fifty years old, I've been an atheist for twenty-four years and it is not a phase – because once you know it, you can't unknow it." Unlike most of the others, though, he does argue about religion with his Saudi relatives. "We have heated discussions regularly but unfortunately many lack the scientific literacy to understand what I'm talking about and have been brainwashed and indoctrinated to the point of no return."[16] But despite being "out" to his family and despite posting frequently on Twitter, Arab Atheist fears he would be threatened if his name became known. "My identity is top secret, and I don't share it with anyone. I take many precautions in protecting it," he told an Emirati journalist.[17]

In Yemen, Ahmad Saeed told his parents he thinks there may be no God, but they just shrugged. "They basically told me: 'You can believe in science, you can believe in evolution theory, you can believe in the Big Bang, but all these scientific theories are the creation of God'. My family are conservative but they are not absolute, so they tell me the more I read about science the more I am going to believe in God in the future." In discussions with Muslim friends, though, Ahmad is more circumspect about his disbelief:

> Usually I tell these friends that I am deist, that I believe in God but I don't believe in Islam. I try not to shock them by saying I don't believe in God, because they will just think that everything I say is ridiculous and that Satan has brainwashed me. So usually I tell them yes, I

believe in God, I think God is awesome, I'm not an atheist so don't worry ... but I think Islam and all the religions in the world have given God a bad name. That's the point of view that I argue with my friends, but I can't talk about being an atheist because they will just think I'm going to hell. That's how much they have been brainwashed. I have just one atheist friend – this is how small the society of atheists is in Yemen.

Spotting other non-believers or striking up conversations about atheism can be a tricky business, as Sarah discovered in Kuwait. She would often become curious about people who seemed to avoid using traditional religious expressions like *"Ma sha' Allah"* ("Whatever God wills") in everyday speech, but appearances could be deceptive:

> I have met people who appeared to be non-religious but when it came down to it they *were* religious. There were a lot of people who would drink and party and listen to all the cool music – the same music that I listened to. People who I thought were just like me ... until religion showed up.
>
> I have a good friend who is the coolest girl ever. She's so badass and westernised and I thought she was my best friend. She once found out my internet account, my Reddit account, and she called me a heathen. She told me how I was going to go to hell and I was like "Ooooooh!"
>
> And then there are people who I am too scared to open the topic with. It's so weird that we don't talk about it. In Kuwait I only know a few people who I can openly talk about this in front of. Definitely less than 10 people.
>
> There are some people who we never say the word "atheist" in front of, but we *imply*. We imply our lack of belief to each other. You might make a joke that's a bit blasphemous – not too much, just a little joke. Even if they laugh at the joke you are still unsure. The laughing, the tone, do they have a sense of humour? Do they think you are just making a joke or do they know that you are trying to say something? Behind every joke there's an element of truth. This is the hard part.

In Bahrain, Nabila says she has gradually become less restrained. "At the beginning it was very hard, and it still is with a lot of people. But as I grow older I'm starting to realise that I have had enough of being quiet about it. I do have conversations and I do have them with a lot of Muslims who are open to conversation. When I joined my job there was a person who didn't want to listen when this kind of conversation came up ... but today we can talk about it normally and joke about it. So there are these people who believe because they are too scared to not believe. It think it terrifies them – the idea of the possibility that it might not be true."

Ramast, the Egyptian ex-Christian, said he does not brag about his disbelief though he has updated the religion section on his Facebook page where friends can find out if they check. He doesn't criticise religion, he said, because it fulfils a human psychological need:

> Religion is not a bad thing. It's a good thing, otherwise people wouldn't have created it. It doesn't matter whether I need it or not, because now I know it's not true.

> I like Santa Claus and wish he would come every year to my house and leave gifts. But I know it's not true any more. I wish I didn't know, but I do know. You cannot undo this. And you shouldn't go telling other people that Santa doesn't exist. Don't criticise religion. Let them be happy unless their religion is affecting them in a bad way, like killing each other. But if they are happy, leave them. If it's working, don't fix it.

His Egyptian compatriot, Reem Abdel-Razek, sees nothing to be gained by keeping quiet, however:

> Eventually, when people start speaking up, these laws [against atheism, blasphemy, etc] are not going to be enforced. They can't enforce it on everybody but if it's just one person saying something then they will lock him up.

> In Egypt I know a lot of people who believe exactly what I believe but they will never come out, and so the general idea is that there are just a few and that if they are locked up or killed there won't be any. But the reality is that there are a lot more and if they start speaking up things will have to change.

NOTES

1. "French Rapper Diam's embraces Islam." Saudi Gazette, undated. http://www.saudigazette.com.sa/index.cfm?method=home.regcon&contentID=2009101951948. The Saudi Gazette was chastised by one of its readers for saying that Diam's had "converted". Many Muslims believe that everyone is born with a natural faith in God, so non-Muslims who

embrace Islam are considered to be returning or "reverting" to their original faith.

2. Ghalib, Mirza: "From Islam to atheism after a stint of employment in Saudi Arabia." http://www.nairaland.com/882035/islam-atheism-after-stint-employment

3. Michael Martin, in his introduction to The Cambridge Companion to Atheism (Cambridge University Press, 2007) described these two types of non-belief as negative atheism and positive atheism.

4. Kayyani, Saeed: "I felt a weight being lifted off my shoulders". Blog post, 11 August 2013. http://www.al-bab.com/blog/2013/august/email-from-an-arab-atheist-2.htm

5. Author's email correspondence with Kayyani.

6. Smith, Jesse M: "Becoming an Atheist in America: Constructing Identity and Meaning from the Rejection of Theism." Sociology of Religion, 2011, vol 72 (2), pp 215-237.

7. "US Religious Knowledge Survey." Rew Research, 28 September 2010. http://www.pewforum.org/2010/09/28/u-s-religious-knowledge-survey/

8. "How Ignorant About Religion Are Religious Americans?" Friendly Atheist blog, 27 September 2010. http://www.patheos.com/blogs/friendlyatheist/2010/09/27/how-ignorant-about-religion-are-religious-americans/

9. Author's interview, April 2014. Gamal is a pseudonym.

10. The story, related by Ibn Khallikan, is quoted in Nicholson, R A: A Literary History of the Arabs. Cambridge: Cambridge University Press, 1985. pp 377-378.

11. Qassem, Abdul Aziz: "Fighting atheist tendencies." English translation from al-Watan newspaper, re-published in English by the Saudi Gazette, 20 February. http://www.saudigazette.com.sa/index.cfm?method=home.regcon&contentid=20140221196390

12. Author's interview, May 2014. Sarah Way is a pseudonym.

13. Author's interview, September 2014. Hashem al-Shamy is a pseudonym.

14. Munajjid, Muhammad: "Atheism is a greater sin than shirk." Islam Q & A website. http://islamqa.info/en/113901

15. Cheruppa, Hassan: "Religion is solution for moral degradation: Scholar." Saudi Gazette, 30 January 2014. http://www.saudigazette.com.sa/index.cfm?method=home.regcon&contentid=20140130194183

16. Author's email correspondence, March 2014.

17. Qassemi, Sultan Sooud al-: "Gulf atheism in the age of social media." Al-Monitor, 3 March 2014. http://www.al-monitor.com/pulse/originals/2014/03/gulf-atheism-uae-islam-religion.html

5: Atheism, gender and sexuality

THROUGHOUT human history, religions have usually been dominated by men: male prophets, male clerics and male theologians, not to mention a male God. Women, meanwhile, have usually been expected to sit back and listen to them. While some churches in the west have tried to address the gender issue and now have female priests, organised religion in the Middle East is still resolutely patriarchal and its teachings provide grounds for discriminating against women and marginalising them. It could therefore be argued that women in the Middle East have more reasons than men for abandoning religion – and some certainly do rebel and leave. For others, though, social conditions created by the patriarchal system make it difficult even to contemplate doing so.

Those who succeed in breaking away come from a variety of backgrounds, as two contrasting stories show: Badra, a Lebanese feminist who rejected patriarchy in both its secular and religious forms, and Noha Mahmoud Salem, an Egyptian Salafi who turned to atheism largely as a result of her husband's behaviour.

Raised in a traditionally religious family, Noha learned the Qur'an by heart and won a prize for reciting it. In high school, she took to wearing a headscarf after being told by a teacher that "a good student should also have good morals". Later, she exchanged her headscarf for the *niqab*, fully covering her face, and it was only after her marriage that doubts started to arise. The *Egypt Independent* continues the story:

> One day, her husband slapped her face. When she complained to her father, he told her God gave husbands the right to beat their wives as stated in the verse of Al-Nisa' *sura*.[1]
>
> Then she began to wonder how God could give the right to a husband to abandon and beat his wife ... How could that be when Islam forbids beating animals? Are women inferior to animals? Is it because women are physically weaker than men and cannot fight back? How could they be allowed to be so humiliated?

The relationship began to deteriorate. Her husband often left her alone at home and refused to buy her a television set, claiming it was *haram* (forbidden).

> Noha once complained to her husband, pointing out his hypocrisy after seeing him watch television at his mother's place. He responded to her complaint by beating her in front of his mother.
>
> This then made her rethink the entire Qur'an, not just one *sura*. She read in a reference book that the said *sura* came under circumstances that no longer exist in modern time and culture.[2]

Questioning her faith also brought an end to her marriage, since her husband believed that Islam forbade him from remaining married to an apostate woman.

Badra, from the Lebanese city of Tripoli, gave a very different account of her journey to non-belief – though one that also involved patriarchy. Part of it was her teenage enthusiasm for the French feminist/existentialist writer Simone de Beauvoir but also the fact that she grew up without a father, which she thinks "freed" her from the need for a divine "father" in heaven. "At the age of five I lost my father and I think that was crucial in determining the role of religion in my life," she said.

> For me as a child, religion was mainly linked to death. The family culture valued mourning rituals – women in black for a long period, TV and radio (which are considered as entertainment) were not allowed in the family during mourning periods. And whenever there was mourning in the family there was the Qur'an.
>
> My first doubt came from listening to the Qur'an when we were mourning. I found it aggressive and sad and negative. I felt really depressed. It was *Surat Ya Sin* that they read all the time for the dead. For me it was really scary because it was full of negative things and warnings against non-believers, who are considered as desperately stubborn, although it is a powerful and somehow beautiful text.

I was a small child and it was something that I received in a very aggressive manner, especially as it was linked to a very sad environment – loss of loved ones, women in black, people crying, visits to the cemetery early in the morning. For a long time, this was my first and main encounter with religion.[3]

Surat Ya Sin – so called because its mysterious first verse consists only of two Arabic letters, *ya* and *sin* – is often described as "the heart" of the Qur'an. Abu al-A'la al-Mawdudi (1903-1979), one of the most prominent Islamist ideologues, wrote that its themes of reprobation, reproof and warning are "presented repeatedly in a highly forceful manner, so that hearts are shaken up and those which have any capacity for accepting the truth left in them should not remain unmoved".[4]

Badra's second major encounter with religion came at school. Her mother was a Shia Muslim and her father had been Sunni but she attended a Christian girls' school managed by nuns.

This lack of a single reference somehow saved me from religion. In school, the Christian students went to their Christian religious lessons but the Muslim students had a free hour ... until the 1980s when there was this Islamist movement in Tripoli called al-Tawhid and things started to change. Suddenly, militiamen were in the streets warning young girls and women not to wear short-sleeve shirts or short skirts.

I was twelve at the time. The school was obliged to give Qur'anic lessons for the Muslim students when Christian students went to their catechism class. So this was basically how I re-discovered religion.

I was first affected by this Islamist cultural movement in the school and I went to the religious courses. It was exciting in the beginning. At first I took it seriously because it was a new thing to discover, and the courses offered a space for reflection and discussion.

There was this event with my grandmother, because she saw me doing the prayers. At a certain stage I wanted to do the five prayers but I was a daydreamer so it was a real pain for me to stick to them. I wanted to be good and to do them but at the same time I also wanted an excuse to stop doing them.

My grandmother saw me and said "What are you doing?" Actually, she didn't want me to do the prayers because she was Sunni and didn't want me to pray in my Shia mother's way.

I think it was more social than religious because the Sunnis look down on Shia Muslims with some contempt. She was afraid of some rituals that the Shia have and she didn't want me to be affected by that. Although I was torn between two loyalties and although I felt the injustice of the judgement against my mother, this helped break my new enthusiasm for religious precepts and the accompanying feeling of commitment.

At school, meanwhile, Badra was discovering French literature – and existentialism.

> This is how I became distanced from religion. I was reading Sartre, de Beauvoir and, later on, Camus – but mainly de Beauvoir, *Mémoires d'une Jeune Fille Rangée* ("Memoirs of a Dutiful Daughter"). She was talking about herself as a teenager so I was really identifying with her and how she slowly left the clan, made different choices other than the one that her family prescribed and expected from her.
>
> This was a pivotal book for me because it is a story about the construction of identity. The story of Simone, the young girl from a conservative family who later became Simone de Beauvoir – and the type of relationship that she later developed with Sartre – was certainly fascinating for me as a girl in Tripoli. It made me dream and want to do like her, to discover the world, discover literature, have friends who think differently and try to completely change her environment and way of thinking.
>
> I had some very interesting teachers in school who never expressed any atheism but introduced us to this kind of literature which was not part of the curriculum. They were keen on developing critical thinking among students. They introduced us to the concepts of cultural diversity and universality of human values, and to ideas (such as existentialism) that were not necessarily those of the school but were nevertheless accepted.
>
> My French literature teacher who used to teach [the classical plays of] Racine, Corneille, Molière, opened a small door for modern texts and this is how I came to know some Sartre *(Huis Clos, Les Mouches)* and Camus *(Caligula)* plays in school.
>
> I stopped believing in hell when I read *Huis Clos*. It had nothing to do with religion but I was simply discovering a new language, a new lexicon. "Hell" was already something else. I was a teenager, and one year after taking those Islamic courses in school my interests completely changed.

Badra thinks the early death of her father contributed to her lack of a need for God. "The fact that I did not have an overwhelming father figure made me somehow free ... I simply knew by experience that it is possible to live and grow up without one."

In a traditional Arab family, Syrian-born sociologist Halim

Barakat wrote, the father sits at the top of a pyramid of authority and requires "respect and unquestioning compliance with his instructions" – in much the same way that God does.[5] Barakat noted that in Arab society the head of the family, the head of state and God are all cast in a similar mould, with many characteristics in common: "They are the shepherds, and the people are the sheep."[6] This "social pyramid" was one of the things that drove another young woman, Egyptian-born Reem Abdel-Razek away from Islam:

> A lot of times when I was reading the Qur'an I would read about slaves, for example. It's mentioned 29 times, and I couldn't understand how a God that is proclaiming to be fair and sending a message that is supposed to be a peaceful one would allow someone to enslave another person.
> Not only that, but if it's a female slave the slave owner is allowed to have a [sexual] relationship with her – and to me this is rape. I couldn't imagine how a God that is claiming to be just would allow something like that. I think that's one of the most important things that made me consider why Islam isn't as I was taught it.

Several male interviewees also cited patriarchal attitudes as one of their reasons for rejecting religion. "I would say the treatment of women in Islam was a major factor," Arab Atheist said. "I noticed how women were in the west and how different they were from all the women I knew back home and I started to see how Islam mistreats women."

Ahmad Saeed added: "Even when I was a Muslim I used believe that although Islam was the true religion and that these were the words of God, there were people who manipulated these words for their own purposes, so they could have power over families or engage in domestic violence without anybody saying anything to them. Look at Saudi Arabia, how it's very misogynistic – we are living in a region where the father has control of the entire family."

For Yahya, a Yemeni, this was one of the things that made him start to "feel disconnected" from religion when he was fourteen or fifteen. "Sometimes when I read the Qur'an I felt it was not the word of God – it was just simple talk that anybody can do. There were things that seemed nonsense to me like how a male is better than a female. When I was a kid I was thinking that this is nonsense – like how can my father be greater than my mother?"

For vast numbers of Arab women, though, choosing between belief and non-belief is simply not a realistic option. Nabila from

Bahrain said: "There is a lot of pressure on women to conform. For instance, something as simple as finding a partner or getting into a relationship. Everything is counted, everything is watched."

Bahrain, she continued, had been a pioneer among the Arab countries in terms of women's rights and women's involvement in politics, but it became more restrictive after the Iranian revolution.

> Before the revolution in Iran things were different ... women were more open, they were more rebellious, they were more feminist than today. Today even my mother, who is a feminist, keeps on asking me to try and compromise, because if I don't compromise I will not be accepted. I do compromise to some extent. For instance in front of my grandparents I have to act like a Muslim because if I don't they won't sleep at night from worrying that they have done something wrong because they can't direct me to the right path.
>
> Me being a *woman* atheist is even worse because, in their heads, I wouldn't be able to find a husband and things like that. I've known a lot of girls here who find it very hard to admit to themselves that they have doubts about religion, because they think that when they do they will ruin their chances of finding someone [to marry].

In Egypt, Reem Abdel-Razek managed to break away but she acknowledges the difficulties that other women face:

> A lot of women are so – I don't want to say they are brainwashed but a lot of women in Egypt really do believe that they are less than men. Of course the pressures can get them to feel that maybe this is unfair, but most of the women I've met would say to an outsider: "This is our choice. This is completely up to us, we are not oppressed."
>
> But when it's just between us [Arab women] they say: "I'd love to take off the hijab but I know I can't." So it's a sort of acceptance of the status more than a rebellion against it.

"You get these thoughts, you get these doubts," Nabila said, "but we are so wired. In this part of the world religion is in the system. It's not only in your household, it's in the whole system – it's in your school, even in your laws. Because of that it's very hard for people to break out."

Sarah, with Syrian parents but raised in Kuwait, described visits to friends of her family:

> We used to go to their house a lot because they were Syrian. His wife

was Alawi but he was Sunni. His wife was all covered up. We would be sitting down in their house and she was always very silent, even though he and his wife had the same level of education in the same field – they were both nurses.

When we were sitting down and talking she was always quiet. His kids were very bright and one of the things that hurt me the most – and one of the main reasons why I despise this man and his religion – was because his wife was so quiet. She couldn't talk much when he was around and she had to sit there and do "women's stuff", whatever that is.

He had a daughter. Now, she's probably 16. She was so beautiful and bright. It kind of hurt me that she was never going to have a voice.

But Sarah has also learned from painful experience about the costs of rebellion:

I got married when I was 18 and my ex-husband was very religious. He was abusive, he wanted me to make babies and cover myself up to the eyes – and I ran away.

No one had any idea where I went. I went to Quebec and disappeared. I was homeless for a year. I was hitch-hiking, I was eating out of trash cans, sleeping on the sidewalks. I'm now sleeping on a friend's floor but at least I'm not homeless. I'm trying to get my life together.

And sometimes she reflects on what she has sacrificed:

I ask myself: do I want to have a voice and freedom or do I want to have a home and family and food in my belly and have a roof over my head and never have to worry about money?

I know it's a cliché when people say freedom is much better but there are so many days when it feels like I'm going to give up my choice in exchange for security.

The popular association of atheism with immorality is a particular deterrent for women who have religious doubts, since in Arab society they are expected to be "virtuous" and not rebellious in order to marry. "It is difficult to come out as an atheist because society immediately considers you to be a person without moral values or ethics. This affects girls the most," the administrator of the "Arab Atheists" Facebook page noted. "We have had to remove names of female members from the page to protect them from families and society."[7]

Social pressures of this kind, obviously, are not the only reason why many women still cling to religion. In the west, the relationship between religion and gender has been the subject of much sociological research, and numerous studies have found women in general to be "more religious" than men. This points to a paradoxical situation in which women may be simultaneously subjugated by religion and sustained by it.

Before looking at possible explanations for this it is necessary to sound a note of caution. Most of the published research – including findings that women are "more religious" than men – relates to people from a Christian cultural-religious background living in the west and is not necessarily applicable to Muslims, especially those living in the Middle East. A comparative study in 2001, looking at Christians, Hindus, Jews and Muslims living in Britain came up with different findings: in the non-Christian groups, women appeared to be "significantly less religiously active" than men. This led the authors to dispute the generality of the view that women are more religious than men, on the grounds that previous research has been culture-specific and contingent on the measurement method used. The authors commented:

> Many religious traditions differentiate between the religious obligations of men and women, placing greater onus upon men to fulfil "religious" duties such as prayer and text study. Traditional Judaism and Islam place less strenuous religious obligations upon women than upon men in some respects, due particularly to the traditional allocation of primary home making and child care responsibilities to women.
>
> For example, attendance at a place of religious worship may be less frequent for Jewish and Muslim women compared to men ... Muslim women should not enter a mosque during menstruation, so the devout woman would be expected to attend a place of worship less often than a man.
>
> Women who are occupied with family responsibilities may be less obligated to pray or to engage in religious study. Thus on measures of religious activity, Jewish and Muslim women may appear less "religious" than Jewish and Muslim men.[8]

The 2001 study, it should be noted, was not concerned with belief but with religious activity – specifically, how often people attended a place of worship, how often they prayed and how often they studied religious texts.

Although there is too little evidence to know for certain whether the maxim that "women are more religious that men" applies to

Arab women, and Arab *Muslim* women in particular, it is still worth considering possible differences between men and women in the factors that attract them to religion and the part religion plays in their lives. Again, most of the research and theorising relates to women in the west but it is easy to see how some of it may be relevant to the Arab countries.

For example, it has been suggested that women's involvement in religion may be shaped by their domestic role. One idea is that mothers, as the primary socialisers of children, would be responsible for instilling moral values – perhaps by setting an example for their children through religious practice. Another idea is that women who are confined mainly to the home "may be placed in fewer situations that challenge them to think critically" about their religious beliefs. A third idea is that women's traditional role as carers – giving birth, nursing babies, looking after sick and dying relatives – puts them "in a more immediate relationship with the ultimate questions of life and death" which may lead some of them to seek comfort in religion.[9]

The "comfort factor" provided by religion appears to be particularly important among marginalised social groups, including ethnic minorities and women. Melanie Brewster writes:

> Religiosity may provide solace from feelings of frustration, fear, and anxiety, but these symptoms of distress stem from holding a marginalised position in society in which discrimination and prejudice are rampant, not from innate personality traits. Indeed, many studies have found that individuals from socially oppressed groups use their religious communities as systems of support ...[10]

Men, Brewster suggests, are less likely to need this kind of support because of their relatively privileged position.

In countries such as Egypt and Lebanon, where changing religion is not against the law and sectarian rivalries are strong, conversions by women – whether actual or merely rumoured – can be far more contentious than conversions by men. In 2012, a Christian priest was kidnapped at gunpoint in the Bekaa region of Lebanon, reportedly for having baptised a Shia woman who fled her home after converting to Christianity. Both sides in the dispute claimed foul play. A Lebanese archbishop told the press that the woman's father, a Shia cleric, had physically and psychologically tortured her following her conversion to Christianity. Her father, speaking on local television, retorted that monks and priests had "practised witchcraft and sorcery" on his daughter to bring about her conversion.[11]

Stories of this kind have little to do with religion itself but reveal a lot about attitudes towards women: old concepts of family and tribal "honour" are extended and applied to faith. Women, as the repositories of virtue, must be guarded jealously since other faiths are assumed to be trying to entice them away.

In 2010, demonstrations broke out in Egypt and continued for several weeks over the case of Camillia Shehata, a Coptic priest's wife who was rumoured to have been incarcerated by the Coptic Orthodox Church after converting to Islam. The affair began when Camillia's husband reported her missing. Although it later became clear she had left home because of a marital dispute, a story circulated that she had been abducted and forcibly converted to Islam – with the result that hundreds of Coptic demonstrators took to the streets. Police investigations revealed that she was not being held against her will and she was said to be staying at an undisclosed location belonging to the Coptic Church. That sparked new rumours and protests – this time by Muslims who believed Camillia had willingly converted to Islam and was now being held captive by the Church. Commenting on the affair, Mariz Tadros wrote:

> It is a truism of study of patriarchal societies that concepts of honour are tied to women. The Coptic demonstrations in Upper Egypt upon the "disappearance" of Camillia were driven by a sense of having lost a priest's wife to a predatory Muslim majority. The phenomenon of abduction is thoroughly gendered in Egypt, since it is always a woman, and never a man, who is thought to have been abducted for the purposes of conversion.
>
> When rallies [by Muslims] took place in every corner of Egypt later, they were driven by a desire to emancipate the Camillia who had ostensibly donned the *niqab* from the clutches of the church. The gatherings were about defending the honour of Muslims in claiming what is rightfully theirs – a sister in Islam. At no time in memory has such a large number of women wearing the *niqab* engaged, week after week, in collective protest.
>
> Certainly, there have been fierce sectarian clashes over land, places of worship and the commentary of religious leaders, but none have so fired the imagination of both Muslims and Christians like cases involving women in this intensely patriarchal society.[12]

In Sudan, 27-year-old Meriam Ibrahim was convicted of apostasy and sentenced to death. In accordance with usual practice, the Sudanese authorities gave her an opportunity to recant but she refused – understandably, since there was nothing to recant. As often happens with "apostasy" charges, the case was not really about theology; it was about patriarchy, sectarianism and a family quarrel.

Ibrahim's Muslim father had been absent since she was six years old and she had been raised by her mother as a Christian. In Sudan, under Islamic law, children inherit the religion of their father and so Ibrahim was officially classified as a Muslim. This meant she was technically an apostate, having supposedly abandoned Islam for Christianity.

In 2011, she committed a further "crime" by marrying a Christian man – which, as a technically Muslim woman, she was not allowed to do. In addition to the death sentence, the court declared her marriage void and therefore sentenced her to 100 lashes for having sex outside marriage. Ibrahim could not be executed immediately because she was pregnant at the time and was sent to prison, along with her 20-month-old son. She gave birth to her second child in jail, reportedly while her legs were chained.[13]

The prosecution had been instigated by her Muslim half-brother and half-sister for motives which are not entirely clear. Her half-brother, Al Samani Al Hadi Mohamed Abdullah, claimed that her husband had bewitched her into leaving Islam by giving her a magic potion. "It's one of two," he told CNN. "If she repents and returns to our Islamic faith and to the embrace of our family, then we are her family and she is ours but if she refuses she should be executed."[14] According to her lawyers, she owned several successful small businesses – a hair salon, agricultural land and a convenience store – and her relatives were hoping to take possession of them.

Following a lot of international pressure (her husband had acquired American citizenship), an appeal court eventually overturned her sentence and she was released from jail. Shortly afterwards, however, she was briefly re-arrested at Khartoum airport, along with her husband and her children, while attempting to leave the country – ostensibly because of a problem with travel documents.

Once again, there were suggestions that the airport arrests had been prompted by Ibrahim's Muslim relatives. Her half-brother complained to a Sudanese newspaper that she should have been handed over to her family rather than her husband when she was released and claimed that she had been "kidnapped" and spirited away against here will after leaving prison. "Our family is not convinced by the decision of the court [to quash the charges]," he said. "The law has failed to maintain our rights, and now it is a matter of honour. Christians deface our honour, and we know how to take revenge for that."[15]

After being released for a second time, Ibrahim took refuge in the American embassy and eventually arrived in the United States.

ACCUSATIONS of patriarchy can be found on the other side too, among non-believers. In the US particularly, there have been complaints that atheism is largely "a boys' club". There is some truth in this, though perhaps not as much as people imagine, and some blame the media for focusing almost exclusively on a group of men dubbed the New Atheists. Among Americans who say they have no formal religious affiliation, women account for about 40% – a minority but a very substantial one.[16] Women have also been activists and not just passive non-believers. In an article published by Bitch magazine, Victoria Bekiempis writes:

> From Madalyn Murray O'Hair, the founder of American Atheists,[17] whose 1963 Supreme Court lawsuit brought an end to prayer in public schools, to Sergeant Kathleen Johnson, who started an organisation for atheists in the United States military, to Debbie Goddard, founder of African Americans for Humanism, countless women have worked as successful atheist activists.
>
> They've penned books, run organisations, and advocated on behalf of religiously repressed citizens. But you might not guess that from the popular portrayal and perception of atheism in America, which overwhelmingly treats the contemporary class of non-God-fearing freethinkers (also known as secularists, sceptics, and nonbelievers) as a contentious, showboating boys' club.[18]

One of the first atheist feminists was Ernestine Rose, born in Poland in 1810. While still in her teens, she fought and won a court battle to save herself from an unwanted marriage which had been arranged by her father, a Jewish rabbi. She later continued her activism in Britain and the US. Listing a large number of currently-active women atheists in an article for *Ms* magazine, Jen McCreight says: "It's undeniable that most of the time men outnumber women, whether you're looking at conference attendees or conference speakers, blog readers or best-selling authors," but she adds: "This problem is compounded when the media fails to mention deserving women atheists – even in articles in feminist publications asking where all the atheist women are."[19]

Some have also argued that the aggressive approach of the New Atheists – that religion should be actively combated rather than tolerated – conveys a macho image which women may find off-putting. McCreight rejects this, however, pointing to a number of female atheists who are "gnashing their teeth even louder than Richard Dawkins and Christopher Hitchens".

The freethinkers of Arab history (at any rate, those who are remembered today) were, of course, men. But among the new wave of non-believers from the Middle East women are not noticeably absent. Iranian-born Mariam Namazie of the Council of Ex-Muslims of Britain points out that the American ex-Muslim organisation was founded by a woman, the German group is headed by two women and her own British group has two female spokespersons. "I personally think it's a woman's club," she continued:

> If you look at the protests [in the Middle East] you do find women at the forefront of many of them. Many of them are freethinkers and atheists even if they don't necessarily call themselves atheists.
> I think the problem is they [women] are invisible in the atheist movement in the west. If you go to atheist conferences, it is very white and male. I hate using those terms because I hate dividing people in that way, but I think it's because it takes time for the grassroots leadership to show ... There's nothing wrong with being white and male. The problem is not that they [white men] are there and speaking – we need that. The problem is that other people are not seen.
> We are organising a conference and the vast majority of speakers are women of colour – from the Middle East, from North Africa, from immigrant backgrounds here in the west – people who are doing amazing work but you wouldn't know about them ... They haven't been recognised because they are working at such a grassroots level and very often it is difficult to see them.[20]

Of the forty-six speakers listed for the conference that Namazie mentioned, twenty-nine were women and seventeen were men.[21]

"THERE IS a big closet population of atheists who need to come out," Richard Dawkins said, endorsing the OUT Campaign which had been launched in 2007 urging atheists – especially in the United States – to show their atheism by wearing a badge in the shape of a red letter "A".[22] It is no coincidence that atheists use the term "coming out" to describe a public declaration of their non-belief. Homosexuality and atheism are two things that people often prefer to keep secret. In an Arab context, both are socially taboo and may also involve law-breaking.

Atheism and homosexuality are linked in other ways too, however. Statistics compiled in the US by the General Social Survey[23] show that lesbian and gay Americans are almost three times more likely than heterosexuals to describe themselves as atheist or agnostic.[24] It has also been reported that 62% of LGBT people in the US feel religion is not an important part of their lives.[25] The obvious explanation is that people who find their sexuality condemned by religious teaching are likely to start asking questions about religion that lead them towards disbelief. [26]

Homosexual acts are illegal in most of the Arab countries, and where no specific law exists there are usually other laws that can be deployed, such as Egypt's law against "debauchery". Being gay is not in itself a crime (unless it involves sex), though men have sometimes been arrested for effeminate behaviour and gay parties have been raided. The usual penalty for sodomy is imprisonment, though it is punishable by death in Mauritania, Saudi Arabia, Sudan and Yemen. On the whole, despite occasional crackdowns, implementation of the law tends to be arbitrary and haphazard – the authorities do not systematically hunt gay people for prosecution. One reason for this is the official line that homosexuality does not exist to any significant degree in Arab countries – it is mainly viewed as a western "disease". In post-Saddam Iraq, however, vigilante groups have often harassed and killed men suspected of being gay or regarded as not "masculine" enough.[27]

As far as religion is concerned, mainstream Islamic teaching condemns homosexuality, and Christian churches in the region generally adopt a similar position. Homosexuality is mostly seen as a "choice" (and therefore sinful), though some – perhaps trying to be more charitable – regard it as a mental illness. No punishment seems to have been established during the Prophet's lifetime, so interpretations of the sharia usually treat sex between people of the same gender as akin to sex outside marriage.

Islamic denunciations of homosexuality often rely heavily on the *hadith* – the possibly spurious "traditions" of the Prophet – since there is little of relevance in the Qur'an itself. Those who invoke the Qur'an focus mainly on the story of Lut, the Biblical prophet known as Lot. The biblical version is recorded in the Book of Genesis where God resolves to punish the people of Sodom and

Gomorrah by raining stones from heaven, and the story is told in similar terms in the Qur'an.

This has traditionally been interpreted – by Christians and Muslims alike – as a divine punishment for homosexuality, though a careful reading of the story shows it is more complicated than that. Multiple sins were involved and, to the extent that these included homosexuality, it was of a non-consensual kind. The traditional interpretations have increasingly been questioned by Christians outside the Middle East but only rarely by Muslims – even though the Biblical and Qur'anic stories are very similar. In a book which examines the scriptural evidence, Scott Siraj al-Haqq Kugle argues that homosexuality is not categorically forbidden by Islam and calls for more acceptance of diversity within the faith. This, obviously, is a reformist view and it has parallels in the way some Muslim feminists have sought to re-read the Qur'an in a less patriarchal light.[28]

In western countries, where not all churches are hostile, LGBT people do sometimes reach an accommodation between their sexuality and religion but in the Arab countries current religious teaching makes that much more difficult. Hasan, a gay Bahraini, said: "You have religious texts condemning gays but then it makes you feel that what's written there is probably not by a god. Why would God create gays in the first place if He condemns them? Should I live a celibate life to please Him and then go to heaven?" When he eventually came out, Hasan judged – correctly – that his sexuality was more likely to be accepted by the less religious members of his family: "Because my father is not religious and my brother and sister are not, they accepted me. I did not tell my mum because she's very conservative and she's sick. I hid it from her because I don't think she would receive it very well."

People who are struggling with their sexuality or preparing to come out are often in need of support – the sort of support that religion, in different circumstances, might be expected to provide. This points to one of the key differences between women and LGBT people in their relationship with religion. Thus, while women may gain some comfort from religion, even if it contributes to their repression at the same time, for gay Arabs the comfort factor is lacking: instead of sympathy and understanding, they are greeted with condemnation.

In Hasan's case, though, this did not immediately turn him against all forms of religion but prompted him to explore other "spiritual" possibilities. "When you go through a hard time you search for spiritual answers or something to give you hope," he said. He was studying in India at the time of his coming out and he drew some comfort from Buddhist ideas – "not the reincarnation aspect but things like impermanence, loving kindness, compassion".

One way that feminists and gay men can sometimes reconcile themselves with religion is through what sociologists call "faith plasticity" – in essence, reshaping orthodox concepts of God and faith to fit their needs. Tareq Sayed Rajab de Montfort is a young Kuwaiti-born artist, and openly gay. He describes himself as devout, though not in a conventional way – a fact which becomes apparent at first sight: the Arabic word for "truth" is tattooed on his throat and other parts of his body are permanently inked with verses from the Qur'an.

Growing up in Kuwait, his first contact with Islam was not through the mosque as might be expected but through his family's museum. The privately-owned Tareq Rajab Museum, founded by his grandfather, contains more than 30,000 items from around the Muslim world.

"I never felt the need to go to a mosque because we had coverings of the Kaaba in our basement," Tareq said.[29] "We have three nineteenth-century ones from when they were still being made in Cairo. Those from the nineteenth century are so much more ornate. The entire front is covered in gold and silver embroidery. They are absolutely amazing. We also have one of the largest private collections of Middle Eastern calligraphy from the earliest scriptures on vellum to Chinese nineteenth-century Islamic calligraphy. So God was very much present, but a much more abstract sense of God, a much more mystical sense of God."

It was from his grandfather and this art collection that he first got an idea of what religion was – that it came from the worship of beauty. "It gave an entire foundation to my understanding of Islamic art. I saw the manifestation of the Prophet's words: 'God is beautiful' and 'God loves beauty'," he told one interviewer.[30] Tareq's growing-up experience was unusual and possibly unique, and it gave him a far more positive perspective than most people acquire from sermons in the mosques. It also made him critical of mainstream Islam.

"I don't mean this in an offensive way," he said, "but it's a bit of a sad result from what Muhammad and Islam were supposed to be and could have been ... the Prophet would be appalled if he saw what it has turned into today." As a *sayyid* – a descendant of the

Prophet – Tareq feels entitled to express these views. "I find there are two extremes of people's identity towards religion now," he continued. "One side is that they completely accept it – 'you must do this' – a lot of the dogma, and I don't mean it in a negative or positive way." On the opposite side there are those who reject religion altogether and turn to atheism but also others who experiment with different forms of religion, with some even turning to Satanism – though he added that this is not "real Satanism" but "the Hollywood version".

In Kuwait, he said, there seems to be a growing (if surreptitious) interest in Buddhism which, as a non-monotheistic religion, is general regarded as less acceptable than Islam, Judaism or Christianity.

> I got into trouble in school once for talking about Hinduism and Buddhism. I don't know if I can say it's a taboo but it is for some people, I suppose. But I've seen that changing, especially with the internet. In Kuwait, now, there are "healing centres" which are Buddhist. The people who run them go to Buddhist events around the world but it's not labelled as Buddhist when they advertise a healing centre or a spa. This started very recently ... and yoga classes. All sorts of things are happening now.

So far, this undercover Buddhist activity has not attracted attention from the authorities or religious vigilantes. "I guess they don't feel threatened because there is no mention of Buddhism – it's all 'health'," he said. "The *mutawa*, the big bearded guys, are probably not in any kind of lifestyle where they will hear about spas or things like that."

Tareq said his homosexuality had never caused him to doubt faith "or that sense of the divine", though he recognised that others go through trauma that makes their sense of divine "decay or disintegrate". That problem would not arise, he suggested, if Muslims heeded the Prophet's advice to "think for yourself":

> If we take things upon ourselves as the Prophet asked us to do ... If people actually did that and did read the Qur'an, there are routes through Islam for us to find beautiful things that don't agree with homosexuality being wrong, or that the hijab must be worn. It's all interpretation, and if we are to follow what the Prophet asked us – interpret with *al-rahim* (compassion), then that will take you to a purer form of Islam. And the purer form of Islam as I consider it is that homosexuality is not a sin, it's not punishable.
>
> If the Prophet Muhammad is the ideal Muslim who we are all meant

to follow, there are no hadiths that ever said he condemned any homosexual men. There are recollections of where he apparently allowed queer men to be in the presence of his wives, unveiled. The Qur'an even says that men who do not have the desire [for women] are permitted to see them as well. [31]

In 2013, Saeed Kayyani came out as both gay and an atheist in a bog post on the internet. This is an extract of what he wrote:

> For me, the process began as soon as I was born. I wasn't born 100% Arab. My father is from the United Arab Emirates and my mother is from Alabama, USA. I was already classified as "different". While others would be able to adapt to this, I wasn't able to cope. Homosexuality changed the dynamic for me right from the start. I wasn't entirely American, truly Arab, or a "real man".

> The first game changer came to me while I was living in Florida with my family. I was a painfully awkward sixth-grader at the time that was doing his best to be a good Muslim and son. Then 9/11 came.

> From then on, life in America wasn't the same. Since my mother wears the hijab, she couldn't go a single day without stares. The kind of stares that say "traitor". I lost friends. I had my beliefs mocked in front of me. People started to treat my family less seriously. This feeling of "otherness" was starting to surface from my insides. However, seeing as I was the good Muslim boy, I defended Islam as much as I could.

> This is significant because it is the first time that I became aware that religion could even have a different interpretation. Unfortunately, my parents weren't much help in clearing things up for me. I was simply told the "We're right and they're wrong," line.

> A year later, we moved to the United Arab Emirates so that my father could put his newly earned PhD in psychology to good use ... Since I was doing good at school work and barely had a social life, not many people questioned why I never had a girlfriend. That is, until I made my first gay friend. As soon as it became obvious that I was friends with him, rumours started spreading.

> I was even approached by a couple of boys saying that I needed God. What's ironic about this is that this point of my life was easily the most religious. Deep feelings of guilt and pain pushed me to try to make peace with God. Around this time, I felt like I was being betrayed. I kept on asking Allah "Why is this happening to me? I don't want to feel like this any more. Help me become clean!"

> I was trying to figure out, through an Islamic perspective, what purpose did Allah have for homosexuality? I didn't buy the "He's only

testing you" line. Why would the creator purposely inflict such emotional pain on his creation? Also, why would homosexuality be created and yet condemned by the very same entity?

Even with all of this though, I was still faithful. Faithful, yet a complete wreck. I was extremely lonely, anxiety-ridden, confused, and suicidal. Especially after hearing degrading anti-gay remarks from my own parents several times.

After learning about apostasy in Islam, I felt a metaphorical light-bulb switch on inside me ... Death to those that leave us? Allah really said this? Really? No. It sounded more like humans projecting themselves into the heavens. Tactics like this served a purpose in medieval times. Human purposes. Why would an all-powerful, all-mighty, and all-knowing being demand death for a lowly, pathetic, and powerless little human being that changed his mind about its existence?

I was honestly dumb-struck by this epiphany. I felt a weight being lifted off of my shoulders when I was finally able to gather enough courage to say to myself: "I don't believe in Islam."

Describing reactions to his blog post a few months later, Kayyani said that in general they confirmed how scared people are to talk about these subjects openly. A handful of Arab friends and acquaintances offered support and some seemed genuinely interested to learn more, since they had never knowingly met an atheist and/or a gay person. Others were more aggressive or condescending, suggesting he was out of touch with reality or too influenced by the west, that he had mental problems or some sort of agenda against Islam. One even said he was possessed. Most of these hostile views came from the younger generation in UAE, he said.

He was still unsure whether his parents knew of his double-coming-out article. He suspected that they did, because their behaviour had noticeably changed. "They've given me several more lectures about marriage and religion and have even pressured me to regularly see a psychologist. Thankfully, the psychologist has been on my side and has been a wonderful source of support."

For Kayyani, belonging to a sexual minority was certainly a factor in becoming an atheist, but there were other considerations too. "Several logical issues with Islam did not hold at all with my values, such as fairness," he said. "People are unnecessarily harmed by the nonsensical aspects of religion every day. I saw a big problem with this and didn't want any part of it. It was easier for me to come to that conclusion since I'm gay." Although not surprised by the statistical linkage of homosexuality with atheism, he felt there were significant differences between the two.

> Being gay makes it fundamentally problematic to conform with societies' expectations. This isn't the case with atheism: one can still be comfortably functional in a religious society and also atheist. Homosexuality is biological. Because of this, it will manifest itself to other people eventually whether anybody likes it or not. This doesn't apply to atheism. It's easier to hide not believing in God than it is to hide emotions for another person.

He continued:

> It goes without saying that LGBT people historically haven't been welcome in institutionalised religion, but there are also those that are genuinely religious and gay. This may be the case with part of the LGBT population, but it definitely is not the entire story. LGBT people are diverse people like everyone else. We have the same complexities, needs, concerns, and faults as everybody else.
>
> In particularly religious environments, survival for LGBT people sometimes means obedience or rebellion. The majority end up in a grey area, leading a double life. A gay, atheist Emirati friend of mine, for example, is having an Islamic marriage to a woman soon. His marriage isn't about Islam, though. It's a cultural expectation that's imposed on Emirati men in order to avoid social stigma for himself and his family. He is going along with it so that his government employment opportunities aren't harmed. This cultural expectation applies to me as well and the social consequences for my family still scare me.[32]

NOTES

1. Qur'an 4:34: "Men are in charge of women, as Allah has made one of them superior to the other, and because men spend their wealth for the women; so virtuous women are the reverent ones, guarding behind their husbands the way Allah has decreed guarding; and the women from whom you fear disobedience, [at first] advise them and [then] do not cohabit with them, and [lastly] beat them; then if they obey you, do not seek to do injustice to them; indeed Allah is Supreme, Great."
2. Adib, Mounir: "Salafi woman turned atheist recounts her journey."

Egypt Independent, 4 November 2013.
http://www.egyptindependent.com/news/salafi-woman-turned-atheist-recounts-her-journey
3. Author's interview, April 2014.
4. http://www.islamicity.com/quran/maududi/mau36.html
5. Barakat: Halim: The Arab World: Society, Culture and State. Berkeley and Los Angeles: University of California Press, 1993. pp. 100–101.
6. Barakat: Halim: op cit, p. 117.
7. https://www.facebook.com/GODS.FACKER/posts/437110759728752
8. Loewenthal, Kate; MacLeod, Andrew and Cinnirella, Marco: "Are women more religious than men? Gender differences in religious activity among different religious groups in the UK." Psychology Department, Royal Holloway, University of London, 2001.
http://digirep.rhul.ac.uk/file/a4d4660e-7408-3162-7ab7-61dd4ee6ad60/3/Are_women_more_religious_than_men.pdf
9. Brewster, Melanie: "Atheism, gender and sexuality." Chapter in The Oxford Handbook of Athiesm. Oxford: Oxford University Press, 2013.
10. ibid.
11. Bureau of Democracy, Human Rights and Labor: International Religious Freedom Report for 2012.
http://www.state.gov/j/drl/rls/irf/religiousfreedom/index.htm?year=2012&dlid=208400
12. Tadros, Mariz: "Behind Egypt's Deep Red Lines". MERIP, 13 October 2010. http://www.merip.org/mero/mero101310
13. "Sudanese woman sentenced to death for apostasy gave birth with her legs chained, her husband says." Telegraph, 29 May 2014.
http://www.telegraph.co.uk/news/worldnews/africaandindianocean/sudan/10861889/Sudanese-woman-sentenced-to-death-for-apostasy-gave-birth-with-her-legs-chained-her-husband-says.html
14. "Meriam Ibrahim's brother turned her in because 'she won't repent'." CNN, SBS, 5 June 2014.
http://www.sbs.com.au/news/article/2014/06/05/meriam-ibrahims-brother-turned-her-because-she-wont-repent
15. "Meriam Ibrahim was 'kidnapped' and I went to police before she boarded flight to America, her brother says." Telegraph, 25 June 2014.
http://www.telegraph.co.uk/news/worldnews/africaandindianocean/sudan/10925293/Meriam-Ibrahim-was-kidnapped-and-I-went-to-police-before-she-boarded-flight-to-America-her-brother-says.html
16. Pew Research: Religous Landscape Survey.
http://religions.pewforum.org/reports#
17. http://www.atheists.org/about-us/history
18. Bekiempis, Victoria: "New Atheism and the Old Boys' Club." Bitch magazine, May 2011. http://bitchmagazine.org/article/the-unbelievers
19. McCreight, Jen: "Where Are All The Atheist Women? Right Here." Ms blog, 3 November, 2010.

http://msmagazine.com/blog/2010/11/03/where-are-all-the-atheist-women-right-here/
20. Author's interview, May 2014.
21. http://ex-muslim.org.uk/2013/12/two-day-international-conference-on-the-religious-right-secularism-and-civil-rights/
22. http://outcampaign.org. See also: MacAskill, Ewen: "Atheists arise: Dawkins spreads the A-word among America's unbelievers." The Guardian, 1 October 2007.
http://www.theguardian.com/world/2007/oct/01/internationaleducationnews.religion
23. http://www3.norc.org/gss+website
24. Self-declared atheists comprised 2.5% of heterosexual respondents and 5.6% of LGBT respondents. Agnostics comprised 4% of the heterosexual respondents are agnostics, 12% of LGBT respondents. Linneman, T and Clendenen, M: "Sexuality and the Secular", chapter in Atheism and Secularity: Volume 1 – Issues, Concepts, and Definitions, edited by Phil Zuckerman. Santa Barbara, CA: Praeger, 2010.
25. Singer, B and Deschamps, D: Gay and Lesbian Stats: A Pocket Guide of Facts and Figures. New York: Harper Collins, 2010.
26 Brewster (op cit) points out that this may also happen in the opposite direction: that atheists, having freed themselves from religion, are more able to explore their sexuality.
27. "They Want Us Exterminated." Human Rights Watch, August 2009. http://www.hrw.org/reports/2009/08/17/they-want-us-exterminated-0
28. Kugle, Scott Siraj al-Haqq: Homosexuality in Islam. Oxford: Oneworld, 2010.
29. The Kaaba in Mecca is covered with a cloth known as the kiswa, which is replaced with a new one annually.
30. Video interview with Huffington Post.
http://live.huffingtonpost.com/r/archive/segment/5363d19efe3444b0130002d9
31. Author's interview, July 2014.
32. Author's email correspondence with Kayyani.

PART TWO:

PROTECTING THE FAITH

6: The privileges of religion

DURING the holy month of Ramadan, adult Muslims fast from sunrise to sunset. Fasting is supposed to encourage self-control but fasting under the threat of arrest is more about obedience than self-control. Using the law to ensure that people fast (as numerous Arab countries do) undermines the moral purpose of Ramadan, just for the sake of keeping up appearances.

Gulf states tend to be the most strict in enforcing Ramadan. The typical penalty is a one-month jail sentence and/or a fine, and the law applies to everyone regardless of religion – on the grounds that seeing someone break their fast is offensive to Muslims even if the fast-breaker is not actually Muslim. In Kuwait, where most of the population are foreigners and non-Muslims account for more than 20% of the total,[1] restaurants and cafes must remain closed during daylight hours, though supermarkets can open. In Dubai, members of the public are officially encouraged to look out for anyone eating, drinking or smoking – even in the relative privacy of their own car – and report them to the police. According to Dubai police, 27 people were arrested for fast-breaking between 2005 and 2009, including a European non-Muslim.

In Egypt, which has a large Christian minority and no law requiring people to fast, the authorities nevertheless embarked on a crackdown in 2009, reportedly arresting more than 150 people in Aswan province and ordering the closure of cafes and restaurants in the Red Sea tourist resort of Hurghada. In the Delta area, seven youths were arrested for smoking in the street (smoking is considered to be fast-breaking) and fined LE 500 ($90) each. The wave of arrests seemed to be mainly the work of some especially religious-minded police officers but the authorities supported them on the grounds that public fast-breaking is a form of "incivility" covered by the Egyptian penal code. Clerics also backed the punishment of those who broke the fast in public. Sheikh Abdel Moati Bayoumi, a member of al-Azhar's Islamic Research Centre, said: "People are free not to fast, but privately; doing so in public is not a matter of personal freedom ... it reveals contempt for those who are fasting, for Ramadan and for the fasting as an obligatory religious duty."[2]

Arrests for Ramadan infringements are a regular occurrence in Algeria, too, though there has also been public debate about whether fasting should be a matter for the law or personal conscience. Six residents in the town of Biskra were arrested for eating and playing cards during the daylight hours of Ramadan in 2008. They were each fined 120,000 dinars ($1,770) though an appeals court judge later quashed the sentences, saying they violated constitutional provisions for freedom of belief. In a separate case, three men convicted of smoking during Ramadan in Algeria had their three-year jail sentences reduced to two months on appeal. In 2011, a group of men working on a construction site were imprisoned for eating during Ramadan even though they insisted they were not Muslims. Arrests usually occur when people break the fast in public but in a more unusual Algerian case police entered a house in Akbou following a tip-off and arrested young men who had been breaking the fast privately inside.

In Morocco in 2009, the *Mouvement Alternatif pour les Libertés Individuelles* (known by its French acronym MALI) set out to challenge Article 222 of the penal code which says:

> A person known as belonging to the Muslim religion who ostensibly breaks the fast in a public place during the time of Ramadan, without grounds permitted by this religion, is punished by imprisonment of one to six months and a fine of 12 to 120 dirhams [$1.50–$15].

The group, organised mainly through Facebook, decided to hold a picnic in a public place, citing the Moroccan constitution which guarantees religious freedom for all citizens, and Article 18 of the Universal Declaration of Human Rights, to which Morocco subscribes. The planned location for the picnic was a forest outside Mohammedia – chosen to minimise the risk of the action being seen as provocative. This was the first recorded protest against the country's Ramadan law, and a Moroccan news website described what happened:

> The meet-up was at the train station of Mohammedia, a few miles from Casablanca. Seventy people indicated their intention to attend but only a dozen made it through a cordon of security personnel ... "We were surprised by the heavy police presence that we encountered" said Ms Zineb Elghzaoui, journalist and a founder of MALI along with Ibtissam Lachgar, a psychologist.
>
> More than a hundred officers, including riot and mounted police and military personnel had besieged the station and its environs. "We had to show our backpacks and when they saw we had food, they [police] forced us to return to Casablanca on the next train," explained Lachgar.
>
> The security forces were also keeping back local youth groups who were attempting to confront the Ramadan fast-breaking protesters ... "Our aim was to show that we are Moroccans, but that we do not fast, and that we have a right to exist," said Ms Elghzaoui. "And although the Moroccan Constitution guarantees freedom of worship, each year there are arrests" for public fast breaking, she added.
>
> Ms Elghzaoui spoke about the case of a citizen who was attacked and denounced in the city of Fez and handed to the police by civilian vigilantes last year for drinking in the street. He was free hours later, after his family showed he was a diabetic.[3]

A more successful protest took place in Algeria in 2013 after security forces questioned three young people for breaking the fast. Angry residents of Tizi-Ouzou, a largely Berber area with a relatively secular outlook and a history of tense relations with the central government, organised a public fast-breaking lunch which was attended by some 300 people. Bouaziz Ait Chebib, head of the local Kabylie Autonomy Movement, explained: "We called this gathering to denounce the inquisition and persecution of citizens who, because of their beliefs, refuse to observe the fast."

MAKING criminals of people who eat in the daytime is just one rather mundane example of the special privileges granted by Arab governments to Islam – privileges that discriminate against those of other faiths and none. Public opinion also generally approves of such practices. Rather than giving a lead in combating discrimination, governments indulge popular prejudices and, in the process, help to legitimise private acts of discrimination by individual citizens.

Domestic workers who are not Muslim, Jewish or Christian are regarded as *najis* (impure) – which, in the eyes of some Muslims, means they cannot be allowed to cook meals for the family. "My mum would not hire a maid if she's not from the Abrahamic religions," Hasan, a Bahraini, said. "Some domestic workers claim to be Christian just to be hired," he continued. "It's quite obvious – they would be from Nepal, from India or Sri Lanka and their names would be clearly not Christian. We had a maid who I think was Buddhist, so my dad printed a picture [from the internet] of Jesus Christ and said 'Just keep it in your room in case mum checks, to show you are definitely Christian'."[4]

That did not satisfy Hasan's mother, however. She continued to voice her suspicions that the maid was Buddhist rather than Christian – eventually causing the maid to leave. The recruitment agency that provided the maid refused to take her back, on the grounds that no other household would employ her because she had left her job. "So dad bought her a ticket to Nepal along with a small sum for financial security to help her, out of kindness," Hasan said. "My uncle's house also returned their Indian maid since she is a Hindu."

Among the members of the Arab League, Islam is "the religion of the state" in Algeria, Bahrain, Egypt, Iraq, Jordan, Kuwait, Libya, Mauritania, Morocco, Oman, Qatar, Saudi Arabia, Tunisia, the UAE and Yemen. In Algeria and Morocco, the official status of Islam is specified as an element of the constitution that can never be amended.

Sharia law, according to Yemen's constitution, is "the source of all legislation" and in Oman it is "the basis of legislation". Sharia is "*the* main source of legislation" in Egypt, while in Bahrain, Kuwait, Syria, Qatar and the UAE it is "*a* main source". The constitution of Iraq, approved by a referendum in 2005, specifies Islam as "a fundamental source of legislation" and says that "no law that contradicts the established provisions of Islam may be established." Rather confusingly, it also says that no law must contradict "the principles of democracy" or "the rights and basic freedoms" stipulated elsewhere in the constitution. These potentially opposing stipulations reflect conflicting political pressures at the time of drafting and it is unclear how they might be reconciled in practice.

Tunisia's post-revolution constitution is similarly inconsistent, promising "liberty of conscience and of belief" while committing the state to "protection of the sacred and the prohibition of any offence thereto". In Tunisia, the drafting of the new constitution generated much debate and, in the words of Amna Guellali of Human Rights Watch, attempted the impossible task of reconciling two radically different visions of society. "On the one hand, it caters to a hyper-religious audience that sees the government as a watchdog and protector of all things sacred. At the same time, [it] describes a society that leaves each person the freedom of religious choice, without intrusion or interference."[5]

Among Arab monarchies, the accession of a Muslim ruler to the throne might be assumed but to make doubly sure, Jordan, Kuwait, Oman and Qatar specify this in their constitutions too. Among Arab republics, the constitutions of Algeria, Mauritania, Syria, Tunisia and Yemen say the president must be a Muslim (a *practising* Muslim in the case of Yemen) – thus applying the principle of religious discrimination to the head of state. In Lebanon the picture is more complicated because of the mix of faiths and sects, but it is nevertheless discriminatory. Although Lebanon has no state religion the president has to be a Maronite Christian, the prime minister a Sunni Muslim and the speaker of parliament a Shi'a Muslim.

Disqualifying non-Muslims from presidential office might seem a fairly trivial matter since in practice it is almost certain that a Muslim will be chosen, but it violates the principle of equal rights for all citizens. This issue cropped up during debates about Tunisia's post-revolution constitution and Nejib Gharbi, a spokesman for the Islamist Ennahda party, failed to see the point. "Islam is the religion of the majority of Tunisians, and the official religion of Tunisia is Islam. It is normal for the president of the country to be Muslim," he said. While it's true that the vast majority of Tunisians are Muslims (nominally, at least), there is a big difference between saying that on the balance of probabilities any Tunisian president is *likely* to be a Muslim and saying that the president *must* be a Muslim. An earlier statement from Ennahda had claimed that members of Tunisia's (tiny) Jewish community "are citizens enjoying all their rights and duties" – but where the presidency is concerned that is clearly not the case.[6]

To place this in a broader context, forty-nine countries worldwide have some kind of religious requirement for their head of state, according to analysis by the Pew Research Center. Nineteen of these (sixteen members of the British Commonwealth, plus Denmark, Norway and Sweden) have a ceremonial Christian monarch without political power. Among countries where the head of state has a more-than-ceremonial role, seventeen require the monarch or president to be Muslim – and these are mostly in the Middle East or North Africa. Meanwhile, Andorra and Lebanon specify a Christian head of state, Bhutan and Thailand specify a Buddhist head of state, and the Indonesian president is required to uphold Pancasila, a monotheistic political philosophy on which the state is based. In eight other countries, including Bolivia, Mexico and El Salvador, the religious requirement is of a secular kind, since it prohibits members of the clergy from becoming head of state.[7]

Worldwide, the existence of official religions is not particularly unusual. A study in 2004 identified seventy-five out of 188 independent countries – 40% – as having a state religion.[8] In some cases, as in most of the Arab countries, this is made explicit in the constitution but the picture is not always so clear-cut. Where it is not explicit, the government may still support a particular religion in various ways, such as financially or through the education system. Having a state religion also means different things in different countries. In some – Britain, for example – the effect on daily life is fairly small but the impact in the Arab countries puts them at the extreme end of the scale.

Although state religions do not conflict directly with international humanitarian law, in practice they almost inevitably lead to the abuse of rights. Examining this problem in 2011, the UN Special Rapporteur on Freedom of Religion or Belief commented:

> While the mere existence of a state religion may not in itself be incompatible with human rights, this concept must neither be exploited at the expense of the rights of minorities nor lead to discrimination on the grounds of religion or belief ... Indeed, it seems difficult, if not impossible, to conceive of an application of the concept of an official "state religion" that in practice does not have adverse effects on religious minorities, thus discriminating against their members.[9]

Apart from the general atmosphere of religiosity there are political explanations for the prevalence of state religions in the Middle East and North Africa. One is that most of the governments are not freely elected and therefore need to seek other sources of legitimacy. Religious credentials, if available, can be a useful alternative. Thus the king of Saudi Arabia is known as the Guardian of the Two Holy Shrines (Mecca and Medina) – a title which according to Saudi protocol should always be mentioned first, before alluding to the fact that he is king. To a lesser extent, the kings of Morocco and Jordan also make use of religious credentials. Jordan's monarch, Abdullah II, boasts of being a "forty-third generation direct descendant of the Prophet Muhammad" and is official guardian of al-Aqsa mosque in Jerusalem, regarded as Islam's third holiest site. The king of Morocco, meanwhile, is known as *Amir al-Mu'minin* – Commander of the Faithful.

Having a state religion also creates a legal pretext for the authorities to meddle in religious affairs and exercise some control over them – for example, by employing clerics who are amenable towards the regime and supervising the content of sermons. Where governments face serious challenges from Islamist opposition movements they sometimes try to claim the moral high ground for themselves as defenders of Islam. The intention, usually, is to appease or even undermine the Islamists but it does not always succeed and can easily lead to Islamists calling the shots where religion is concerned.

In 1991 the unsaintly Saddam Hussein changed Iraq's flag by inserting the words *Allahu akbar* ("God is Greatest"), allegedly in his own handwriting. This was seen as an attempt to boost the regime's Islamic credentials just a few days before the start of the war that ousted Iraqi forces from Kuwait.

Syria under the Assads provides an interesting example of a relatively secular regime that nevertheless shaped and promoted a specific view of religion. Although the Baathist regime was never particularly religious, the dominant position occupied by followers of the minority Alawi sect (which is generally regarded as an offshoot of Shia Islam) was potentially a weakness that could be exploited by the regime's opponents. Put simply, the Alawites were at risk of being portrayed as heretics.

Hafez al-Assad responded to this in several ways. The first was to try to control the Sunni majority by channelling them into "acceptable" forms of Islam that posed no threat to his regime or the Alawis, as Torstein Worren explains:

> He realised that in order to stabilise the country, he would have to make concessions to the Sunnis. Through his Corrective Movement, he sought to redo the most radical secular reforms of the earlier Baath regimes. In order to limit the clergy's influence in the political sphere, he co-opted them by giving them increased power in the social realm. Therefore, instead of building a true secular society, the state was

secular on the surface, but not in matters of family and personal law. Instead, this was governed by religious legislation for each religious community, meaning that Muslims are governed by Islamic sharia law and Christians by their churches' religious rules.

The other side of the coin was to redefine the Alawis as ordinary, mainstream Muslims. Thus, for example, the Alawis were not allowed their own religious courts but were brought under the same sharia rules as the Sunnis.

This also helps to explain the official (but misleading) view of Islam that has been taught in Syrian schools. Worren continues:

> The Islam presented in the schoolbooks is that of orthodox Sunni Islam, and there is no mention of the Islamic minorities living in Syria or of Shia Islam as a whole, or even of the different schools of thought within Sunni Islam. According to the schoolbooks, there is no diversity within Islam. This means that Alawism is never mentioned in schools in Syria – the epitome [of] the Official Discourse – and it falls implicitly under Islam. Syrians, therefore, learn nothing about each other's beliefs and differences, and what they know or think they know is based on rumours and stories passed on from friends and relatives.[10]

In the opinion of Syrian atheist Hashem al-Shamy, pursuing this policy has contributed to the sectarian rivalries that have since risen to the surface. "Basically, by not educating people about the other sects, the regime held everyone hostage to its version and deterred sects from learning about each other," he said. "The less you know about someone the harder it is to accept them as peers. The continuing civil war, with increasing sectarianism, is the product of such decades-long policies."[11]

WORLDWIDE, the linkage between religion and states has a long history, not least in Europe. Although church attendance in Europe has declined steadily and society is now largely secular, the formal separation of church and state is not complete. In Britain, for example, the head of state is also head of the Anglican church. Britain, incidentally, retained a blasphemy law until 2008, but in the century before its abolition prosecutions had been extremely rare. In many parts of Europe churches enjoy privileges granted by the state, such as tax benefits or funding through taxes collected on their behalf, and religious schools exist in parallel with state education. In Europe, though, the continuing links between religion and the state are far less significant than in the Arab countries today. In contrast to much of Europe, the US has a formal separation of religion from the state but remains very religious socially (and even politically). The American example also seems to disprove the idea that religion automatically declines in a modern, technologically advanced society. If so, there must be some other explanation for the popularity of religion in the US and its relative unpopularity in Europe.

Various theories have been put forward to account for this difference. A number of factors seem to be involved but the "comfort factor" may be particularly relevant: there is plenty of evidence from around the world that feelings of insecurity draw people towards religion. Although the US is a prosperous country, social welfare services provided by the American government are far less extensive than they are in Europe. Thus it might be argued that while Europeans are more likely to look to the state for their welfare needs Americans are more likely to look to religion. Others have pointed to ethnic and cultural diversity in the United States where, again, the comfort factor may be important. The popularity of religion among black Americans has often been noted: black churches provide communal support and solidarity in what can often be a hostile environment.[12]

In terms of the religion providing a "comfort factor", Arab countries are more similar to the US than to Europe. Religion clearly flourishes in the Middle East where there is turmoil, social insecurity or poverty, and Islamist movements have gained strength by providing welfare services that governments failed to provide. The exception to this may be the wealthy Gulf states which have more extensive welfare provision – implying, perhaps, that religion would decline there without strong government support.

Another theory which may be of some relevance to the Arab countries looks at religion in terms of a marketplace where state religions are granted a monopoly or protected from competition. One of the first to view religion in this light was Adam Smith, the eighteenth-century economist:

> According to Smith, the key aspect of state religion is its promotion of the monopoly position of the favoured religion. This promotion works partly through limitations on entry of competitors and partly through subsidies. Smith's analysis focuses on the adverse consequences from the monopoly positions of the Anglican Church in England and the Catholic Church in other countries. He argues that monopoly providers of religious services tend – as monopolies do generally – to

become non-innovative and indolent. Consequently, service quality and religious participation decline.[13]

This has been explored further in recent times, notably by Rodney Stark and Roger Finke in their book, *Acts of Faith*.[14] The other side of the argument is that while state-sponsored religions are ultimately doomed to lose followers, a "free market" in faith forces religions to become self-reliant and allows them to flourish, so long as they make the effort to satisfy their "customers". A prime example of that is the United States. As far as Arab countries are concerned, the marketplace argument suggests that state support does not serve the long-term interests of Islam – though serving the interests of Islam is not necessarily the intention behind state support. In practice, governments rarely embrace religion out of the goodness of their hearts but because of the political benefits they hope to gain from doing so.

THE PRIVILEGES granted to religion by Arab governments raise specific issues in connection with education. States which are parties to the International Covenant on Civil and Political Rights have a duty to ensure the religious and moral education of children "in conformity" with their parents' convictions. Among other things, this means there is a right to opt out if the type of religious education provided by the state conflicts with parents' beliefs. All Arab countries are parties to the convention, with four notable exceptions: Oman, Qatar, Saudi Arabia and the UAE.

There is an important distinction to be made here between religious *education* and religious *instruction*. Religious instruction is the teaching of a specific religion or belief based on its tenets, and there is often public demand for this, as a UN report acknowledged:

> In the understanding of many parents, the development of knowledge and social skills of their children through school education would be incomplete unless it includes a sense of religious awareness and familiarity with their own religion or belief. Hence the provision of religious instruction in the public [state] school system may be based on the explicit or implicit wishes of considerable currents within the country's population.[15]

However, the report went on to say that religious instruction in state school systems "must always go hand in hand with specific safeguards" for religious minorities and respect for the convictions of parents and guardians who do not believe in any religion. It added that the possibility of opting out should not be linked to "onerous bureaucratic procedures" or penalties.

While the purpose of religious *instruction* is to familiarise pupils with their own religious tradition, religious *education* aims to broaden their knowledge about different religions and beliefs: "In this sense, providing information about religions is not part of theological teaching, but instead comes closer to other disciplines, such as history or social sciences." This kind of teaching, if delivered in a neutral way, has the positive effect of encouraging tolerance and combating prejudice, in the view of the UN report:

> Information about religions and beliefs should always include the crucial insight that religions – as a social reality – are not monolithic; the same applies to non-religious belief systems. This message is particularly important, because it helps to deconstruct existing notions of a collective mentality that is stereotypically, and often negatively, ascribed to all followers of various religions or beliefs ...
>
> It is important that textbooks and other materials draw a sufficiently complex picture of the various religions or beliefs and their internal pluralism. Furthermore, existing alternative voices within religious traditions, including voices of women, should always have their appropriate and fair share of attention ...
>
> Only by overcoming monolithic perceptions can we become aware of the real diversity among human beings.[16]

There are fundamental – probably irreconcilable – differences between this idea of using religious education to broaden the minds of students and what actually happens in many Arab schools where teaching can have the opposite effect of promoting intolerance and monolithic perceptions. Saudi Arabia's Basic Law openly declares use of the education system for "instilling the Islamic faith in the younger generation" and attempts elsewhere to adopt a different approach can meet with stiff resistance. Following the overthrow of the Gaddafi regime in Libya, for example, Grand Mufti Sadeq al-Ghariani demanded changes in the new school textbooks – including the removal of a paragraph suggesting that people were free to choose their own religion.[17]

Kuwait, despite being a party to the International Covenant on Civil and Political Rights, does not provide the opt-out required by the covenant (unless parents pay for private education). The government requires Islamic religious instruction for all students in state schools, largely based on the Sunni interpretation of Islam even though Kuwait has a substantial Shia minority unofficially estimated at 30%-40% of the population. Some textbooks "refer to certain Shia religious beliefs and practices as heretical".[18] Iraq, another party to the covenant, does not require non-Muslim students to take part in religious instruction in state schools – at least in theory. However, there have been reports of non-Muslim students feeling pressurised to do so by teachers and classmates: "There were also reports that some non-Muslim students were obligated to participate because they could not leave the classroom during religious instruction."[19]

CITIZENS' religious affiliation is recorded on national identity cards in a number of Arab countries. This is a controversial practice which, in the words of a UN special rapporteur, "appears to be somewhat at variance with the freedom of religion or belief that is internationally recognised and protected". The justification usually given is that the authorities need to know people's religion because different legal systems apply to different faiths in the area of personal status law – marriage, divorce, inheritance, child custody, etc – but in the case of religious minorities recording it on ID cards also opens the door for discrimination by officials, police and others.

Apart from the question of whether anyone should be forced to disclose their religion, at a purely practical level serious difficulties can arise if people change their religion or choose not to be linked with any particular faith. In Egypt, by law, everyone must obtain an identity card on reaching the age of sixteen. This places officials in an extremely powerful position regarding the issuing of ID cards and the religion that is recorded on them. Without a card, Egyptians effectively become non-citizens, unable to work legally, study beyond secondary school, vote, operate a bank account, obtain a driver's licence, buy and sell property, collect a pension, or travel.

It is not uncommon for Egyptians to change their religion – sometimes out of conviction but often because of marriage to someone from a different faith (since Egypt has a large Christian minority and, under sharia, a Muslim woman cannot marry a non-Muslim man). Christians also sometimes convert to Islam for the purpose of divorce, since the Coptic Orthodox Church has restrictive rules about divorce.

In practice, registering a conversion to Islam is very

straightforward in Egypt but conversion from Islam to another faith is much more problematic. Egypt's Civil Status Law says that citizens can change information on their identity documents, including their religious affiliation, simply by registering the details with the interior ministry. In theory the ministry cannot refuse but the courts and officials have sometimes argued that registering a conversion from Islam would amount to endorsing the "sin" of apostasy – which they claim would be unconstitutional because the constitution says Islam is the religion of the state. Some have also argued that converting from Islam to Christianity shows "contempt" for a "divinely-revealed religion" (which is against the law in Egypt) or that it poses a threat to public order. Conversions do sometimes lead to violence if they become public knowledge but that is partly a result of the government's failure to tackle sectarianism and promote tolerance of religious diversity. In a report examining state interference with religious freedom in Egypt, Human Rights Watch commented:

> Egyptians who are born Muslim but convert to Christianity face considerable social opprobrium as well as official harassment. For these reasons, very few if any Muslim converts to Christianity have initiated the necessary formal steps to revise their identification documents to reflect their change in religion, as permitted by the Civil Status Law. An undetermined number have emigrated to other countries, or live anonymously and surreptitiously with forged documents ... Some who nonetheless have made their conversion public say that security officials have detained them on charges of violating public order and, in some cases, have subjected them to torture.[20]

Human Rights Watch also found Christians in Egypt who had been involuntarily converted to Islam by officialdom, sometimes without their knowledge. Officials might even assign them a new name if their original name indicated they were not Muslim.

One such case involved Fadi Naguib Girgis who had been born into a Christian family in Alexandria. When he was five years old his father converted to Islam, left home and adopted a Muslim surname (since Girgis, the Egyptian equivalent of George, is a name that clearly identifies its holder as Christian). Fadi, however, continued to use Girgis as his surname – it was the name shown on his birth certificate – and he regarded himself as Christian. At the age of nineteen he moved to Cairo for work and applied for a new ID card:

My [paper] ID was falling apart, and I wanted the national identity card ... They pulled up my name; it was listed not as Girgis but as Abd al-Hakim [his father's new Muslim surname]. And the religion was wrong [listing Fadi as a Muslim]. They charged me with forging my ID, my birth certificate, my diplomas, said I was trying to convert from Islam to Christianity. They confiscated my documents and transferred me to the public prosecution office.[21]

He was detained for five days then released after intervention by the Coptic pope. The public prosecutor eventually dropped the forgery charges for lack of evidence and advised him to reapply for an identity card; he did so and the application was again refused.

In the days when government officials filled in identity cards by hand it had often been possible to persuade them to enter a dash in the "religion" section or leave it blank. But in 1995 Egypt began introducing computerised ID cards and the computer system was set up to allow only three options in the "religion" section: Muslim, Christian or Jew (the three "heavenly" religions as they are referred to in Arabic). This meant that anyone who refused to accept one of these options could not be issued with an identity card.

Apart from those who would prefer not to be associated with any religion, the people most affected by this were members of the Baha'i faith, thought to number around 2,000 in Egypt. In 2006, Hossam Ezzat Mahmoud and his wife went to court and initially won the right to register themselves and their two daughters as Baha'is. This upset conservatives and Islamists, so the government decided to appeal. The Supreme Administrative Court then overturned the lower court's decision, on the grounds that Baha'ism is not a recognised religion and that Muslims who adopt it are apostates. The verdict was greeted with shouts of "Allahu Akbar! Islam is victorious!" from members of the public in court and a columnist for *al-Gomhouriya* newspaper declared: "If Baha'ism is officially recognised, worshippers of cows, the sun and fire will want to jump on the bandwagon."

Apart from being regarded as a heretical offshoot of Islam, the Baha'i faith is unpopular in Egypt because of its accidental connections with Israel. In 1868, after being banished from his native Persia, the founder of the faith, Baha'u'llah, was exiled with his family and a small band of followers in the Turkish penal colony of Acre. As a result of this, the faith's international headquarters was established in the Acre/Haifa area which later became part of Israel. In the 1960s, President Nasser withdrew state recognition from the Baha'i community and confiscated their property. Nasser's decree was reaffirmed by the Supreme Court in 1975 in a ruling which said that only the three "revealed" religions were protected by the constitution: the Baha'is were entitled to their beliefs but practice of the Baha'i faith was a "threat to public order".

Meanwhile, the Baha'is continued their legal battle over identity cards and in 2008 the Court of Administrative Justice ordered the interior ministry to place a dash in the religious affiliation section for Baha'i citizens on their ID cards and birth certificates. On that occasion the Egyptian government did not appeal.

MARRIAGE in Lebanon is regulated according to the customs of the country's 18 officially-recognised sects. Some types of mixed-faith marriage are not allowed (the rules are very complicated) and there is no provision for marriages involving people of unrecognised faiths (Hindus and Baha'is, for example), people who have no religion or those who simply want a non-religious ceremony. Lebanon does, however, recognise marriages made abroad and this has resulted in an endless succession of couples trekking across the sea to get married in Cyprus.

In 2012, rather than taking the Cyprus option, Khouloud Sukkariyeh and Nidal Darwish, who had been born into different sects (Sunni and Shia), decided to challenge the system – and the result was the first officially-recognised civil marriage in Lebanon.[22]

They began the process by having their sectarian affiliations removed from their identity documents – a step that has been permitted in Lebanon since 2009. According to an almost-forgotten decree issued in 1936 under the French Mandate, their newly-acquired lack of a religious affiliation made them "subject to civil law" but this placed them in uncharted territory as far as their proposed marriage was concerned since Lebanon had no secular version of its sectarian personal status laws and there were no existing rules for other aspects of civil marriage, such as inheritance and divorce.

A lawyer drew up what they hoped would be a legally-valid marriage contract citing various documents, including the Lebanese constitution and Article 16 of the Universal Declaration of Human Rights ("the right to marry and to found a family"). They also had to obtain a form signed by the local mayor saying there were no objections to their marriage and post a public announcement 15 days before the wedding. There were still doubts, though, over whether the interior ministry would officially recognise it.

News of the civil marriage ignited fresh debate about Lebanon's confessional system, with President Michel Sleiman declaring his support for it and prime minister Nijab Mikati opposing it. The Grand Mufti of Lebanon then joined the fray, threatening to excommunicate any Muslim member of parliament or government minister who supported the legalisation of civil marriage:

> Every Muslim official, whether a deputy or a minister, who supports the legalisation of civil marriage, even if it is optional, is an apostate and outside the Islamic religion ...
>
> [Such officials] would not be washed [for burial when they died], would not be wrapped in a shroud, would not have prayers for their soul in line with Islamic rules, and would not be buried in a Muslim cemetery. [23]

In an apparent threat to resist any legislation allowing civil marriage, the mufti, Sheikh Mohammad Rashid Qabbani, warned that religious scholars would not hesitate to do their duty. "There are predators lurking among us, trying to sow the bacteria of civil marriage in Lebanon," he said. A prominent Christian Maronite MP, Sami Gemayel, hit back denouncing the mufti's comments as "a violation of the civil state and every Lebanese person's right which is stipulated in the constitution".[24]

Despite the prime minister's insistence that "civil marriage is a sensitive issue and we cannot afford a new dispute in this country", in April 2013 – almost six months after the wedding ceremony – the country's caretaker interior minister, Marwan Charbel, finally approved the contract, making the marriage official.

The following September, Khouloud Sukkariyeh gave birth to a son, Ghadi, who reportedly became Lebanon's first sect-free baby. President Sleiman welcomed the news with a message on Twitter: "Congratulations to Nidal and Kholoud and to all Lebanese on the birth of Ghadi, first newborn registered without a sect".

NOTES

1. CIA World Factbook. https://www.cia.gov/library/publications/the-world-factbook/geos/ku.html
2. "Furore as 155 arrested for not fasting." The National, 10 September 2009. http://www.thenational.ae/news/world/middle-east/furore-as-155-arrested-for-not-fasting
3. "Death Threats and Arrests for Facebook Ramadan Fast Break Protesters." Morocco News Board, undated. http://www.moroccoboard.com/news/34-news-release/664-death-threats-and-arrests-for-facebook-ramadan-fast-break-protesters
4. Author's interview, April 2014.
5. Guellali, Amna: "The Problem with Tunisia's New Constitution." Human Rights Watch, 3 February 2014. http://www.hrw.org/news/2014/02/03/problem-tunisia-s-new-constitution
6. Whitaker, Brian: "Tunisia's discriminatory new constitution." Blog post, 12 December 2011. http://www.al-bab.com/blog/2011/blog1112a.htm#tunisia_discriminatory_new_constitution
7. "In 30 countries, heads of state must belong to a certain religion." Pew Research Center, 22 July 2014. http://www.pewresearch.org/fact-tank/2014/07/22/in-30-countries-heads-of-state-must-belong-to-a-certain-religion/
8. Barro, Robert and McCleary, Rachel: "Which countries have state religions?" Working Paper 10438, National Bureau of Economic Research, Cambridge, MA. 2004. http://www.nber.org/papers/w10438
9. Report of the Special Rapporteur on freedom of religion or belief, Heiner Bielefeldt. A/HRC/19/60, 22 December 2011. http://daccess-dds-ny.un.org/doc/UNDOC/GEN/G11/175/41/PDF/G1117541.pdf?OpenElement
10. Worren, Torstein: Fear and Resistance: The Construction of Alawi Identity in Syria. Master thesis in human geography. University of Oslo, Dept of Sociology and Human Geography, 2007. pp 49-52. https://www.duo.uio.no/bitstream/handle/10852/16035/fear_and_resistance.pdf?sequence=2
11. Author's interview, September 2014. Hashem al-Shamy is a pseudonym.
12. For further discussion, see: Zuckerman, Phil: "Secularization: Europe Yes, United States No." Skeptical Inquirer, March/April 2004. http://www.skeptic.ca/secularization.htm
13 . Barro and McCleary, op cit.

14. Stark, Rodney and Finke, Roger: Acts of Faith: Explaining the Human Side of Religion. Oakland: University of California Press, 2000.
15. Report of the Special Rapporteur on freedom of religion or belief, Heiner Bielefeldt A/HRC/16/53. 15 December 2010. http://daccess-dds-ny.un.org/doc/UNDOC/GEN/G10/177/93/PDF/G1017793.pdf?OpenElement
16. ibid.
17. "Grand Mufti calls for changes to school textbooks." Libya Herald, 18 October, 2012. http://www.libyaherald.com/2012/10/18/16414/#ixzz35YjCCGVB
18. US State Department: "International Religious Freedom Report for 2012." http://www.state.gov/j/drl/rls/irf/religiousfreedom/index.htm?year=2012&dlid=208398#wrapper
19. US State Department: "International Religious Freedom Report for 2012." http://www.state.gov/j/drl/rls/irf/religiousfreedom/index.htm?year=2012&dlid=208390#wrapper
20. "Prohibited Identities: State Interference with Religious Freedom." Human Rights Watch/EIPR, November 2007. http://www.hrw.org/en/reports/2007/11/11/prohibited-identities.
21. Ibid.
22. Whitaker, Brian: "Sects and marriage in Lebanon." Blog post, 28 January 2013. http://www.al-bab.com/blog/2013/blog1301a.htm#sects-and-marriage-in-lebanon
23. Whitaker, Brian: "Mufti's threats over civil marriage in Lebanon." Blog post, 29 January 2013. http://www.al-bab.com/blog/2013/blog1301a.htm#mufti-threats-civil-marriage-lebanon
24. "Gemayel slams Lebanon mufti over civil marriage remarks." Daily Star, 29 January 2013. http://www.dailystar.com.lb/News/Politics/2013/Jan-29/204185-sleiman-defends-civil-marriage-at-cabinet-meeting.ashx

7: Once a Muslim, always a Muslim

WHEN Saudi Arabia decided to use Chinese labour for railway construction in Mecca controversy broke out because Mecca is a holy city where non-Muslims are barred. But that did not deter the Saudi authorities or the Chinese railway company, a former branch of the People's Liberation Army which had been eager to secure the lucrative contract. The Saudis neatly solved the problem by presenting each of the workers with a small gift: a book printed in Chinese explaining about Islam. At that point something which can only be described as a miracle occurred. Within twenty-four hours, more than 600 Chinese workers had decided – apparently of their own volition – to convert to Islam and they were received into the faith at a mass ceremony witnessed by Dr Abdul Aziz al-Khudhairi, undersecretary of the Mecca governorate.[1]

Becoming a Muslim is extremely easy (though becoming an ex-Muslim can be far more difficult). All that is required for conversion is a recitation of the *shahada* – a short, simple statement testifying that there is no god but God and that Muhammad is the Messenger of God. To be valid, the *shahada* is also supposed to be said with sincerity, which perhaps was not the case with the 600 Chinese labourers in Mecca.

Most religions welcome new members and Muslims are enjoined to take part in *da'wa*, the call to Islam, through proselytising. Several verses in the Qur'an encourage it: "Call unto the way of thy Lord with wisdom and fair exhortation,"[2] "Let there arise out of you a band of people inviting to all that is good."[3]

Taking these verses to heart, Saudi Arabia has been one of the world's largest exporters of religion since the early 1980s. This was triggered partly by fears about the spread of Shia Islam after the Iranian revolution and partly by the Soviet invasion of Afghanistan which, among other things, led to the creation of large numbers of Saudi-influenced religious schools in Pakistan. Saudi-based foundations and individuals also made vast quantities of Islamic literature available in many parts of the world, either cheaply or free of charge. Some of this missionary work was aimed at steering other Muslims in the direction of Wahhabi Islam and in many countries it found a receptive market. The kingdom, after all, was the Prophet's homeland, and so Saudi – i.e. Wahhabi – religious ideas and practices were often perceived as the most "correct" or authentic. Other material was aimed at a securing new converts, with books such as *A Brief Illustrated Guide to Understanding Islam* which can be read on the internet and also freely reprinted by anyone, so long as nothing is altered.[4] In the United States, English translations of the Qur'an, printed under the auspices of the Iqraa Charitable Society in Jeddah, became widely available free of charge.

In most of the Arab countries, however, *da'wa* is a one-way street. While proselytising by Muslims is encouraged, proselytising by non-Muslims is regarded as inflammatory behaviour and forbidden by law or government policy. In Algeria, for instance, anyone who "incites, constrains, or utilises means of seduction tending to convert a Muslim to another religion" faces a possible fine of one million dinars ($12,900) and five years' imprisonment. The law also forbids making, storing, or distributing printed or audiovisual materials with the intention of "shaking the faith" of a Muslim. In Kuwait, the law not only outlaws proselytising but also prohibits organised religious education for faiths other than Islam. One effect of that has been to prevent British schools in Kuwait from teaching comparative religion – which is a required part of the curriculum in Britain. Proselytising in Qatar for any religion other than Islam can result in a jail sentence of up to ten years, while the penalty for possessing missionary materials of a non-Islamic variety is two years' imprisonment and a fine of 10,000 riyals ($2,740). In practice, though, suspected foreign proselytisers are likely to be summarily deported.

What this amounts to is old-fashioned protectionism – the religious equivalent of governments shielding uneconomic industries from competition through subsidies or restrictions on imports. The idea that a religion needs to be protected in this way does not say much for the convictions of its followers or the merits of its creed, and it is surely not the job of governments to prevent people, in the words of the Algerian law, from having their faith shaken.

Some would no doubt defend this on the grounds that Islam is entitled to unique and special treatment because it is the only "true" religion. Arab governments, on the other hand, usually try to justify it in terms of cultural exceptionalism or even security concerns – fears that the free exchange of ideas about religion would result in *fitna* (discord or strife). If that were to happen it would be largely their own fault because they have tried, over many years, to maintain social harmony through compulsion rather than consent and have not allowed the public to learn to address differences in an open and mature way. Citing potential troublemakers as a reason for suppressing religious dissent in effect gives the troublemakers a veto over what may or may not be said.

As far as freedom of belief is concerned, the policies and practices of most Arab governments are fundamentally at odds with international principles established by the United Nations. Article 18 of the Universal Declaration of Human Rights states that everyone has "the right to freedom of thought, conscience and religion". And in the view of the UN, this right is absolute and unconditional; it cannot be modified in any way by individual states: "Article 18 ... does not permit any limitations whatsoever on the freedom of thought and conscience or on the freedom to have or adopt a religion or belief of one's choice."[5]

Although the article can be assumed to include various forms of *dis*belief along with belief, this was made explicit by the UN Human Rights Committee in 1993 when it said: "Article 18 protects theistic, non-theistic and atheistic beliefs, as well as the right not to profess any religion or belief."

Article 18 also explicitly states that people have the freedom to change their religion or belief – a point which is of particular importance to Muslims who wish to leave Islam. By rejecting Islam they expose themselves to possible charges of apostasy, a "crime" which in the eyes of many Muslims – and, indeed, some Arab governments – warrants the death penalty.

Interestingly, the mention of freedom to change religion was included in Article 18 at the behest of Charles Malik, a Lebanese Christian who was a member of the international committee drafting the declaration shortly after the Second World War. Although "freedom of belief" implies freedom to change beliefs, Malik's insistence on spelling it out stemmed from his experiences in Lebanon, "a country then known for the relatively harmonious coexistence of its many ethnic and religious groups, which had served as a haven for people fleeing religious persecution".[6] The phrase about changing religion was opposed by several Muslim countries, partly because of sharia rules against apostasy but also because of fears about Christian missionary activity. Saudi Arabia, which had general objections to what it saw as western cultural influences in the draft declaration, was especially critical of Article 18, arguing that the right to change religion would "open the door to proselytism, political unrest, and perhaps even war".[7] Eventually, though, other Muslim countries accepted it and Saudi Arabia was the only one among them not to vote in favour of the declaration.[8]

A few years later Article 18 was incorporated word-for-word into the European Convention on Human Rights which is binding on all 47 states belonging to the Council of Europe. However, moves to incorporate it into the International Covenant on Civil and Political Rights (ICCPR) were again resisted by Muslim countries – notably, Afghanistan, Saudi Arabia, Yemen, Iraq and Egypt – with the right to change religion as the main sticking point.

The draft of the International Covenant finally adopted by the UN General Assembly in 1966 omitted the word "change". Instead, it said that everyone shall have freedom "to *have* or to *adopt* a religion or belief *of his choice*", adding that "no one shall be subject to coercion which would impair his freedom to have or to adopt a religion or belief of his choice". This was a diplomatic fudge in order to secure agreement. Essentially it conveyed the same meaning as Article 18, allowing people to choose their religion without resorting to use of the objectionable word "change". In 1981, the UN's Declaration on the Elimination of all forms of Intolerance and of Discrimination based on Religion or Belief softened the language a bit further by omitting the word "adopt". Regardless of semantics, though, both documents clearly indicate that people have a right people to change their religion.

Among the Arab League members, the ICCPR has since been ratified by Algeria, Djibouti, Iraq, Jordan, Lebanon, Libya, Morocco, Somalia, Sudan, Syria, Tunisia and Yemen. They are thus legally bound by its terms. Bahrain, Egypt, Kuwait and

Mauritania have ratified but tabled reservations (which in the case of Bahrain and Mauritania appear to claim that sharia over-rides the treaty). Comoros has signed but not ratified. Oman, Qatar, Saudi Arabia and the United Arab Emirates have neither signed nor ratified.

A growing emphasis internationally on human rights issues has prompted several efforts by Muslims to formulate alternative rights systems. These are partly intended to counter the idea that Muslims are not particularly concerned with human rights but also, and perhaps mainly, to challenge what they regard as "western" concepts by developing alternatives which purport to be no less valid. In reality, though, they are attempts to create a more limited rights framework using the sanctity of Islam as its justification.

One particularly egregious example is the 1981 Universal Islamic Declaration of Human Rights. This was circulated with an English translation which, as Ann Elizabeth Mayer has demonstrated, disguises some of the more restrictive parts found in the Arabic version.[9] Article 12a, in the English translation, begins by saying: "Every person has the right to express his thoughts and beliefs so long as he remains within the limits prescribed by the Law." As translated, this appears consistent with international norms, since the *expression* of beliefs – as opposed to the *holding* of beliefs – can, under certain circumstances, be limited by law [see next chapter].

The English translation is inaccurate and deceptive, however. What the Arabic actually says is this: "Everyone may think, believe and express his ideas and beliefs without interference or opposition from anyone as long as he obeys the limits set by the sharia." The first problem here is that the Arabic text makes no distinction between holding and expressing beliefs; both are subjected to legal controls – contrary to the internationally accepted view. The second problem, as the Arabic text makes clear, is that "the Law" mentioned in the English translation is not statute law (*qanun*) but religious law (sharia). In effect, the document is not so much a declaration of rights as a declaration that sharia determines what rights people shall have. Furthermore, these rights cannot be specified precisely because sharia is not a codified legal system and is subject to a variety of interpretations by religious scholars.

The Cairo Declaration on Human Rights in Islam suffers from similar problems. Adopted in 1990 by the Organisation of the

Islamic Conference[10] representing 57 countries, this document is described as "a guide for member states in all aspects of life". It refers to "fundamental rights and freedoms according to Islam". It does not talk about freedom of belief but it does say there should be no discrimination on grounds of religious belief. Freedom of expression is allowed "in such manner as would not be contrary to the principles of the sharia". It ends by saying: "All the rights and freedoms stipulated in this declaration are subject to the Islamic sharia" and "The Islamic sharia is the only source of reference for the explanation or clarification to any of the articles of this declaration."

While these "alternative" formulations illustrate a certain style of approach to human rights issues, their importance should not be over-estimated. "Islamic human rights declarations," Ziya Meral points out, "are known to a small circle of Muslim statesmen, activists and scholars and are almost never referred to by Muslims in discussions over human rights abuses in the Islamic world."[11]

APOSTASY – the abandoning of faith by former believers – is something that Muslims either welcome or condemn, depending on the circumstances. They welcome it when an ex-Christian converts to Islam but when a Muslim leaves Islam it is often regarded as a serious crime.

There are differences of opinion, however, over what constitutes apostasy in Islam and what punishments, if any, should apply. The Qur'an provides no clear-cut ruling and a much-quoted verse says: "There is no compulsion in religion."[12] Others counter with a remark attributed to the Prophet: "He who changes his religion should be killed." Some argue that apostasy (*irtidad* or *ridda* in Arabic) involves more than simple disbelief and should be viewed in its historical context during the lifetime of the Prophet. Tariq Ramadan, for example, writes:

> The Prophet took firm measures, only in time of war, against people who had falsely converted to Islam for the sole purpose of infiltrating the Islamic community to obtain information they then passed on to the enemy. They were in fact betrayers engaging in high treason who incurred the penalty of death because their actions were liable to bring about the destruction of the Muslim community.[13]

According Professor Abdelmouti Bayoumi of the Islamic Research Academy in Cairo, renouncing Islam is not enough, on its own, to merit execution. Interviewed by the BBC, he said the death penalty would only apply if an apostate was found to be working against the interests of a Muslim society or nation. In effect, the apostate would not be punished for disbelief but for treason. While agreeing that disbelief is not necessarily a crime in itself, Abdelsabour Shahin, an Islamist writer and academic at Cairo University, expressed a more limited view of what might be acceptable: "If someone changes from Islam to *kufr* (unbelief), that has to remain a personal matter, and he should not make it public," he said. But if someone goes public with his apostasy it "amounts to *fitna* [sedition, or civil strife]; he is thus like someone fighting Islam, and should therefore be killed". The implication of that is that apostates automatically forfeit their right to free expression – on pain of death.[14]

Attitudes of this kind are not uniquely Islamic. The ancient Greek philosopher Plato, for example, regarded atheism and impiety as a cause of vice, and therefore as a problem to be dealt with by the law. Book X of Plato's *Laws* advocated putting religion under state control, with punishments for "those who speak or act insolently toward the gods" – an idea that would not sound unfamiliar to Arabs today:

> There should be one law, which will make men in general less liable to transgress in word or deed, and less foolish, because they will not be allowed to practise religious rites contrary to law.

Plato identified two kinds of unbeliever who should be punished by the law. One was "the hypocritical sort", while the other was the misguided kind who needs "bonds and admonition":

> Let those who have been made what they are only from want of understanding, and not from malice or an evil nature, be placed by the judge in the House of Reformation, and ordered to suffer imprisonment during a period of not less than five years. And in the meantime let them have no intercourse with the other citizens, except with members of the Nocturnal Council, and with them let them converse with a view to the improvement of their soul's health. And when the time of their imprisonment has expired, if any of them be of sound mind let him be restored to sane company, but if not, and if he be condemned a second time, let him be punished with death.

R F Stalley, in his *Introduction to Plato's Laws,* comments: "No doubt Plato expects members of the Nocturnal Council to convert the atheist through philosophical argument. But since the atheist's only hope of freedom (and indeed survival) lies in agreeing with his instructors, the conditions are hardly those of a fair and free discussion. 'Brainwashing' might be a more adequate description."[15] Meanwhile, the more serious type of offender who combines atheism with "contempt of mankind" is to be imprisoned for life:

> Let no freeman ever approach him, but let him receive the rations of food appointed by the guardians of the law from the hands of the public slaves; and when he is dead let him be cast beyond the borders unburied.[16]

In Thomas More's *Utopia* – an imaginary picture of an ideal society written in the early sixteenth century – religious tolerance is viewed with approval, though tolerance of atheists is specifically excluded. Among the inhabitants of Utopia, belief in an afterlife where vice will be punished and virtue rewarded is considered essential for good order; people will "openly despise all the laws and customs of society, if not prevented by fear":

> Who can doubt that a man who has nothing to fear but the law, and no hope of life beyond the grave, will do anything he can to evade his country's laws by craft or to break them by violence, in order to gratify his own personal greed?

On that basis, unbelievers cannot be treated as full citizens:

> A person who holds such views is offered no honours, entrusted with no offices, and given no public responsibility; he is universally regarded as low and torpid. Yet they do not punish him, because they are persuaded that no one can choose to believe by a mere act of will.

This is not unlike the concept of "civil death" in modern Jordan, where apostates from Islam can be stripped of basic social rights in the areas of marriage, inheritance and custody of children.

The seventeenth-century English philosopher John Locke was an advocate of religious freedom. In 1689, in *A Letter Concerning Toleration,* he wrote: "No private person has any right in any manner to prejudice another person in his civil enjoyments because he is of another church or religion ... Neither single persons nor churches, nay, nor even commonwealths, have any just title to invade the civil rights and worldly goods of each other upon pretence of religion."[17]

Locke considered religious diversity to be beneficial and not in itself a cause of civil strife, arguing that civil strife was more likely to be the result of efforts to suppress religious diversity. Nevertheless, he found it difficult to accept atheists: giving them free rein could weaken the nation's religious faith and, consequently, its morals. Locke also doubted their honesty: "Promises, covenants, and oaths, which are the bonds of human society, can have no hold upon an atheist. The taking away of God, though but even in thought, dissolves all."

The idea that atheists could not be trusted – since they had no fear of God's punishment if they lied or broke promises – provided a legal basis for discrimination which continued in England for two centuries after Locke. Atheists were prevented from holding certain public offices and from giving evidence in court because of the requirement for a religious oath. This was eventually overcome by allowing non-religious "affirmation" as an alternative to the oath, but not without a struggle. In 1880 Charles Bradlaugh, an atheist and a republican, was elected as the Member of Parliament for Northampton and, on arriving at the House of Commons, asked to affirm rather than taking the religious Oath of Allegiance. Parliament rejected this and in the ensuing dispute Bradlaugh was deemed to have forfeited his seat. A fresh election was called which Bradlaugh contested and won – only to be disqualified once again. This process was repeated for a third time and it was not until 1886, after Bradlaugh's fourth re-election, that he was finally allowed to affirm and take up his seat.

THE EXACT legal position regarding apostasy in the Arab countries today is often difficult to determine. This is partly because their systems are based on a mixture of secular and religious law. In some countries Islamic sharia law predominates; in others it is confined to personal status matters – marriage, divorce, etc. Sharia law, since it is not formally codified, can also be inconsistent because it relies heavily on the interpretations of individual judges. In addition to that, what the law says – or appears to say – does not necessarily reflect actual practice; the way suspected apostates are treated may be determined more by social pressures than the law itself.

Algeria, Egypt, Jordan, Lebanon, Libya, Morocco, Oman and Tunisia have no statutory laws against conversion from Islam. Bahrain does not specifically outlaw apostasy, though the constitution's statement that sharia is "a principal source" for legislation implies that it could be illegal. In Iraq, government laws and regulations prevent conversion away from Islam but the country's civil and penal codes prescribe no penalties for doing so.

In Kuwait, Qatar, Saudi Arabia, Sudan, the United Arab Emirates and Yemen apostasy is a crime and in theory the death penalty can apply. As far as the state in these countries is concerned, though, "death for apostasy" is more of a myth than a reality. No recent executions for apostasy have been reported in any of them and in Saudi Arabia there have been none for well over twenty years, according to the US State Department.[18] On the rare occasions when an execution for apostasy becomes a possibility, these countries usually resort to avoidance mechanisms.

In 1996, for example, the authorities in Kuwait were confronted with their first apostasy case since independence. Hussein Ali Qambar, a Shia Muslim, converted to evangelical Christianity and adopted "Robert" as his first name. Qambar had separated from his wife and his conversion came to light during a court case about custody of their children. In accordance with Islamic custom, efforts were made to persuade him to recant – but to no avail. Islamists then began agitating and filing lawsuits seeking to have him condemned for apostasy. The case went to court and a judge recommended the death penalty. This put the Kuwaiti authorities on the spot, since there was no doubt (in sharia terms) that Qambar was indeed an apostate. Looking for a way to defuse the situation, they issued him with a passport and allowed him to quietly leave the country.[19]

A similar case arose in Yemen in 2000 when Mohammed Omer Haji, a Somali refugee who had converted from Islam to Christianity, was arrested and charged with apostasy. Once again, there were behind-the-scenes activities to avert his execution which ended with him being granted emergency resettlement in New Zealand with his wife and son.[20]

Among the 22 Arab League members, Saudi Arabia and Sudan are designated under the US International Religious Freedom Act as "countries of particular concern". Since the southern part of Sudan became independent in 2011, the north – still known as Sudan – has assumed a more strongly Islamic character. According to government estimates, Muslims (almost all of them Sunnis) make up 97% of the population and Christians 3%. Among the Muslims there are various religious traditions, including Shia, Sufi orders, the Republic Brothers and apparently growing numbers of Salafis. Discrimination and abuse is prevalent, though what appears to be religious intolerance often has an ethnic dimension too. Amidst this maelstrom, accusations of apostasy are fairly common but they rarely result in formal charges. Sudan's vaguely worded apostasy law criminalises acts that encourage apostasy as well as apostasy itself.

Apostasy in Sudan tends to be more about religious and ethnic differences than actual renunciation of belief. In 2011, for example, police in South Khartoum arrested 150 men, women, and children, mostly of Hausa ethnicity, for apostasy – based on the way they performed their Islamic prayer. Some of them were detained for almost two months but all were eventually released after instruction on "proper religious practice".[21] Although apostasy in Sudan is potentially a capital offence, the law insists that anyone who is convicted must be given an opportunity to recant. This no doubt helps to explain the lack of executions but also, perhaps, how the apostasy law has come to be used in such a trivial fashion.

There are some, on the other hand, who think the apostasy law is not used nearly enough – as a news item from the Sudan Tribune showed:

> The chairman of the Islamic Centre for Preaching and Comparative Studies, Ammar Saleh, said that cases of apostasy and atheism are on the rise in the country and accused authorities of negligence in addressing this issue.
>
> At a press conference on Tuesday, Saleh claimed that the number of converts from Islam in Khartoum has reached 109 apostates, stressing that these figures are growing in a "continuous" and "scary" fashion, especially with the presence of atheists and homosexuals.
>
> The Islamic figure slammed the government for not taking decisive action against missionaries operating "boldly" in the country. He said that anyone who denies the existence of proselytising or the increase in people converting to the Shiite faith are either "living on Mars" or are in denial.
>
> Saleh appealed to the official bodies and the community to take a stand against Christianisation and find a long-term solution to the problem, arguing that government's efforts in this regard are timid compared to missionaries' efforts.[22]

Much of this may be paranoia but it's also a sign of Sudan's multi-dimensional religious ferment. In its report on religious freedom for 2012, the US State Department noted:

In December unknown persons put up posters throughout Khartoum urging Muslims not to celebrate Christmas and the New Year, asserting that celebrating the holidays of unbelievers was akin to being an unbeliever.

The growing proportion of Salafists in the Muslim population created conflict with non-Salafist Muslims. On January 29, members of the Ansar al-Sunna group in Khartoum urged the public to refrain from celebrating the Prophet Mohammed's birthday. Sufi activists harassed Ansar al-Sunna group members. Violent clashes between the two groups the next day left between 35 and 50 injured.

At the other end of the scale, the situation in countries without an official line on apostasy can be more problematic than it appears on paper. Jordan has no explicit law preventing Muslims from leaving Islam, and no formal legal penalties. Regardless of that, though, the government does not recognise conversions away from Islam and this can have serious consequences for those affected. Muslims who leave Islam continue to be treated as apostate Muslims rather than converts to some other religion (or none).

Personal status law in Jordan is dealt with by two types of court: sharia-based courts for Muslims and others for those of recognised non-Muslim religions. Defectors from Islam can be taken to the sharia courts (by relatives or others) and stripped of important rights – in effect being punished with "civil death":

> During 2005 and 2006 two apostasy cases were heard by the sharia courts in Jordan. In January 2005, the sharia appeals court, declaring a Muslim convert to Christianity to be a ward of the state, stripped him of his civil rights and annulled his marriage.
>
> The court stated that he no longer had any inheritance rights and that he could not remarry his wife unless he returned to Islam. He was also forbidden from being considered an adherent of any other religion. The verdict also implied the possibility that legal and physical custody of his child could be assigned to someone else. The convert has since left Jordan, received refugee status, and resettled in another country.
>
> A similar decision in 2006 left another Jordanian man without identification cards, thus depriving him of basic social rights."[23]

Egypt, like Jordan, has no specific law forbidding apostasy but in another "civil death" case a 73-year-old Egyptian Muslim was awarded custody of his seven-year-old grandson because the boy's parents changed their religion, converting to the Baha'i faith. The grandfather, Mohammad Abdul Fatah, said he had gone to court after seeking advice from Egypt's Grand Mufti: "He advised me to consider my daughter dead, and to file a lawsuit to demand the guardianship of my grandchild." The court ruling could not be enforced, however, as the parents had already emigrated with their son.[24]

The use of lawsuits in religious disputes has been taken to extreme lengths in Egypt and used by Islamists in particular to harass those they disagree with – people who are not necessarily unbelievers. For Nasr Abu Zayd, a teacher of Arabic literature at Cairo University in Egypt, the trouble began in 1992 when he applied for a professorial post. The committee responsible for promotions considered three reports on his work – two of which were favourable. But the third report, prepared by the Islamist Dr Abdel-Sabour Shahin, questioned the orthodoxy of Abu Zayd's religious beliefs, claiming that his research contained "clear affronts to the Islamic faith", and the committee rejected his appointment by seven votes to six. Not content with having deprived Abu Zayd of a promotion, Shahin then wrote a newspaper article accusing him of apostasy. This in turn prompted a group of Islamist lawyers to file a lawsuit seeking to divorce Abu Zayd from his wife, on the grounds that a Muslim woman cannot be married to an apostate. They eventually won their case and Abu Zayd fled the country along with his wife.[25]

The Egyptian writer and feminist, Nawal el Saadawi, faced a similar situation in 2001 when Islamists sought to have her divorced after thirty-seven years of marriage, on the grounds that her views had placed her outside Islam. The case seems to have been prompted by an interview in which she said kissing the black stone of the Kaaba (which Muslims do on the pilgrimage to Mecca) is a "vestige of pagan practices".[26] Fortunately for Saadawi, the divorce claim was rejected.

Both these cases were made possible by *hesba*, an Islamic legal principle based on notions of collective responsibility – the idea that every Muslim has a part to play in promoting good and opposing evil. Following the Islamists' success in the Abu Zayd case, *hesba* in Egypt became a busybodies' charter, allowing countless vexatious lawsuits to be brought – mainly (but not always) by those of a religious disposition against high-profile figures whose beliefs were suspect.

In effect, these were private prosecutions and many of them never reached the courts. But they did have an intimidating effect.

In 2009, the Cairo-based Arabic Network for Human Rights Information accused the Mubarak government of allowing cases to go ahead where the plaintiffs had no real interest or legal status, and complained: "These primarily illegal cases are becoming a hovering threat over the heads of all intellectuals in Egypt. Instead of conducting an open, reasonable dialogue based on intellectuals' opinions, *hesba* experts [would] rather start the legal chase and a chain of lawsuits."[27] One lawyer, Nabih el-Wahsh, was reported to have initiated more than 1,000 *hesba* cases over a ten-year period.[28]

Legal proceedings aside, there is always the possibility of hotheads taking matters into their own hands. In 1992 Farag Fouda, an outspoken secularist who ruthlessly mocked many of Egypt's leading Islamists, was shot dead by two members of the militant group, al-Gama'a al-Islamiyya. The Muslim Brotherhood publicly welcomed his killing and during the trial of his assassins a scholar at al-Azhar who was also a former Brotherhood member argued in court that their action was justified because the authorities had failed to punish Fouda for his apostasy.[29] Two years later, Naguib Mahfouz, the only Arab ever to win a Nobel prize for literature, was stabbed in the neck outside his home after being accused by militants of apostasy. Mahfouz, who was eighty-two at the time, survived the assassination attempt but with his right arm partly paralysed.

Clearly, the Arab countries have a very long way to go before freedom of belief can become a reality. The problem is not merely one of government policies but of societies which do not yet accept that what individuals choose to believe is their own personal business – and nobody else's.

NOTES

1. "Over 600 Chinese nationals working in Saudi embrace Islam." Gulf News, 27 September 2009. http://gulfnews.com/news/gulf/saudi-arabia/over-600-chinese-nationals-working-in-saudi-embrace-islam-1.540965
2. Qur'an 16: 125. http://www.multimediaquran.com/quran/016/016-125.htm
3. Qur'an 3: 104. http://www.multimediaquran.com/quran/003/003-104.htm
4. http://www.islam-guide.com/
5. CCPR General Comment No. 22: Article 18 (Freedom of Thought,

Conscience or Religion).
http://www.refworld.org/docid/453883fb22.html
6. Kristine Kalanges: "Religious Liberty in Western and Islamic Law: Toward a World Legal Tradition." OUP USA, 2012, p 60.
7. ibid, p61.
8. Mayer, Ann Elizabeth: Islam and Human Rights – Tradition and Politics. Boulder, Colorado: Westview Press 2007. p. 150.
9. Mayer, Ann Elizabeth: op. cit. Mayer's book discusses these Islamic rights schemes extensively.
10. It was renamed in 2011 and is now known as the Organisation of Islamic Cooperation.
11. Meral, Ziya: "No Place to Call Home: Experiences of Apostates from Islam, Failures of the International Community." Christian Solidarity Worldwide, 2008.
http://www.academia.edu/2462595/No_Place_to_Call_Home_Experiences_of_Apostates_from_Islam_Failures_of_the_International_Community
12. Qur'an 2:256. http://www.multimediaquran.com/quran/002/002-256.htm
13. Ramadan, Tariq: "Muslim Scholars Speak out on Jihad, Apostasy and Women", 2007.
http://pa.cair.com/files/Muslim_Scholars_Speak_Out.pdf
14. Abdelhadi, Magdi: "What Islam says on religious freedom". BBC, 27 March 2006.
http://news.bbc.co.uk/1/hi/world/south_asia/4850080.stm
15. Stalley, R F: An Introduction to Plato's Laws. Indianapolis: Hackett Publishing, 1983. pp 177-178
16. Plato: Laws. Translated by Benjamin Jowett. Internet Classics Archive. http://classics.mit.edu/Plato/laws.10.x.html
17. Locke, John: A Letter Concerning Toleration. 1689. Translated from Latin by William Popple. http://www.constitution.org/jl/tolerati.htm
18. Bureau of Democracy, Human Rights and Labor: International Religious Freedom Report for 2012.
http://www.state.gov/j/drl/rls/irf/religiousfreedom/index.htm?year=2012#wrapper
19. Longva, Anh Nga: "The apostasy law in the age of universal human rights and citizenship". Fourth Nordic conference on Middle Eastern Studies, Oslo, 1998. http://www.hf.uib.no/smi/pao/longva.html
20. Barbara Baker: "Yemen Court Sentences Somali Convert to Death", Christianity Today, 7 July 2000.
http://www.christianitytoday.com/ct/2000/julyweb-only/55.0.html
21. Bureau of Democracy, Human Rights and Labor: International Religious Freedom Report for 2011.
http://www.state.gov/j/drl/rls/irf/2011/af/192763.htm
22. "Sudanese centre says incidents of apostasy, atheism increasing in

country". Sudan Tribune, 15 May 2013.
http://www.sudantribune.com/spip.php?article46577
23. Meral, Ziya: "No Place to Call Home: Experiences of Apostates from Islam, Failures of the International Community." Christian Solidarity Worldwide, 2008.
http://www.academia.edu/2462595/No_Place_to_Call_Home_Experiences_of_Apostates_from_Islam_Failures_of_the_International_Community
24. Sherbini, Ramadan al-: "Bahai daughter, Muslim father locked in court battle over child's custody." Gulf News, 9 August 2009.
http://web.archive.org/web/20090815013038/http://archive.gulfnews.com/region/Egypt/10338696.html
25. For more details see: Whitaker, Brian: What's Really Wrong with the Middle East. London: Saqi Books, 2009, pp. 126-128.
26. Szymanski, Tekla: "Battling Bigotry". World Press Review (Vol. 48, No. 9), September 2001. http://www.worldpress.org/Mideast/311.cfm
27. ANHRI press release, 1 October 2009.
http://www.anhri.net/en/reports/2009/pr1001.shtml
28. Whitaker, Brian: "The biter bit". Blog post, 10 October 2009.
http://www.al-bab.com/blog/blog0910a.htm
29. Soage, Ana Belén: "Faraj Fawda, or the cost of freedom of expression." Middle East Review of International Affairs, Volume 11, No. 2, June 2007.
http://meria.idc.ac.il/journal/2007/issue2/jv11no2a3.html.

8: The right to offend, shock and disturb

SHARING thoughts and beliefs is a natural human activity. Without people trying out ideas, expressing opinions and others disagreeing, civilisation would scarcely have moved beyond the Stone Age. It is not enough, therefore, simply to say that we are all entitled to our own thoughts so long as we keep them to ourselves; we also need to be allowed to express them and, sometimes, to do so in conjunction with others. The rights to freedom of thought and belief, to freedom of expression and to freedom of association are inter-linked and they are grouped together consecutively in articles 18, 19 and 20 of the Universal Declaration of Human Rights.

Unlike freedom of belief, freedom of expression and freedom of association are not considered absolute rights, because exercising them can sometimes interfere with the rights of others. It may therefore be necessary, on occasions, to impose some restrictions in order to strike a balance between competing rights. According to the International Covenant on Civil and Political Rights, though, such limitations should be kept to a minimum. For example, it says that any restrictions on freedom of expression must not only be specified by law but must also be *necessary* in order to respect the rights or reputations of others or to protect national security, public order, public health or morals.

In the view of the European Court of Human Rights, the demands of pluralism, tolerance and broadmindedness are so great – at least, in democratic societies – that freedom of expression should be protected even when it causes offence. In a landmark ruling in 1976, the court decided that freedom of expression applies not only to ideas "that are favourably received or regarded as inoffensive or as a matter of indifference, but also to those that offend, shock or disturb the state or any sector of the population". This is a view that most Arab governments and many Muslims flatly reject. As far as they are concerned, religious people need to be protected from remarks that cause them offence or expose them to ridicule. Had this been applied in the past, it would have required the imprisonment of many of the most important thinkers and writers in Islamic history. Trying to apply it today results in all sorts of discriminatory practices and, since all that is required is for someone to claim they have been offended, creates opportunities for score-settling, either through the courts or on the streets, and often over extremely trivial matters.

A few years after the European Court gave its ruling on the right to offend, a Muslim organisation known as the Islamic Council of Europe was pushing in the opposite direction. In 1981 it issued the Universal Islamic Declaration of Human Rights which, said, among other things, that no one should be allowed to "hold in contempt or ridicule the religious beliefs of others", "incite public hostility against the religious beliefs of others" or "disrespect the religious feelings of others". In other words, the Islamic Declaration sought to give specially-protected status to religious beliefs as distinct from other forms of belief. Replace the word "religious" in the declaration with "political" and the problems become more obvious: the effect on public debate would be stifling. With unintended irony, the Islamic Declaration also sought to prohibit the dissemination of "falsehood" – in which case atheists might well argue that religion itself would have to be banned.

Between 1999 and 2011, mainly at the behest of Muslim countries, the UN General Assembly, the UN Commission on Human Rights and the UN Human Rights Council passed a series of resolutions to combat "defamation of religions". These resolutions, which were often criticised as interfering with free speech, can be seen partly as a reflection of international politics at the time: a response to growing prejudice against Muslims in general, especially in the west, the stereotyping Muslims as terrorists, etc – but in terms of addressing that problem they were mis-directed and ill-conceived.

"The very concept of defaming religion is unclear and lacks a sufficient basis in international law," Article 19, an organisation that defends freedom of expression, complained. "Defamation, in its ordinary meaning, refers to unwarranted attacks on one's reputation. Religions, like other beliefs, cannot be said to have a reputation of their own." Quoting a UN Special Rapporteur, it noted that in international law protection of reputation is "designed to protect individuals, not abstract values or institutions".[1]

International law addresses religious and other forms of prejudice mainly in terms of hate speech. The International Covenant on Civil and Political Rights, for example, calls on governments to prohibit "advocacy of national, racial or religious hatred that constitutes incitement to discrimination, hostility or violence". Article 19 continued:

> While it is appropriate to sanction certain forms of hate speech, limiting debate about contentious issues, including religion, will not address the underlying social problems of prejudice that undermine equality. Instead, open debate about these issues is needed to expose the harm created by prejudice and to combat negative stereotypes.

In 2009, three UN Special Rapporteurs issued a joint statement which reinforced this point:

> We should never lose sight that our ultimate goal is to find the most effective ways through which we can protect individuals against advocacy of hatred and violence by others. Hate speech is but a symptom, the external manifestation of something much more profound which is intolerance and bigotry. Therefore, legal responses, such as restrictions on freedom of expression alone, are far from being sufficient to bring about real changes in mindsets, perceptions and discourse.
>
> To tackle the root causes of intolerance, a much broader set of policy measures are necessary, for example in the areas of intercultural dialogue or education for tolerance and diversity.[2]

They added that these policies should include strengthening freedom of expression rather than restricting it: "The strategic response to hate speech is more speech". The rapporteurs also cautioned against viewing "defamation" of religion as equivalent to racism. Racism is often based on demonstrably false ideas of racial superiority and religions often make claims of superiority for themselves, they said. "Consequently, the elements that constitute a racist statement may not be the same as those that constitute a statement 'defaming a religion' as such."

At a purely practical level, a UN study found, national laws protecting religion fail to safeguard the religious rights of individuals, stifle debate that can be "constructive, healthy and needed", and are often applied in a discriminatory manner by favouring whichever religion happens to predominate in any particular country:

> There are numerous examples of persecution of religious minorities or dissenters, but also of atheists and non-theists, as a result of legislation on religious offences or overzealous application of laws that are fairly neutral.
>
> Moreover, the right to freedom of religion or belief, as enshrined in relevant international legal standards, does not include the right to have a religion or a belief that is free from criticism or ridicule.[3]

A further point to note is that in many countries religious leaders and institutions wield significant power and influence that goes well beyond straightforward matters of faith. It is therefore not in the public interest to have laws that protect them from scrutiny and criticism.

At the UN Human Rights Council, support for protecting religions from "defamation" gradually waned and in 2011 the council approved a resolution which did not mention "defamation", "vilification" or "denigration" of religions at all. Instead, it talked more constructively about ways of combating intolerance, negative stereotyping, stigmatisation, discrimination, incitement to violence, and actual violence against persons based on religion or belief. The resolution, put forward by Pakistan on behalf of the Organisation of the Islamic Conference, was accepted without a vote.

At the international level this was a significant victory for free expression, but as far as the Islamic countries were concerned it was probably due more to a recognition that they were outnumbered in the council than to a change in their views. At a national level, it made little impact and some countries moved the other way.

Tunisia, for example, had been relatively secular during President Ben Ali's 23 years in power though freedom of expression was severely curtailed. The popular uprising that overthrew Ben Ali in January 2011 created an opening for both secularist and ultra-religious elements. On the religious side, militants described as Salafis sought to impose their own version of Islam, attacking Sufi shrines (which they regarded as idolatrous) and events organised by Shia Muslims. They also attacked some hotels and individuals selling alcohol and harassed the Russian Orthodox Church. Five people, including a police officer, were arrested for allegedly plotting to kidnap Jews.

The post-revolution authorities in Tunisia seemed unsure how to respond or were perhaps reluctant to do so. "Government investigations of attacks on religious sites resulted in arrests and prosecutions in only a minority of cases," the US State Department reported. The authorities were also accused of providing inadequate security for Christian and Jewish places of worship, and of failing to protect Sufi sites. They did, however, take steps to remove "divisive" imams from some of the mosques, including Salafi imams.

In October 2011, Nessma, a privately-own Tunisian TV channel, broadcast *Persepolis* – an animated film which had won a prize at the Cannes festival and had previously been shown in Tunisian cinemas without much fuss. Based on an autobiographical graphic novel by Marjane Satrapi, it depicts the last days of the Shah and Iran's 1979 Islamic revolution through the eyes of a young woman. In one short scene she imagines herself talking to God, who is shown as an old man with a white beard.

In Islamic teaching, depictions of God are generally regarded as idolatrous, and a group of around 300 protesters reportedly attacked the TV station and attempted to set fire to it. The station's owner, Nabil Karoui, was later fined 2,400 dinars ($1,500) for "disturbing public order" and "threatening public morals". Two of his staff were also fined. Prosecutors had been seeking a prison sentence and at least two Islamist lawyers had called for the death penalty: "Anything related to God is absolute," one of them told the Washington Post.

Commenting on the trial, Amnesty International accused the Tunisian government of a "lack of will" to defend free expression. "While protecting public morals or public order may sometimes be a legitimate reason for restricting freedom of expression, such restrictions may only be imposed if absolutely necessary. This is clearly not the situation ... people should not be convicted and sentenced for their views, even if these views are seen as controversial or offensive," a spokesperson said.

Around the same time, two Tunisian atheists were each

sentenced to seven-and-a-half years in jail and fined 1,200 dinars ($800) after posting material on the internet that was deemed "liable to cause harm to public order or public morals". Jabeur Mejri and Ghazi Beji, both in their late twenties, were friends from Mahdia, a coastal area south of Monastir, and apparently quite well known locally for their atheistic views. Mejri had written several short books which could be downloaded from the internet. One of them, mainly about sex and its effects on health, mentioned various sexual practices including homosexuality, which it said is increasingly accepted "in open minded regions", and paedophilia, which was accompanied by a cartoon showing "The Prophet Muhammad aged 50 trying to seduce Aisha aged six". The shape of the Prophet's robe in the drawing suggested very clearly that he was sexually aroused. Another of Mejri's self-published books, called *Guidance and Light,* began with this question:

> Is it possible that the Muslim Qur'an is nothing more than an entire book of Satanic lies and verses that "tickle the ears" of Arabs?

None of this appears to have caused a fuss at the time but a lawyer in Mahdia, Fouad Sheikh Zouali, took exception to some images on Mejri's Facebook page and asked him to remove them. Mejri refused. Zouali then filed a lawsuit against Mejri, who was duly arrested.

Meanwhile, Ghazi Beji was concerned for his friend and went to check the court file about the case – only to discover that he himself was named as a co-defendant. He fled the country before he could be arrested, and was tried and convicted in his absence.

Beji travelled to Algeria and Turkey before sneaking illegally into Greece, where he told an atheist website that his views on Islam had started to cause problems while he was at university. After graduating in 2007, he could not find work to suit his qualifications so he took a job selling tickets for the Tunis metro. Colleagues taunted him when they learned of his atheism and he was eventually fired "due to the numerous accusations of heresy". He was fired from another job in a factory, according to the website, after colleagues noticed he was not fasting during Ramadan and began questioning him about why he did not pray or read the Qur'an. They nicknamed him Abu Lahab ("the father of flame" – presumably because of his "inflammatory" views) and rumours circulated about his sexuality. Summoned by the management and questioned about his religious views, he said he had come to the factory to work and his religion was not relevant.[4]

In 2011, Beji had spent four months recovering from a knee operation and used the time to write a book in Arabic called *Wahm al-Islam* ("The Illusion of Islam") which he self-published on the internet – thinking, as he told the atheist website, that after the Tunisian revolution he was living "in a new era". One of Beji's chapters included reproductions of four cartoons: two of them associating Muslims with terrorism and one showing a pig labelled "Muhammad" writing in a book labelled "Qur'an". The fourth was the cartoon of Aisha and the sexually-aroused Prophet which had also appeared in Mejri's book on sex.

Zouali – the lawyer who initiated the case – said he considered insulting the Prophet to be a more serious crime than murder. "This affair has nothing to do with freedom of expression, or with freedom at all," he told the Tunisian website Nawaat. "I hope that the new constitution will institute a serious penalty for this kind of crime in order to protect religion and the feelings of Tunisian Muslims."

Beji's father told Nawaat that as a result of the trial he was thinking of selling his house because the family had been shunned by neighbours. "I go to a mosque in a neighborhood far away and I can't spend time in the cafe any more," he said. "In court, they warned us not to contact any journalists or human rights groups and that if we did the public opinion against us might be violent." He added that his son had received death threats from Salafis and his wife had received a message that Mejri would not escape the Salafis' punishment, even in prison. The imam of one of the largest mosques in Mahdia told Nawaat that while he was not responsible for the threats, he considered Mejri's "crime" unpardonable. "We cannot blame Muslims who are offended if they react violently," he said. Following an international campaign on his behalf, Mejri received a presidential pardon and was released in March 2014 – exactly two years after his arrest. Beji was eventually granted asylum in Romania.

In June 2012, disturbances over a contemporary art exhibition in Tunisia left 100 people injured and 160 under arrest, with a night-time curfew imposed on eight regions of the country. At the centre of this trouble was the *Printemps Des Arts* [Springtime of the Arts] fair in La Marsa, a chic seaside town on the outskirts of Tunis which serves as a summer retreat for wealthier Tunisians. The ten-day show, authorised by the Ministry of Culture, featured a large number of artists and was aimed mainly at a liberal/secular crowd.

On the eve of its opening a small group of Salafis turned up, apparently to protest, but they left after discovering that it was not – as they had thought – an event celebrating homosexuality. The show then continued normally until it was about to end. Héla Ammar, one of the exhibitors recalled:

> Everything went well until the closing day, when a local official came to assess certain paintings that he personally found shocking. According to his own testimony [in a television interview], he also shared the images online, adding his own interpretations and warned imams in certain mosques of their supposedly blasphemous nature.[5]

A video circulated on the internet urged "all followers of Islam" to "rise in anger" and about 20 protesters arrived at the exhibition – as well as a larger number of its supporters who had been summoned by the organisers. After some heated discussion, police separated the two groups peacefully and also removed a few of the more controversial artworks on the grounds that this would reduce the tension.

Later that evening, however, a much larger group of protesters assembled to march on the exhibition. One witness reported seeing hundreds of people, some brandishing swords, who turned on a small contingent of police: "They were throwing rocks at the police. I was very afraid. I ran to the car and locked the door." Some of them gained entry to the building, slashing at least two paintings and throwing one piece of sculpture on to the roof. A large installation was removed from the courtyard and taken outside to be burned. Among the graffiti daubed on the walls, one said "Let God be the judge", and another said: "Tunisia is an Islamic state; with the licence of the Ministry of Culture, the Prophet of Allah gets insulted." Some of the artists also received threatening and abusive messages after their names were listed on Facebook.

There's no doubt that much of the art on display was provocative and ridiculed extreme forms of Islam. One showed a Superman figure in a Salafi-style beard, cradling another bearded man in his arms. Another showed an angry, bearded face with steam coming out of the ears. A naked female figure, with a plate of couscous covering her private parts, was seen surrounded by dark and menacing male figures. A sculpture had statues of three veiled women buried up to their chests with stones. One artwork depicted lines of ants creeping into a child's schoolbag. The formation of the ants spelled "Subhan Allah" ("Glory to God") in

Arabic. Another piece incorporated a crescent, a cross and a Star of David with the words: "République Islaïque de Tunisie" – "Islaïque" being a made-up term combining "Islam" with "laïque", the French word for "secular".

In Héla Ammar's view, however, the artists had become scapegoats in a bigger struggle over the future of Tunisia. She told al-Jazeera:

> This affair has been entirely manufactured to eclipse more serious issues. We are in the middle of a war between several political movements, with the Salafists and other reactionary movements which are pressuring the present government against moderation and appeasement.
>
> The debates over identity and religion are false problems which distract from a precarious security situation, grave economic and social problems that have not yet been resolved, and a transitional justice system which is proving difficult to set up ...
>
> Under Ben Ali, we suffered most of all from self-censorship when it came to tackling political subjects. Now, the censorship is based on religious and moral questions, which has made things even worse.

The *Printemps des Arts* affair led to calls for a new Tunisian law to protect "the sacred". Nessma TV and the two atheists had been prosecuted under existing laws from the Ben Ali era – laws which the previous regime had often used against its political opponents. Ennahda, the religious party dominating the Constituent Assembly, complained about the lack of a law specifically dealing with blasphemy – "Religious symbols are above all derision, irony or violation," it said in a statement – and in August it introduced a draft law listing God, prophets, the Qur'an, Bible and Torah, the Sunnah (the sayings and teachings of the Prophet Muhammad), churches, synagogues, and the Kaaba in Mecca as sacred. "Cursing, insulting, mocking, undermining, and desecrating" any of these symbols could lead to a two-year jail term and a fine of 2,000 dinars fine ($1,265P). The bill also proposed to forbid pictorial representations of God and prophets.

The plan was later dropped following representations from Tunisian and international civil society groups. One of the objectors, Article 19, complained that the draft violated international human rights standards and left "far too much discretion to the police and judiciary to decide what behaviour constitutes an 'insult' or 'mockery' of sacred values." [6]

"BLASPHEMY" is a broad term used in a religious context to describe any display of contempt for sacred figures and things. It is derived from a Greek verb, *blasphemein* – "to speak evil of" – but in Arabic several different words may be used: *sabb* (insult), *shatm* (vilification), *la'an* (cursing), *takdhib* (denial), and more. Sometimes in Islam, blasphemy is considered a form of apostasy.

Arab states use several different mechanisms, either separately or in combination, to prevent unwanted discourse about religion. Aside from the sharia, these can include constitutional declarations giving Islam privileged or protected status, specific laws against blasphemy and general laws about public order, media, telecommunications, etc, which can be applied to blasphemy. There are often also similar laws against what might be called "secular blasphemy" which violates the "sanctity" of the state – damaging the country's reputation, insulting the head of state, defaming government officials and the military, spreading "false" news, and so on. In Algeria, for example, the constitution combines religion with the political system by forbidding "practices that are contrary to the Islamic ethics *and* to the values of the November Revolution". Morocco's 2002 media law prohibits criticism of "Islam, the institution of the monarchy, or territorial integrity".

Oman, Qatar and the United Arab Emirates all have specific anti-blasphemy laws with established penalties. In Oman, it is a criminal offence to defame any faith and the maximum penalty for inciting religious or sectarian strife is ten years' imprisonment. Sentences of up to three years and a fine of 500 rials ($1,300) are prescribed for anyone who "publicly blasphemes God or His prophets", commits an affront to religious groups by spoken or written word, or breaches the peace of a lawful religious gathering. Use of the internet in ways that "might prejudice public order or religious values" is an imprisonable offence. In Qatar, the penalty for defaming, desecrating, or committing blasphemy against Islam, Christianity, or Judaism is up to seven years in prison. The law also provides a one-year sentence or a fine of 1,000 riyals ($275) for producing or circulating material that defames these three religions. In the UAE, offenders can be fined, imprisoned or deported for swearing, profanities, insults, and all types of vulgar language and behaviour. The law also imposes penalties for using the internet to preach against Islam, proselytise Muslims, "abuse" a holy shrine or ritual of any religion, insult any religion, and incite someone to commit sin or contravene "family values".

Although most Arab countries seek to protect Christianity and Judaism along with Islam (at least on paper) – since all three are monotheistic faiths – other religions are not usually protected and the penalties for attacking Islam are sometimes higher than for attacks on Judaism and Christianity. In Yemen, for example, the maximum sentence for "ridiculing" religion is longer if the religion concerned is Islam.

Several countries have special provisions in their media laws to protect religion. Jordan outlaws material that slanders or insults "founders of religion or prophets" or shows contempt for "any of the religions whose freedom is protected by the constitution", with a possible fine 20,000 dinars ($28,000) for offenders. Yemen's 1990 Press and Publications Law prohibits, among other things:

- Anything that prejudices the Islamic faith and its lofty principles or belittles religions or humanitarian creeds;

- Anything that might cause tribal, sectarian, racial, regional or ancestral discrimination, or which might spread a spirit of dissent and division among the people or call on them to apostasies;

- Anything which leads to the spread of ideas contrary to the principles of the Yemeni Revolution, prejudicial to national unity or distorting the image of the Yemeni, Arab or Islamic heritage.

Kuwaiti law imposes jail sentences for journalists who defame any religion or denigrate religious figures, and private citizens are allowed to bring criminal charges against suspected offenders. An "emergency" decree issued by the emir in 2012, known as the National Unity Law, extended the law to include social media and also greatly increased the penalties. Offenders can be jailed for up to seven years and fined up to 200,000 dinars ($720,000). However, the government has resisted pressure from parliament to introduce the death penalty for Muslims who blaspheme.

Ironically, only a small proportion of blasphemy cases in the Arab countries involve atheists and unbelievers. Mostly, they are the result of quarrels between Muslims, between Christians and Muslims, between Sunni Muslims and Shia Muslims, or simply a case of people pursuing grudges. Often, it's impossible to know exactly what the offender said, since the words cannot be repeated in newspaper reports. Above all, many of the cases that go to court are extraordinarily trivial and sometimes purely vexatious.

In 2013 Musab Shamsah, a Kuwaiti teacher, was jailed for five years over a tweet about the theological role of imams which was deemed to have insulted religion. Shamsah denied the accusation, claiming that his tweet – which mentioned the Prophet's grandson and apparently referred to theological differences between Sunni and Shia Islam – had been misinterpreted. According to his lawyer, he had deleted the tweet ten minutes after posting it and clarified what he meant in two subsequent tweets. On the specific charge of mocking religion, which was brought under Article 111 of Kuwait's penal code, Shamsah received the maximum sentence of one year. But the court added a further four years for publishing offensive material contrary to the National Unity Law and for "misusing" a mobile phone – since he had posted the offending tweet from his phone.

In the Algerian city of Biskra, 26-year-old Samia Smets was sentenced to ten years' imprisonment – the maximum allowed by the law – for desecrating the Qur'an. She was already in jail (over a civil matter) at the time of the alleged offence and was accused by other prisoners of having torn a copy of the holy book. Smets, who was not legally represented in court, denied tearing it and said she had accidentally dropped the book in water during an argument. A year later, a judge hearing her appeal overturned the conviction for lack of evidence – including the prosecution's failure to produce the supposedly torn Qur'an.

In Egypt during the first couple of years after the fall of the Mubarak regime, at least 17 cases alleging contempt of religion were filed with the courts – many of them rooted in Christian-Muslim rivalries. In one case, a female Coptic teacher was summoned for interrogation and detained overnight after students accused her of offensive remarks in class about the Prophet Muhammad. In another case, a Muslim preacher went on trial for destroying a copy of the Bible during a protest against the 14-minute video, *Innocence of Muslims*.

One of the most bizarre Egyptian cases involved two Coptic Christian boys, aged nine and ten, who spent fifteen days in juvenile detention after being accused of urinating on pages of the Qur'an. The boys, living in a mixed Muslim/Christian village were said to have been seen taking the pages behind a mosque where they committed the alleged offence. A neighbour told the Associated Press the boys were illiterate and could not have recognised the pages as coming from the Qur'an.[7]

In cases such as these it seems that blasphemy can be committed even if it exists only the mind of the beholder. There is no evidence that the Egyptian boys, the Libyan prisoner or the Kuwaiti tweeter actually intended to show contempt for religion. Given the context of these three cases – sectarian tensions in Egypt and Kuwait, and an argument among prisoners in Libya – questions might also be raised about the motives of the accusers. Often, there seems to be a "Gotcha!" factor at work, where those who complain are not so much offended as delighted to have found something they can pin on the person they are accusing.

In 2005 *Jyllands-Posten*, a Danish newspaper, published some offensive cartoons depicting the Prophet Muhammad – triggering a campaign which led to worldwide protests by Muslims several months later. Yemen was one of the countries where thousands of demonstrators took to the streets and shops announced they were refusing to sell Danish products. The *Yemen Observer*, an English-language weekly, reported these protests along with an editorial comment and tiny reproductions of three of the offending cartoons – each partly obliterated with a thick black X.

A week later Mohammed al-Asadi, the paper's editor, was arrested on charges of offending Islam. Prosecution lawyers called for the execution of Asadi, the closure of the Yemen Observer and confiscation of its assets. The government suspended the paper's licence and it was unable to print for more than six months, though staff continued to publish on the internet.

According to Asadi, the real problem was not the cartoons (which the paper had condemned) but an editorial which had annoyed hardliners by calling for Muslims to accept Danish apologies and act with "calm and dignity". However, prosecution lawyers and the Yemeni attorney-general insisted that the charges rested on the images alone, and neither the news report nor the editorial could be used in evidence.

As mentioned earlier, Arab legal systems sometimes provide opportunities for citizens to involve themselves in court cases if they happen to have an axe to grind, and the *Yemen Observer* trial was no exception. Abdul Majeed al-Zindani, the erstwhile friend of Osama bin Laden who had been listed by the US as a Specially Designated Global Terrorist, who in the 1980s had tricked western scientists into endorsing the Qur'an's "scientific knowledge" and who later announced that he had discovered a cure for HIV/AIDS, joined the legal fray with a massive claim for damages, alleging that reproduction of the cartoons had violated Muslims' civil rights.

Zindani's claim was eventually dismissed but the court fined

Asadi 500,000 rials ($2,320), saying that he had handled the cartoons "inappropriately".

NOTES

1. "UN resolutions on combating defamation of religions." Statement by Article 19 and the Cairo Institute for Human Rights Studies. 11 September 2008. http://www.article19.org/data/files/pdfs/press/un-resolutions-on-combating-defamation-of-religions.pdf
2. "Freedom of expression and incitement to racial or religious hatred." Joint statement by Githu Muigai, Asma Jahangir and Frank La Rue, 22 April 2009. http://www2.ohchr.org/english/issues/religion/docs/SRJointstatement22April09.pdf
3. "Rabat Plan of Action on the prohibition of advocacy of national, racial or religious hatred that constitutes incitement to discrimination, hostility or violence." 5 October 2012. http://www.ohchr.org/Documents/Issues/Opinion/SeminarRabat/Rabat_draft_outcome.pdf
4. Ghazzali, Kacem el-: "Tunisian Atheists sentenced to seven and a half years of prison." Atheistica blog, 1 April 2012. http://atheistica.com/2012/04/01/tunisian-atheists-sentenced-to-seven-and-a-half-years-of-prison/
5. Ryan, Yasmine: "Tunisia's embattled artists speak out." Al-Jazeera, 15 June 2012. http://www.aljazeera.com/indepth/features/2012/06/2012615111819112421.html
6. "Tunisia: Draft law criminalising offending religious values is repressive and vague." Article 19, 16 August 2012. http://www.article19.org/resources.php/resource/3420/en/tunisia:-draft-law-criminalising-offending-religious-values-is-repressive-and-vague
7. "Egypt frees 2 Coptic boys held for Quran defiling." The Associated Press, 4 October 2012. http://news.yahoo.com/egypt-frees-2-coptic-boys-held-quran-defiling-190054905.html

9: A taste of freedom?

THE EGYPTIAN uprising that overthrew President Hosni Mubarak in 2011 created an opportunity for non-believers to emerge from the shadows – more so than in any other Arab country. Atheists appeared on TV talking about their disbelief, they were interviewed in newspapers, they held meetings in public and even called for their rights to be taken into account in the drafting of a new constitution.

A taboo had clearly been broken. Egyptians could no longer avoid the fact that non-believers did exist, even if the vast majority still found the whole idea repugnant and even if the media tended to portray atheists as examples of the moral depths to which Egypt had sunk.

This undoubtedly had some connection with the spirit of revolution that swept the country though opinions differ as to what the exact connection was, and there is probably no single explanation. A distinction should also be made between the visibility of disbelief, a phenomenon that had scarcely been seen since the rise of political Islam, and disbelief itself which in some cases may have existed for years without finding a voice.

To some extent, the uprising and the spread of atheistic discourse in Egypt are not so much cause and effect as two products of a single process – a process of questioning and challenging authority in which social media played an important part by facilitating the exchange of information and ideas. But the uprising does seem to have contributed to religious questioning too, perhaps because it brought together so many disparate groups of activists in pursuit of the regime's overthrow and created an ideological melting pot.

"During the revolution," said Gamal, an atheist who was also a political activist, "young people in general started feeling empowered and were questioning every established idea or institution that there was before the revolution, including religion itself." But this questioning could not have emerged entirely out of the blue. If the revolt against Mubarak encouraged doubters to shed their inhibitions and brought them into contact with like-minded individuals, the seeds of disbelief had probably been sown earlier – and Gamal regards access to information as a key factor in that. He continued:

> I've heard people on television or in newspaper columns saying the internet has resulted in the rise of atheism and religious scepticism in general – and I guess that's a very honest evaluation because the spread of the internet from the early 2000s up until now in Egypt has resulted in immense access to information without any sort of filtering. So if you want to go and read about Christianity from a first-hand source you can go [and find it]. If you want to read about atheism, if you want to read about Islam, or other versions of Islam, if you want to read about the people being vilified by Islamic preachers you can just go and Google them.[1]

Gamal's own journey towards atheism was shaped mainly by his political activism. "My point of departure was not specifically a departure from Islam; it was a departure from religion in general," he said. "I thought this whole business of religion is harmful and unnecessary."

He had grown up in what he describes as a typical conservative Egyptian family. For the first few years of his education he attended a religious school. His father was a teacher who also preached in local mosques on Fridays and Gamal, as a child, would often go with him to hear the sermon. In his mid-teens, Gamal had been inspired by the preaching of Amr Khaled, a former accountant who built a huge popular following by adopting the style of American televangelists. Unlike the often dour imams found in Egyptian mosques, Amr Khaled wore smart suits, talked in plain language with a friendly tone and even cracked jokes. But Gamal's enthusiasm didn't last. Within a few years he had become an atheist – though he still hasn't told his parents and when interviewed he asked not to have any details revealed that could lead to him being identified.

"The cracks started when I was 19 or 20, as a result of politics, mainly," he said. "I was trying to understand what was wrong with Egypt in terms of governance, its human rights record, the lack of democracy, the corruption, etc, and I was drawn more into the worldly perspective of reforming society. So I started joining protests. We were a bunch of young people from all parties and movements regardless of ideology – with the exception of any Islamist movements of course. We would all get together and organise demonstrations, print leaflets together, hold meetings together. We all had the same basic interest in overthrowing the Mubarak regime and bringing about democracy."

But the more Gamal became involved in political activism the more he saw religion as an impediment to change.

> We would do all these [protest] efforts and then, for example, I would go to a mosque for a Friday sermon and find a Salafi preacher saying it is wrong to protest against a ruler because he is sanctioned by God, or that we have to reform ourselves not the government, and all that trash. He would be really brown-nosing the government. I started seeing the harm in the mixing of religion and politics, and how religious discourse could harm all the efforts that we made as activists trying to better the lives of people and bring about democracy.
>
> Religious teachers would just tell people that this is *haram*, forbidden – you cannot protest, you cannot question what Hosni Mubarak is doing. They kept diverting attention towards individualistic solutions where people need to pray more, to fast more, to reform their own lives.
>
> When we argued with people who were getting convinced by these arguments it was very hard. We tried to present a logical argument to them based on empirical evidence but they would just bring up verses from the Qur'an and the *hadith*, or the words of some sheikh or imam.

In Gamal's view, the Islamist movements – their leaders though not necessarily their grassroots supporters – were far too willing to make compromises with the Mubarak regime:

> You have to remember that a central tenet of the Salafi movement and the Muslim Brotherhood prior to 2011 was that they didn't want to overthrow Hosni Mubarak and his government and they didn't believe in the option of a revolution. Both of them were very hypocritical towards the figure of Hosni Mubarak and they would just cut deals with him to join the parliament or have some more freedom at mosques and stuff like that.

The insistence that prayer rather than politics would solve Egypt's problems led Gamal also to reconsider his previous enthusiasm for Amr Khaled who was fond of quoting a verse from the Qur'an which says: "Allah changeth not the condition of a folk until they [first] change that which is in their hearts."[2] Although Amr Khaled's style was different from that of traditional preachers, Gamal judged that his underlying message was basically the same:

> Two-thirds of what he was talking about was personal development but he was packaging it with religious values and religious inspiration from Islamic history. So he was giving motivational speeches, inspirational stories to make you work hard, to make you study better at school, to make you give charity to the poor.
>
> I am not convinced that there are "moderate" versions and "radical" versions within Islam. There are different preachers who are trying to appease or present religion in certain ways in order to accommodate the concerns or fears of certain segments of society.
>
> So, for example, when Amr Khaled was preaching he was appealing to the middle classes and the upper classes in Egypt who had their kids educated at the American University in Cairo, for example, who had a very liberal lifestyle. If he had come to them and said that men and women have to be separated, that women shouldn't go to school or work, they wouldn't comprehend.

Another eye-opening experience came when Gamal started at university, studying western civilisation and thought. "For the first time I was getting exposed to many of the foundational texts in human civilisation – the history and culture of ancient Greece and Rome, along with classical Arab culture, the Renaissance period, the Enlightenment and all those thinkers," he recalled. He noticed too that the writers he was studying at university were often the same ones that were "getting defamed from the pulpits of mosques during Friday sermons or whenever a preacher was talking about western civilisation as corrupted". Reading them first-hand, he realised that the texts condemned by preachers were "just about liberty, advancing humanity, human progress, secularism – very normal concepts."

Hosni Mubarak's presidency finally came to an end in February 2011, after almost 30 years in power, and the Supreme Council of the Armed Forces temporarily assumed control. In parliamentary elections a few months later, the Muslim Brotherhood's Freedom and Justice Party (and its allies) won 235 of the 508 seats in the People's Assembly. Another group, headed by the Salafi Nour party, won a further 123 seats, giving the assorted Islamists an overwhelming majority. This was followed in June 2012 by a presidential election in which the Brotherhood's candidate, Mohamed Morsi, defeated Ahmed Shafik, a former air marshal who had briefly served as Mubarak's last prime minister.

It was a moment of hubris for the Islamists but Morsi's victory was not really the triumph that it seemed. The final round of the presidential election had presented voters with an invidious choice between the Brotherhood and a figure from the old regime. Consequently, many had voted for Morsi more out dislike for Shafik and a desire for change than any particular enthusiasm for the Brotherhood. At first, Morsi seemed to recognise that he owed his presidency to voters outside the Brotherhood's traditional support base. Speaking in Tahrir Square after the result was announced, he hinted at inclusivity:

> I affirm to all segments of the Egyptian people that I have today, by your choice and your will, through the favour of Allah, become the president of all Egyptians, wherever they are, at home or abroad, and in all the provinces of Egypt, on its eastern borders and the west, and in the south and north and central Egypt.
>
> I turn to you all on this historic day, in which I have become president of all Egyptians, equally. Everyone will be afforded due respect, without any privilege, except that rendered by their service to our nation and their respect for the constitution and the law.[3]

Any pretence of inclusivity soon evaporated, however, and the Islamists rapidly lost support. Just five months into his presidency, Morsi issued a decree granting himself what many regarded as dictatorial powers. Although these were said to be temporary, pending the election of a new parliament, the effect was to prevent any of his presidential decisions from being challenged through the courts. Writing in the *Guardian*, Peter Beaumont noted: "Morsi already has both executive and legislative powers since the dissolution of the parliament's lower assembly, and has now added what appears to be a monopoly of judicial authority, placing himself beyond the courts while appointing a hand-picked prosecutor without consultation."[4] A few weeks later, *The Economist* gave this assessment of his presidency:

> Mr Morsi had promised effective government, an improved economy and a progressive constitution, arrived at by consensus, that addressed the concerns of all. Egyptians now complain instead of a

stalled economy, erratic government and a deterioration in already crumbling public services.

Non-Islamists have also been offended by the president's failure to include them. He even shrugged off an invitation to attend the inauguration of a new Coptic pope, the leader of Egypt's 10% Christian minority. Islamists also ignored the withdrawal in protest of liberal and Christian members from a 100-person constitution-writing body, which then rushed out its draft, including last-minute sweetener clauses to appease the army.[5]

The new constitution needed broad public support in order to serve as the foundation for post-Mubarak Egypt but instead it became a source of division and continuing controversy. Amid complaints about a lack of proper consultation it was approved in a referendum with 64% of the votes – less than the Brotherhood had been hoping for. The relatively low turnout of just under 33% meant that only about 20% of eligible voters had said "yes" to it and three of Egypt's 27 provinces actually delivered a majority "no" vote, most notably in Cairo governorate where almost 57% voted against.

In June 2013, Morsi appointed 17 new provincial governors and his choice of Adel al-Khayyat as governor of Luxor, a popular tourist destination, proved especially controversial. Khayyat belonged to the political wing of Gamaa Islamiyya, which had been widely blamed for the 1997 Luxor massacre in which 58 tourists and four Egyptians were killed. Although the Gamaa had since renounced violence, putting one of its members in charge of Luxor seemed an extremely provocative move. The Gamaa, which was regarded as hostile to tourism and pre-Islamic monuments, had once posted a notice on its website saying: "Because tourist villages have aspects that anger Allah, including alcohol, gambling and other forbidden things, building these hotels and villages is considered aiding their owners in sin and aggression, and is not permitted." *Al-Masry al-Youm* newspaper wrily suggested that Morsi chose Khayyat to appease the Gamaa "because it is the only party that stands beside the Brotherhood *against* the people" [italics added].[6]

In another move that many regarded as provocative, Morsi appointed an Islamist minister of culture, Alaa Abdel-Aziz, who promptly dismissed the heads of the General Egyptian Book Organisation, the Fine Arts Sector, the Cairo Opera House, and the National Library and Archives.[7]

Meanwhile, several entertaining scandals led to Islamist figures being publicly mocked for their less-than-holy behaviour. Anwar al-Balkimy, a Salafi member of parliament, attempted to explain his heavily-bandaged face by reporting to police that he had been attacked by robbers who stole $16,000 from him and also tried to take his car. It later emerged that he invented the story to conceal the fact that he had had cosmetic surgery on his nose.[8] Another Salafi politician, Ali Wanis, was convicted of public indecency after police found him sitting in his parked car "caressing" a female student who was sitting on his lap.[9]

A year after taking office as Egypt's first democratically-elected president, as a wave of protests swept through Egypt Morsi was overthrown by the military and imprisoned. This marked the start of a concerted and often brutal effort to suppress the Muslim Brotherhood – an effort which also had public backing from some of the Arab Gulf states. With the military in control, Morsi and his twelve months of mis-rule provided a convenient scapegoat for Egypt's problems – including what many saw as the "problem" of atheism.

"This atheist movement has occurred, for the first time in the history of Egypt, during the year that Morsi and the Muslim Brotherhood were in power", columnist Helmi al-Namnam claimed in an interview on *Dream TV*. "Oppression and religion became equated in the minds of the people. So what we are seeing [with the emergence of atheism] is ... a response against a failing, intellectually poor, Muslim Brotherhood government. This government was weak and too old-fashioned in its beliefs and actions, even when compared with modern Islamic thoughts and jurisprudence."[10]

Khaled Diab, a journalist who has written about atheism in Egypt and who is himself an atheist, disagrees. "For people who abandoned their faith or never really had it to begin with, I don't think Morsi's presidency had any impact on their abandoning their faith. If that were the case there wouldn't be a centuries-long history of non-belief in Egypt and the Arab world. Quite a few of them lost their faith long before the revolution and what came after it. Some have been atheists for a very long time."

Interest in atheism among Egypt's mainstream media seems to have developed for political reasons as a result of the Islamists' strong performance in the first post-Mubarak parliamentary elections, then growing during Morsi's presidency and in the wake of his overthrow by the military, Diab said:

The media started dealing with it quite intensely, especially following Morsi's ousting. It seems they were trying to suggest or say that that interpretation of Islam had driven people to non-belief. The government seemed to be using it for propaganda purposes – that Egypt was undergoing a crisis of faith, mainly because of the Muslim Brotherhood – which, to be charitable, is oversimplifying to the nth degree and to be non-charitable is absolute bollocks.

All the atheists I've interviewed didn't make a real connection between the Brotherhood and their loss of faith, though the Brothers certainly did not lure them to "repent". Their loss of faith was usually an intellectual, or even a spiritual, process. Quite a number of them were [initially] looking to deepen their faith or understand their faith.

Nevertheless, Diab agrees that the overthrow of Mubarak and its aftermath did make a difference where belief and non-belief are concerned, though not in the way the military's propagandists suggest. He continued:

The revolution made non-believers bolder and more open, it led others to question everything and it made society (not the establishment) more open to tolerating difference. Egyptians generally, even if they are believers, have become a lot more open-minded about other belief systems – they accept that not everyone has to be on the same line. You can still be a good person and a non-believer, for example. You can be a bad person and a believer.

I think that's where the Muslim Brotherhood perhaps had a bit of an influence in that a lot of people may have voted for them because they saw them as pious men who were well organised and would take care of the country. The realisation that just because you are pious doesn't mean you are good has also switched on a light bulb in a lot of people's heads. It follows that not being pious doesn't mean you are bad.

Another factor is that because the Salafists and the Muslim Brotherhood have a holier-than-thou attitude and think they are the only ones who have the right version of Islam. One effect of that has been not so much to drive people away from religion but to make them aware that anyone could be branded a *kafir* [unbeliever], potentially. If someone who is a practising Muslim can be branded a *kafir* by these extremists, people will ask: "Where is it going to stop?"[11]

Judgmental attitudes are not by any means the exclusive preserve of preachers and organised religious movements. There is also what Egyptian journalist Magdi Abdelhadi refers to as "micro-vigilantism" by individuals which on a day-to-day basis causes much annoyance to Egypt's less-devout citizens. In a blog post, Abdelhadi described how the cashier at a car service centre objected to writing his father's first name on the paperwork because the spelling shown on his identification documents was allegedly un-Islamic. A female friend had also been harangued by a taxi driver for not covering her hair. When she replied that she was a Coptic Christian the driver insisted that she should still wear hijab because the Virgin Mary had covered her hair. This kind of harassment, incidentally, was a tactic adopted in the 1920s by Hassan al-Banna, the founder of the Muslim Brotherhood, who used to pester neighbours with anonymous notes if he thought they were not observant Muslims. Abdelhadi continued:

> My neighbour, who has turned his garden into a small mosque with a loudspeaker strung up on the lamppost outside his house, has been joined by yet another neighbour, a few blocks away, with *two* loudspeakers perched on the roof of his villa and pointing to two different directions.
>
> He occasionally lets his little boy exercise his call-to-prayer skills on the neighbourhood – which could mean four in the morning with the added exhortation that "prayer is better than sleep".
>
> I suspect the local council official could not enforce the law after I lodged a complaint – either because he, like my neighbours, believes they are right and the state is wrong, or that he couldn't care less. Or both. I may never find out. However, when I again called to remind him that the problem has not been resolved, I noticed he had an Islamic ring tone on his mobile ...
>
> For those who don't know, the call to prayer is actually broadcast on Egyptian state radio and TV (and most private networks). The prayer times are also published in all daily newspapers. You can also get a smartphone app with recorded calls to prayer with the exact timing for each ... five times a day for your entire life. So there is something else at work here other than reminding people. It's more about bullying and claiming the public space.[12]

While cracking down on the Muslim Brotherhood, the military regime set about establishing its own religious credentials. Another new constitution, approved by a referendum in January 2014, retained Islam as the religion of the state and "the principles of Islamic sharia" as "the main source of legislation", though the personal and religious affairs of Christians and Jews were to be regulated by their own versions of "sharia". The constitution also stated that "the family is the nucleus of society, and is founded on *religion*, morality, and patriotism". These provisions did not go unchallenged, however. A group of Egyptian atheists made formal representations to have them removed from the draft – but to no avail.[13]

Nevertheless, other sections of the constitution said there should be no discrimination based on religion or belief. Freedom of belief was described as "absolute", though the practice of Abrahamic religions was to be regulated by law (there was no mention of non-Abrahamic religions) and everyone would "have the right to express his/her opinion verbally, in writing, through imagery, or by any other means of expression and publication".[14] Writing for *Daily News Egypt*, Rana Alam argued that this was self-contradictory:

> How can one guarantee "freedom" when it is limited to the three Abrahamic religions, ignoring the 1,100 million followers [worldwide] of Hinduism or the 488 million Buddhists, to name just two? It also ignores that not following a religion should also be counted as a freedom ... one cannot be an atheist in Egypt.
>
> One of the strangest things we have here is having our religion documented in our national ID cards (bizarre!) and one cannot get married (for example) without being a follower of one of the three Abrahamic religions. There is no civil marriage in Egypt.
>
> On top of this, even within the three Abrahamic "revealed" religions, Egypt discriminates against Shi'as. Talk of how devious the Shi'as are is all over the TV and newspapers, how Egypt needs to "stop the expansion of the Shi'a beliefs". In a striking move, Egypt refused Shi'a pilgrims from entering the country several times, even after passing the "progressive" constitution.[15]

But Shi'a Muslims were not the only ones to feel the effects of this dubious new freedom; Sunni mosques felt it too. Just two weeks after the constitution was approved the government began setting the "theme" for each week's Friday sermons. Preachers in government-run mosques who failed to comply were threatened with disciplinary action, while non-government mosques were threatened with being taken over by the state.[16] Meanwhile, the army was building a huge new mosque, to be named after Mohamed Tantawi, the military chief who had been forcibly retired in 2012 by President Morsi.[17] In essence, what this amounted to was the replacement of one authoritarian form of religion with another.

In June 2014, little more than a week after Sisi had been elected as Egypt's new president, *al-Ahram* reported that the government was preparing a national plan to "confront and eliminate" atheism. According to the newspaper, the plan was being developed by the Ministry of Youth and Sports – apparently reflecting the popular view that atheism is a "youth problem" – and would be multi-faceted, involving "religious, psychological, educational and social" specialists.[18]

TOWARDS the end of 2013, the Cairo newspaper *El Badil* posted a video on its website which showed eight young Egyptians speaking about their lack of religious belief and the prejudice they faced as a result. "It is not easy for other people to accept that I am irreligious," one said. "At work, if people knew about it, I would be jobless," another added. "Our demands are very simple and basic," said a third (an ex-Salafi). "We wish only to have the same rights that any other Egyptian citizen has."[19]

The non-believers – six men and two women – were named in the film and all but one showed their face to the camera. The 12-minute video presented their views in a matter-of-fact way without commenting on them. In many countries this would be scarcely worth noting but in terms of Egypt's Arabic-language media it was highly unusual – some say unprecedented. If reported at all, such views would normally be condemned or, at a very least, countered with others opposed to them.

When an Arabic satellite channel known as *Honest TV* decided to tackle atheism in its Redline talk show, the host, Mohamed Moussa, explained that the programme was part of a war against "destructive ideas", since atheism is a foreign plot. Mostafa Zakareya, an atheist from Alexandria who had bravely (or perhaps foolishly) agreed to appear in the programme told viewers he had no desire to "insult religions" but simply wanted Egyptians to accept him as an atheist. "I'm not here to say that Islam is bad or to criticise religion, I'm here to say that everyone is free to choose his faith, and that people should understand that religious beliefs should remain personal," he said. "We need to deal with each other as humans."

Responding to Zakareya's remarks, Sheikh Gomaa Mohamed Ali, a well-known cleric, called for him to be arrested and executed. The sheikh claimed that atheism is a "new phenomenon" that has been "coined by the Zionists". Not to be outdone – and despite the fact that atheism is not actually illegal in Egypt – the head of Alexandria's Security Directorate also told the programme he was forming a special task force of police officers specialised in tackling such "crimes" to round up atheists.[20]

Egyptian TV discussions of atheism are generally so tilted towards belief as to be unfair, according to Amira Nowaira, professor of English literature at Alexandria University:

> Even when they say "Today we will talk about atheism", they see it as a problem, as something to be combated, not something that exists. It's very much like the way they talk about homosexuality, for example. If they do, it is always with the implication that it should be fought.
>
> The whole argument is tilted towards the necessity of having belief and making young people stick to their beliefs. I have never seen anything that was really fair to people with doubts. The person conducting the interview is never neutral. I think they are worried in case they are seen to be encouraging atheists, so they go too far the other way in order to stress that they are not in favour of atheism.[21]

When atheist Ismail Mohamed appeared on *al-Mehwar* channel in 2013, a theologian from al-Azhar University was on hand to explain to viewers why atheism is a crime:

> Firstly, it goes against the law of sovereignty regarding the state. That's number one.
>
> Secondly, propagating atheism only results in doubting the revealed religions, and is considered a form of contempt for religions. That's number two.
>
> Number three: ... Intellectual deception is considered in itself a form of crime against the mind, and that is when you intentionally mislead someone naïve ... that there is no God and that life is material ... [22]

Ostensibly, the purpose of the programme was to discuss a call by Ismail Mohamed and several other atheists for the rights of non-believers to be taken into account in the drafting of Egypt's new constitution. But the discussion did not get very far. As Mohamed attempted to respond to the theologian, the programme's presenter, Reham al-Sahli repeatedly pressed him to explain how he had "benefited" from atheism:

> **Sahli:** Excuse me Mohamed, but I'm asking you a question, how have you benefited –
>
> **Mohamed:** Not at all.

Sahli: I have to ask you –

Mohamed [to interviewer]: How have *you* benefited from religion?

Sahli: Everything, my whole life has benefited from religion –

Mohamed: Firstly, I too have benefited in every way, I have very beautiful and wonderful humanity ...

Sahli: Ah –

Mohamed: But that's not the question

Sahli: You mean you benefited from atheism?

Mohamed: The idea the whole idea is, there are things which have to be clarified a bit, we're not making clear –

Sahli: How have you benefited from atheism?

Mohamed: I've not benefited, there is no benefit ... All there is to it is that I have changed, I used to believe something particular and now I believe something else. I'm a human being just like you, I'm an Egyptian citizen, in society, and that's my freedom in my opinion. As for the idea that we're propagating (atheism), we're not propagating anything at all. We don't want people to become atheists, to leave their religions, but –

Sahli: Are you happy with your atheism, Mohamed?

Mohamed: Excuse me, please, let me speak a bit.

Sahli: mm –

Mohamed: Talk about atheism and that it's a crime and so on ... If that's the case then we should confiscate the many books by philosophers in our libraries and universities because there are many philosophers whose philosophy we study, philosophers today say things like that, when we study for instance the books of Nietzsche, someone who said "God is dead" – I mean, just as an example, does that mean that now –

Sahli [interrupting, apparently horrified at the mention of God being dead]: May God forgive me.

Discussion then turned to the new constitution:

Sahli: What do you want from the constitution?

Mohamed: We want a state of the Egyptian citizen.

Sahli: That's the first question you've answered today.

Mohamed: Yes, Madam, yes, the question is very important, the question is about destiny, it concerns the future of us all –

Sahli: Destiny? What –

Mohamed: We're calling for a state of the citizen, where there's no difference between Muslim and Christian, where a Christian for example can become president of the republic, where there's no ... it was forbidden for a while, I think until now, for a Christian person to become President of the Republic ...

Sahli: ... Christians are represented by the church which calls for their rights, what do *you* want?

Mohamed: We're against giving preference to the priesthood or we're against control ...

Sahli: You as an atheist, what do you want from the constitution?

Mohamed: I'm speaking as an Egyptian citizen

Sahli: Ah.

Mohamed: I'm speaking as an Egyptian citizen-

Sahli: ... but also as an atheist

Mohamed: No, madam, I'm speaking as an Egyptian citizen, I ... I'm not concerned with what people believe, I'm not concerned with what you believe ...

Sahli: You, as atheists, you've asked to be heard, so what do you want to propose that's different to the rest of the Egyptians citizens, all of whom are represented in the constitution?

Mohamed: As I told you, that's a very clear and simple example, it was forbidden for a Christian citizen to be nominated as candidate to the presidency ...

Frustrated by the course of the discussion, Mohamed complained that he was not being given a proper opportunity to speak and apologised to viewers and "all my friends". This provided a cue for Sahli to introduce the familiar meme of atheism as a foreign plot. Were these friends *outside* Egypt, she asked.

Mohamed: No, madam, we're Egyptians, all of us are Egyptians, let me –

Sahli: You are not in touch with anyone abroad?

Mohamed: No, madam, we're Egyptian young people. I mean, we're not stooges or spies –

Sahli: No one said you were a spy, but let me move to the break.

Viewers calling in to the programme poured further scorn on Mohamed, some accusing him of causing social "strife" and/or being involved in a foreign plot (though one also thought he was part of a devious scheme concocted by the Muslim Brotherhood). Among the callers was Mohamed's own mother who blamed "the computer" for his atheism and said his siblings were too upset to watch the programme.

Not everyone regarded Mohamed's TV appearance as a disaster, however. Hisham Kassem, a prominent journalist and rights activist suggested that allowing him to appear at all was a breakthrough of sorts. "I was sitting there amazed," he said. "I never thought I would see this in my lifetime."

In a similarly unenlightening fashion, Ayman Ramzy Nakhla, a college librarian who had abandoned Christianity, was interviewed by Reham Said for *al-Nahar* TV:[23]

> **Said:** What's your religion?
>
> **Nakhla:** I'm from a Christian background.
>
> **Said:** What do you mean by "background"?
>
> **Nakhla:** I *was* a Christian, but now I'm a humanist. When I was born my parents were Christians so they put "Christian" on my birth certificate. I was Christian for many years, now I'm a humanist.
>
> **Said:** No one said you were an animalist ... [Laughter]
>
> **Nakhla:** I don't place religion in the circle of my interest – it's not something I'm interested in or concerned with ...
>
> **Said:** Don't you believe in God?
>
> **Nakhla:** It's not something I'm concerned with. My concern is human beings.
>
> **Said:** So you mean *I* fall within your concern?
>
> **Nakhla:** Yes, of course ...

The interview continued with Nakhla insisting that divinity and religions were "outside my circle of concern" and that his only concern was how to live as a decent human being. This prompted Said to ask him repeatedly "Who created humans?" and then to suggest he had become "confused" by reading books.

> **Said:** I want to know – what happened that made you take this

decision?

Nakhla: It was an intellectual development.

Said: Or was it sitting in the library reading?

Nakhla: I've read thousands of books.

Said: So who confused you?

Nakhla: There's no confusion. I consider that my intellectual development brought me to this point.

Said: Aren't you afraid?

Nakhla: Of what?

Said: Suppose there's a one per cent chance you are wrong?

Nakhla: That's my personal decision.

Said [continuing her question]: ... and you went down into your grave and discovered that actually there is a God?

Nakhla: This is my personal decision. And no one is going to impose death on me, and decide that I am wrong and therefore kill me, because he is not the one who gave me life.

Said: So who did?

Nakhla: My parents gave birth to me.

Said: So who created them?

Nakhla: Their parents and grandparents ...

Said: I'm going to cry now

Nakhla: Why? No don't

Said: Because I'm affected by what you said – so you really do have this boldness.

Nakhla: I'm not afraid of tomorrow or the future.

Said: But aren't you afraid people think you are a *kafir* [unbeliever]? Does the word worry you?

A few weeks later, the education minister announced that Nakhla was being suspended from work in the college library and referred to the public prosecutor for spreading ideas that were "atheistic and abnormal for Egyptian society". He was accused of "denying the existence of God and denying religions, prophets and holy books, directly by satellite and indirectly within the educational institution".[24]

Even when television programmes attempt to generate more

light than heat, the dice are still heavily loaded in favour of belief. Moez Masoud is a TV preacher but, unlike many of the traditional religious figures, is willing to engage with doubters in a less judgmental way. Modern, cosmopolitan and still relatively young, having been born in 1978, he talks more about God's compassion than divine punishments and emphasises the spiritual side of Islam.

Masoud seems to have recognised three simple points that old-fashioned clerics mostly fail to grasp. One is that threats of God's punishment don't necessarily scare doubters into submission and may actually increase their doubts. Another is that doubters tend to resent being told that their questions are taboo or being urged to trust God and stop worrying. The third is that people who have given up on organised religion still often yearn for something "spiritual" in their lives.

For Masoud, doubts about religion are not the work of Satan or the result of foreign plots. They are understandable if mistaken, and should be confronted rather than instantly dismissed. With this more subtle approach Masoud presented a series of programmes on Egyptian TV during Ramadan 2012, under the tile *Rihlat al-Yaqiin* ("The Journey of Certainty"). In the 15-minute broadcasts Masoud debated the ideas of such "prominent atheists" as Nietzsche, Darwin and Dawkins – though always with the aim of refuting them. Commenting in the Lebanese newspaper al-Akhbar, Mohammed Kheir wrote:

> Masoud tends to confuse scientists and philosophers, such as Darwin and Nietzsche, to whom atheism was not the main cause *per se*, with public figures who openly advocated atheism throughout their lives – such as Richard Dawkins, author of *The God Delusion*, and Sir Anthony Flew.
>
> This ... has led the show to often explain atheism as either the result of psychological problems, such as "when Darwin lost his young daughter," or as causing psychological problems itself, such as Nietzsche's "mental breakdown in his later life" ...
>
> But the positive trait that sets Masoud's television programme apart is that it has not repeated common mistakes such as claiming that the theory of evolution holds that "humans are descended from monkeys".
>
> [Masoud] did not claim, either, to have the scientific background that allows him to debate evolution, and was honest with his viewers when he spoke about the fact that Darwin did not directly clash with the

fundamental beliefs of the Christian faith ... Such a rare "logical" explanation in the world of religious television programmes is probably the most distinguishing feature ... as well as the fact that it also allows for counter-arguments rather than ignoring them as was the case in the past.[25]

Al Mulhid ("The Atheist"), released in 2014, is said to be the first film in the history of Egyptian cinema to tackle the subject of atheism. It aroused controversy while still being made – mainly because of its title – but, in an interview with *al-Ahram* newspaper, director Nader Seif El-Din insisted the film was not "pro-atheism" and would discuss "a major social problem we have today".[26] He elaborated on the film's purpose in an interview with *al-Arabiya*:

> When asked why he decided to tackle an issue that is likely to cause a lot of problems if only because of the film's name, Seif al-Din replied that he had noticed that the number of atheists in Egypt is increasing and that they have started calling for their rights. This, he said, made him feel that it is necessary to make a film that addresses the problem and that highlights the misconceptions endorsed by atheists.[27]

Al-Mulhid was eventually approved by religious scholars at al-Azhar (who had earlier been consulted about the script) as well as the Egyptian government's censors but by then it was already doomed – apparently because of the contentious nature of its title. Fearing protests, cinemas were reluctant to show it and reportedly only 15 copies of the film were produced for distribution.[28] It tells the story of a Muslim preacher and his atheist son, Nadir: "The preacher is also the presenter of a religious programme on a satellite channel and starts becoming the laughing stock of viewers after his son's beliefs become known. He gets calls on air telling him he is not fit for preaching since he is unable to make his son believe in God."[29] Far from advocating atheism, however, the message of the film appears to be that disbelief can kill: Nadir's father dies, unable to cope with the horror of having an atheist son.

While Arabic-language media tend to sensationalise atheism, feeding off popular prejudices and also reinforcing them, Egypt's English-language media often approach it in a more factual and balanced way. Material produced in English, almost by definition, is aimed at a fairly select market and normally goes unnoticed by the masses. This often gives publishers a bit more latitude where sensitive topics are concerned. In 2012, for example, the *Egypt Independent* reported critically on the trial of Alber Saber who was eventually convicted of blasphemy and "contempt of religion".[30] Other articles have taken a straightforward look at the phenomenon of atheism in Egypt and the problems non-believers can face. One article, which quoted ex-Christians as well as ex-Muslims, began:

> In a religious country such as Egypt, despite atheism being a taboo highly frowned upon, atheists say their numbers are on the rise. But with any new movement taking hold, a cultural backlash is bound to ensue.
>
> "In an attempt to understand the tribulation faced by Egypt's atheists, Egypt Independent met with 15 atheists, mostly in their twenties, at a café in downtown Cairo ...

It went on to explain that "being young and atheist can be particularly difficult, especially [for] those currently financially dependent on their families, for fear that revealing their true beliefs will cause them to be alienated and financially cut off from their parents".[31]

These interviews were the work of Mounir Adib, a journalist who has also written a book in Arabic about atheism in Egypt. While presenting debates between atheists and believers and exploring "the relationship between political rebellion and religious rebellion", Adib makes clear, however, that he is not encouraging atheism. The book also presents "scientific and religious refutations" of atheist ideas and provides examples of doubters who eventually became believers.[32]

At the end of 2013, *Daily News Egypt* listed the fourteen most-read columns that had appeared on its website during the year – and three of them dealt specifically with atheism. One, headed "A generation of atheists" and written by a concerned mother whose twelve-year-old son had "suddenly started disrespecting sheikhs", accused the clerics of giving Islam a bad name:

> Although I am not exactly a model of religiosity myself, it pained me to see such disdain from my boy towards those who are supposed to be holy men. And the worst part was that I could not defend the sheikhs, given that I do not want him to listen to the monstrosities these men utter. We are now all torn between the reality of our religion, and the message coming from the bearded bunch. What are we supposed to tell our kids?[33]

Another column discussed the case of a former Muslim Brotherhood member who announced on his blog that he was putting religion "on hold". Young people, it said, are "feeling alienated by every Friday sermon that lacks substance or labels all non-Islamists as heretics and un-Egyptian".[34]

Blaming extremism and out-of-touch preachers for the rise of atheism serves a political purpose and may to some extent reassure more moderate believers. Religious extremism may be a factor but imagining that the atheist "problem" will disappear if extremism is dealt with is self-delusion and fails to recognise that atheists have fundamental objections to religion itself. Khaled Diab, an Egyptian living outside the country, addressed these core issues directly in a column headed "Confessions of an Egyptian infidel". Childhood doubts over why his English friends would be going to hell when they eventually died had "matured into questions over the status of women and sexuality, as well as the contradictions and scientific errors in the Quran", he said, adding:

> That's not to mention the more metaphysical and philosophical questions, such as why a just and loving God would intentionally create a flawed being whom he places in a test of which the omnipresent, omniscient deity already knows the outcome. Of course, I'm not singling out Islam – the same and similar questions apply to other religions.[35]

Diab stated in his column that this was the first time he had declared his disbelief in an Egyptian newspaper and he expected some readers to be offended. "Although I do not wish to insult people's most intimate beliefs," he wrote, "I believe I also have a right to express my heartfelt convictions, and ones which I arrived at after years of doubt, questioning, hesitation and thought." Interestingly though, and perhaps because of the article's carefully non-inflammatory tone, there were no untoward repercussions. Asked later about the response, Diab replied:

> All in all, the reaction was positive. The article was widely read and it generated a lot of curiosity and interest. What was noteworthy, given all the buzz around Muslim attitudes to atheism and apostasy, was the absence of fanatical condemnation. The general reaction seemed to be that even if we don't agree with you we accept your right to express your views. The article even enabled me to connect with the growing community of non-believers.[36]

A sign of changing times, perhaps. Or possibly Diab was just fortunate that nobody complained. The events of 2011 opened up a space for non-believers but the law keeps them guessing as to what can be safely said and Egypt still has a very long way to go before atheists can hope to be regarded as normal, rational people.

NOTES

1. Author's interview, April 2014. Gamal is a pseudonym.
2. Qur'an 13: 11, Al-Rad (Pickthall's translation). For repeated use of this verse see, for example, Amr Khaled's message 'To the Youth of the Muslim Omma'.
http://english.islamway.com/bindex.php?section=article&id=263.
3. Speech by President Morsi in Tahrir Square, 24 June 2012.
http://www.al-bab.com/arab/docs/egypt/morsi_speech_120624.htm
4. Beaumont, Peter: "Morsi 'power grab' angers Egypt opposition groups." The Guardian, 23 November 2012.
http://www.theguardian.com/world/2012/nov/23/morsi-power-grab-angers-opposition
5. "Egypt's constitutional referendum: A dubious yes." The Economist, 22 December 2012. http://www.economist.com/news/middle-east-and-africa/21568756-flawed-constitution-will-be-endorsed-argument-far-over
6. Whitaker, Brian: "Egyptian provinces need elected governors." Blog post, 18 June 2013. http://www.al-bab.com/blog/2013/june/egyptian-provinces-need-elected-governors.htm
7. Whitaker, Brian: "Artists versus Islamists in Egypt's culture war." Blog post, 20 June, 2013 http://www.al-bab.com/blog/2013/june/artists-versus-islamists-in-egypt-culture-war.htm
8. "Egypt MP quits over nose job cover-up." Al-Jazeera, 6 March 2012.
http://www.aljazeera.com/news/middleeast/2012/03/201235224452570454.html
9. "Egypt Salafist ex-MP convicted of public indecency." BBC, 21 July 2012. http://www.bbc.co.uk/news/world-middle-east-18937515
10. Quoted by Samaan, Magdy: "Atheists Rise in Egypt." Zam Magazine, 13 October 13. www.zammagazine.com/chronicle-3/38-atheists-rise-in-egypt
11. Author's interview, April 2014.
12. Abdelhadi, Magdy: "The age of unreason." Blog post, 16 April 2014.
http://maegdi.wordpress.com/2014/04/16/the-age-of-unreason/
13. Adib, Mounir: "Atheists call for reduced religious footprint in constitution." Egypt Independent, 19 September 2013.
http://www.egyptindependent.com/news/atheists-call-reduced-religious-footprint-constitution
14. "Constitution of the Arab Republic of Egypt, 2014." Unofficial English translation. http://www.sis.gov.eg/Newvr/Dustor-en001.pdf

15. Allam, Rana: "A constitution not worth its ink." Daily News Egypt, 19 February 2014. http://www.dailynewsegypt.com/2014/02/19/constitution-worth-ink/
16. "Egypt mosques: Weekly sermon themes set by government." BBC, 31 January 2014. http://www.bbc.co.uk/news/world-middle-east-25983912
17. Abdelhadi, Magdy: "The age of unreason." Blog post, 16 April 2014. http://maegdi.wordpress.com/2014/04/16/the-age-of-unreason/
18. Al-Ahram (in Arabic), 18 June 2014. http://gate.ahram.org.eg/UI/Front/Inner.aspx?NewsContentID=506013
19. https://www.youtube.com/watch?v=rVPdVS-eImE 20 December 2013.
20. "Police vow to arrest Alexandria-based atheists." Mada Masr, 26 March 2014. http://madamasr.com/content/police-vow-arrest-alexandria-based-atheists
21. Author's interview, April 2014.
22. http://www.masress.com/en/video/3063055 and https://www.youtube.com/watch?v=OOF375-NZhc, 10 November 2013
23. https://www.youtube.com/watch?v=oESeyFgtpbE&list=PLx2EFu656F-ErXUFQaZ6ywgMFFm2zB__r, 15 April 2014.
24. Elwatannews, 13 May 2014, https://www.elwatannews.com/news/details/480971 and Sout al-Umma, 13 May 2014, http://www.soutalomma.com/articles/72748 (both reports in Arabic).
25. Kheir, Mohammed: "Egyptian TV: Darwin, Nietzsche, and a Certain God." Al-Akhbar, 1 August 2012. http://english.al-akhbar.com/content/egyptian-tv-darwin-nietzsche-and-certain-god. See also: Kazim, Butheina: "In the company of Moez Masoud." Al-Jazeera, 17 August 2012. http://www.aljazeera.com/indepth/opinion/2012/08/201281694821594437.html
26. Montasser, Farah: "Al-Molhid (The Atheist) Egyptian film praises Islam, says film crew." Ahram Online, 25 November 2012. http://english.ahram.org.eg/NewsContent/5/32/59125/Arts--Culture/Film/AlMolhid-The-Atheist-Egyptian-film-praises-Islam,-.aspx
27. "Controversial Egyptian film 'The Atheist' gets go ahead by censors." Al-Arabiya 14 March 2012. http://english.alarabiya.net/articles/2012/03/14/200689.html
28. Al-Arabiya in Arabic, 3 February 2014. http://www.alarabiya.net/ar/culture-and-art/2014/02/03/%D8%AF%D9%88%D8%B1-%D8%B9%D8%B1%D8%B6-%D9%85%D8%B5%D8%B1%D9%8A%D8%A9-%D8%AA%D8%B1%D9%81%D8%B6-%D8%A7%D8%B3%D8%AA%D9%82%D8%A8%D8%A7%D9%84-

%D8%A7%D9%84%D9%85%D9%84%D8%AD%D8%AF-.html
29. "Controversial Egyptian film 'The Atheist' gets go ahead by censors." Al-Arabiya 14 March 2012.
http://english.alarabiya.net/articles/2012/03/14/200689.html
30. Shams El-Din, Mai: "Rights groups condemn detention of atheist on blasphemy charges." Egypt Independent, 24 September 2012.
http://www.egyptindependent.com/news/rights-groups-condemn-detention-atheist-blasphemy-charges
31. Adib, Mounir: "While atheism in Egypt rises, backlash ensues." Egypt Independent, 30 September 2013.
http://www.egyptindependent.com/news/while-atheism-egypt-rises-backlash-ensues
32. Dawakhly, Sherif al-: "New book at Cairo's book fair tackles atheism." Egypt Independent, 25 January 2014.
http://www.egyptindependent.com/news/new-book-cairo-s-book-fair-tackles-atheism
33. Allam, Rana: "A generation of atheists." Daily News Egypt, 7 January 2013. http://www.dailynewsegypt.com/2013/01/07/a-generation-of-atheists/
34. Abdelfattah, Mohamed: "Leaving Islam in the age of Islamism." Daily News Egypt, 24 January 2013.
http://www.dailynewsegypt.com/2013/01/24/leaving-islam-in-the-age-of-islamism/
35. Diab, Khaled: "Confessions of an Egyptian infidel." Daily News Egypt, 15 August 2013.
http://www.dailynewsegypt.com/2013/08/15/confessions-of-an-egyptian-infidel/
36. Author's email correspondence, March 2014.

10: Politics of disbelief

IN THE Arab countries, abandoning religion is a decision that usually comes at a cost, and if the religion happens to be Islam it is a decision that also comes with political baggage. Besides the social and legal consequences of apostasy, ex-Muslims risk being paraded as trophies by Islamophobes or condemned as stooges in battles that were not of their choosing. Thus when a young Palestinian is arrested for posting his atheistic thoughts on the internet police automatically assume he is in the pay of Zionists – and check his bank account in search of evidence. Similarly, an atheist who appears on Egyptian television is asked whether he is "in touch with anyone abroad", prompting him to deny that he is a spy.

Viewing ex-Muslims as the agents of some foreign power removes any need to take their philosophical arguments seriously but the suspicions of a conspiracy against Islam and Muslims, though often exaggerated, are not entirely fanciful. There are plenty of unsavoury organisations in western countries that seek to stir up prejudice against Muslims for racial or other motives, and who regard ex-Muslims as useful fodder for their cause.

In Europe, extremists of the political right focus especially on Islam in their campaigns against immigration, claiming that Europe is about to be taken over by Muslims. The "Stop Islamisation of Europe" movement, which originated in Denmark, calls for "a permanent stop to immigration from Muslim countries and a temporary stop from other countries", along with "repatriation of disaffected Muslim and other immigrants and all immigrant criminals".[1] The former leader of the British National Party, Nick Griffin, who claims that Britain and Ireland are being turned into "a Third World Islamic slum"[2] has spoken nostalgically of "the traditional, upright, decent and honest Christianity that defended Europe from Islamic conquest, the Christianity of the Crusades and the Christianity of our forefathers".[3] In the US, the far right also engages in fear-mongering about "Islamisation" but its focus is less on immigration and more on terrorism. Robert Spencer's Jihad Watch website, for example, has long promoted the idea that the essence of Islam is terrorism:

> There is no distinction in the American Muslim community between peaceful Muslims and jihadists. While Americans prefer to imagine that the vast majority of American Muslims are civic-minded patriots who accept wholeheartedly the parameters of American pluralism, this proposition has actually never been proven.[4]

At the opposite end of the political spectrum is a leftist strand that supports Islamist movements under the guise of combating imperialism. The result is an Orientalist perspective where Islamists and religious conservatives are regarded as culturally authentic while those with a more progressive outlook are dismissed as westernised and agents of imperialism. Abuses based on religion that would never be accepted by leftists if applied in western countries are thus considered acceptable in an Arab context. Mariam Namazie of the Council of Ex-Muslims of Britain describes this as the politics of betrayal: "It's a betrayal of the dissenters and victims of Islamism but also of the very principles that the left has historically defended" – social justice, egalitarianism, secularism, universalism, etc.[5]

Namazie sees little difference between Islamists in the Middle East and the far right in the west, even though the latter "attack mosques and people just because of their background and issue collective blame on entire populations". Both come from the same sort of background, she said:

> Obviously there are variations, given the differences in power, but their politics and their philosophy and their politics of hate are quite similar to each other. So from our perspective we fight on both fronts, particularly in the west.
> You can't just fight one, particularly as the far right are scapegoating Muslims and immigrants. They are using the issue of sharia, the issue

of apostasy laws – in a sense they are feigning support of apostates and women under Islam, whereas in fact they couldn't care less about women and people in the Middle East and North Africa. And they are very happy to deport everyone and deny those very people that they show concern for the right to asylum and protection.[6]

Like its British counterpart, Ex-Muslims of North America sees itself as standing between the two extremes: political Islam and its apologists on one side and the far right on the other – and resisting them both. A statement on its website headed "No Bigotry and No Apologism" explains:

> There are those who propagate racist, bigoted and xenophobic ideas against Muslims, against anyone who comes from a Muslim background, and even against people who are not Muslim at all (e.g. Sikhs). These types of people (the bigots) tend to treat all Muslims (or all those perceived to be Muslim) as a monolith, a horde without internal differences or dissent.
>
> On the other hand, there are those who react to the bigoted, xenophobic types by trying to justify the violent parts of Islam and the harsh actions of some Muslims. This second type (the apologists) often shields Islam and Muslims from any and all critique and scrutiny, even the kinds of critique and scrutiny they themselves apply to other ideologies like Christianity, Capitalism, Communism, and others.
>
> As people who were raised Muslim, or converted to Islam of our own choice, and then left Islam because we could not believe in it any more, we stand between this polarity, and we refuse to cater to either the bigots or the apologists. We do not wish to promote hatred of all Muslims. We ourselves were Muslim. Many of our families and friends are Muslim. We understand that Muslims come in all varieties and we do not and will not partake in erasing the diversity within the world's Muslims.
>
> Most of us have researched and continue to research many of the world's religions, and we are, as a group, very well-versed in the horrors committed by other religions throughout history. We reserve the right to focus on Islam because it is the religion with which we have the most experience, it is the religion in which many of us were raised, and the religion some of us who are former converts tried to believe in with all our hearts.
>
> While we denounce the bigotry of those who promote their racist and xenophobic ideas under the guise of criticising Muslims, we also denounce the cultural and moral relativism of those who propagate the idea that all people of Muslim backgrounds are the same and want

to follow Islam, and that Islam is somehow less capable of being scrutinised than other belief systems.[7]

ONE OF the challenges for ex-Muslims is how to avoid providing more fuel for prejudice in the west. The contentious term "Islamophobia" has existed for more than a century. Its first recorded use was in 1910 in French – as *islamophobie* – referring to the attitude of French colonial administrators. Its first recorded use in English appears to have been in 1985 by Edward Said who linked it to antisemitism, saying that "hostility to Islam in the modern Christian west has historically gone hand in hand" with antisemitism and "has stemmed from the same source and been nourished at the same stream".[8] The term gained wider currency following a report by the Runnymede Trust in 1997, *Islamophobia: A Challenge for Us All,* which looked at attitudes towards Muslims living in Britain.[9] A few years later "Islamophobia" also began to be used by various international bodies, including the United Nations. It is important to mention this historical background because of false (but often-repeated) claims in the US that the term was coined by Islamists with the specific purpose of portraying themselves as victims. For instance, one misinformed article on a right-wing American website says:

> The neologism "Islamophobia" did not simply emerge *ex nihilo*. It was invented, deliberately, by a Muslim Brotherhood front organisation, the International Institute for Islamic Thought, which is based in Northern Virginia.[10]

The idea that Islamophobia doesn't really exist and that the term was concocted to suppress free-ranging criticism of Islam persists, however. This is exacerbated by the lack of a generally accepted definition of Islamophobia, and there are many without a political axe to grind who regard the term as problematic. The late Professor Fred Halliday suggested that "Anti-Muslimism" would be more accurate, since it usually refers to hostility directed against Muslims rather than Islam and its tenets. Robin Richardson, who edited the 1997 Runnymede report, later acknowledged the criticisms and offered a rather complex re-definition of Islamophobia as ...

> A shorthand term referring to a multifaceted mix of discourse, behaviour and structures which express and perpetuate feelings of anxiety, fear, hostility and rejection towards Muslims, particularly but

not only in countries where people of Muslim heritage live as minorities.[11]

At a less abstract level it is worth noting that the Runnymede report concerned the situation of Muslims in Britain and had a specific brief "to counter Islamophobic assumptions that Islam is a single monolithic system, without internal development, diversity and dialogue" and "to draw attention to the principal dangers which Islamophobia creates or exacerbates for Muslim communities, and therefore for the well-being of society as a whole".

Regardless of debates about the word "Islamophobia", prejudice of the kind identified in the Runnymede report does exist and is usually not difficult to recognise. Typically, it involves sweeping and misleading generalisations about Islam and/or Muslims (along with others who are presumed to be Muslim) in order to portray them in a negative light. There is widespread agreement, though, that the term "Islamophobia" cannot sensibly be applied to genuine critiques of Islam as a religion. Tackling Islamophobia should not become a mandate for stifling free and fair comment, as the British-based Forum Against Islamophobia and Racism (FAIR) has made clear:

> It is not Islamophobic to disagree or disapprove of Muslim beliefs, practices or actions. Indeed, within the Muslim community, both in Britain and globally, it is recognised that disagreements, discussions and debates are an important part of contemporary Islam and Muslim societies, and absolute requisites to maintain the relevance of Islam. Legitimate disagreement and criticism by non-Muslims, is therefore, not only expected but appreciated. However, we would urge that this is done sensibly and sensitively.[12]

Unfortunately, this is sometimes also interpreted as a licence for crude forms of abuse. In a speech about Islam, Nick Griffin of the far-right British National Party said: "This wicked, vicious faith has expanded from a handful of cranky lunatics about 1,300 years ago till it's now sweeping country after country before it, all over the world. And if you read that book [the Qur'an], you'll find that that's what they want."[13] Griffin was later tried on several charges of using words or behaviour intended or likely to stir up racial hatred but in court he denied the words were racist. He told the court: "There's a huge difference between criticising a religion and saying this is an attack on the people who follow it. When I criticise Islam, I criticise that religion and the culture it sets up, certainly not Muslims as a group ..." Following a retrial he was eventually cleared of all charges.[14]

There are certainly differences between race and religion. Race, for example, is inherited and unchangeable whereas religion, at least in theory, is not. But it is also necessary to recognise that a religion can be far more than a belief system; it is often also an identity and a cultural (and sometimes political) affiliation. There is an old joke about the sectarian troubles in Northern Ireland where a man is dragged out of a car by an assailant who demands to know if he is Catholic or Protestant. The man, hoping to avoid trouble, replies that he is a Jewish atheist. His assailant, not satisfied with this, then asks if he is a Protestant Jewish atheist or a Catholic Jewish atheist. This is one of the reasons why the European Commission Against Racism and Intolerance defines racism as "the belief that a ground such as race, colour, language, *religion*, nationality or national or ethnic origin justifies contempt for a person or a group of persons, or the notion of superiority of a person or a group of persons".

References to cultural "markers" such as religion, language or dress often become a substitute for more overt forms of racism. "Racism is almost never a direct discussion of something on explicitly racial grounds," Hiba Krisht, an Arab atheist, pointed out during a discussion with other members of Ex-Muslims of North America (EXMNA):

> Most racist attitudes are at the surface level not towards explicit races. Racist attitudes about single moms, rap music, food stamps, hoodies, football mascots abound. None of those are races *per se*. Racist discussions of them are reducible to generalised beliefs regarding the customs and communities of those who engage/partake in them.
>
> Anti-Muslim bigotry is very, very much about race. Even discussion of white converts involves concepts of theft and seduction by brown people taking over white values. We do no one favours by hiding behind the "Islam is not a race" card ...[15]

In the west, she added, ex-Muslims face the same kind of prejudice as Muslims. "The racism that allows others to assume that we adopt Muslim sentiments or beliefs because of our ethnicities, and despite our actions and words, is the same racism that Muslims suffer from."

Members of EXMNA were discussing what terminology to use in order to distinguish between "undue discrimination against

Muslims and reasoned critique of Islam". The reason for this, Krisht explained, was that "the term 'Islamophobia' has become a catch-all phrase used to silence legitimate critique of an ideology in addition to condemning bigotry towards Muslims, and the two concepts need to be differentiated, perhaps deserving their own neologisms".

The discussion failed to come up with a solution but for ex-Muslims this is clearly a difficult problem.

"I feel that criticism of any ideology should be OK but discrimination against people because of their beliefs is where I draw the line," Egyptian Reem Abdel-Razek said. "It's OK to criticise an idea but to discriminate against someone because he is a believer of that religion is what constitutes Islamophobia." She added that she would not poke fun at people because of their religious style of dress. "I have friends that do things that are just sort of mocking and I feel that being outrageous just for the sake of it really accomplishes nothing."

Not judging by appearances may be a good general principle – people have been questioned as terror suspects simply because they "looked" Arab or Muslim – but is it always wrong to do so? Within the general category of "Muslim appearance" certain styles of dress signal a certain way of thinking – and are meant to do so by those who adopt them. Kiran Opal, a co-founder of EXMNA, cited the example of a Muslim man in a thobe and a six-inch beard walking with two women in niqabs and six children behind him. When she sees a scene like that, Opal continued, "I *do* judge the people involved. I *do* think that they are living in a way that is oppressive to women, that is supremacist, that is abusive to LGBTQ people, to religious minorities ... Does that mean I am Islamophobic?"[16]

As ex-Muslims struggle to distance themselves from anti-Muslim bigotry, interventions by a number of prominent western atheists have been distinctly unhelpful. Richard Dawkins, for example, posted a controversial tweet saying:

> All the world's Muslims have fewer Nobel Prizes than Trinity College, Cambridge. They did great things in the Middle Ages, though.[17]

Although this was factually accurate, it is difficult to see a reason for posting it other than as a general disparagement of Muslims. The lack of scientific achievement by Muslims in modern times is a valid (and important) topic for discussion, and the explanations are complex,[18] but raising it on Twitter, where posts are limited to 140 characters, is scarcely an invitation to nuanced debate. Instead, it merely feeds anti-Muslim tropes. Dawkins also re-tweeted an article perpetuating the myth that the term "Islamophobia" was invented by the Muslim Brotherhood, though he deleted it shortly afterwards – apparently when he realised his mistake.[19] On his own website, where space is presumably not a limitation, Dawkins has made a habit of taking snide swipes at Islam without elaboration, such as "the menacing rise of Islam",[20] and suggesting that in Europe the word "multiculturalism" is "code for Islam".[21] He has also said: "It is well arguable that Islam is the greatest man-made force for evil in the world today",[22] and: "If you see a Muslim beating his wife, there would be little point in calling a policeman because so many of the British police are terrified of being accused of racism or 'Islamophobia'."[23]

Dawkins, along with Sam Harris and the late Christopher Hitchens, is regarded as one of the "New Atheists" who are noted for their populist and strident – sometimes bellicose – approach. In a critical article for *Salon* magazine, Nathan Lean wrote:

> Though Dawkins, Harris and company have been around for years, their presence on the public scene used to be more muted. An atheist then was something you simply were. It wasn't a full-time career. But in 2001 a man named Mohammed Atta and his Middle Eastern comrades decided to fly jetliners into the Twin Towers and everything changed ...
>
> Until 9/11, Islam didn't figure in the New Atheists' attacks in a prominent way. As a phenomenon with its roots in Europe, atheism has traditionally been the arch-enemy of Christianity, though Jews and Judaism have also slipped into the mix. But emboldened by their newfound fervour in the wake of the terrorist attacks, the New Atheists joined a growing chorus of Muslim-haters, mixing their abhorrence of religion in general with a specific distaste for Islam ...
>
> Conversations about the practical impossibility of God's existence and the science-based irrationality of an afterlife slid seamlessly into xenophobia over Muslim immigration or the practice of veiling. The New Atheists became the new Islamophobes, their invectives against Muslims resembling the rowdy, uneducated ramblings of backwoods racists rather than appraisals based on intellect, rationality and reason.[24]

The problem with this approach, as the Australian writer/philosopher Russell Blackford has noted, is not only that it puts critics of Islam at risk of being tarred with the same brush as the extreme right but also that it helps to make the extreme right seem more respectable. One prominent American atheist, Sam Harris, has even gone so far as to say that "the people who speak most sensibly about the threat that Islam poses to Europe are actually fascists".[25]

"The extreme right benefits from the availability of politically respectable criticisms of Islamic thought and associated cultural practices," Blackford writes. This includes adopting what have traditionally been viewed as liberal causes, such as opposition to forced marriages, "honour" killings, female genital mutilation, and the enforcement of dress codes for women.

"There are reasons why extreme-right organisations have borrowed arguments based on feminism and secularism," Blackford continues. "These arguments are useful precisely because they have an intellectual and emotional appeal independent of their convenience to extreme-right opportunists. Regardless of who uses these arguments, they plausibly apply to certain elements of Islam, or at least to attitudes and practices associated with it."

At a practical level, Blackford suggests, "opponents of Islam who do not wish to be seen as the extreme-right's sympathisers or dupes would be well-advised to take care in the impression that they convey. Where practical, they should explain their positions with as much nuance as possible, distance themselves from extreme-right figures making similar arguments, and avoid sharing platforms with them." But he adds: "The words 'where practical' are important, because what is practical in, say, a philosophical essay may not be practical in a satirical cartoon, or even in a polemical book aimed at a popular audience. We mustn't exclude the talents of people whose training or temperament does not suit hedged, half-apologetic communication. Nor must we always communicate in ways that most people find boring and bland. Beyond a certain point, there is too much disadvantage in walking on eggshells."[26]

Regardless of the reaction, some ex-Muslims argue that the New Atheists are saying things that need to be said – things that ex-Muslims themselves may not be in a position to say.

"You can make a lot of arguments that the approach they are taking is not the most intellectual, maybe not the most valid in a lot of ways, but from the perspective that we are coming from it doesn't seem bigoted and it doesn't seem racist in any way," Sarah

Haider of EXMNA said. Among ex-Muslims, the criticisms tend to come from those living in the west who "have adopted liberal sensibilities of being hypersensitive to bigotry, or anything that can be perceived to be bigotry," she added. "Those who are not living in the western world or those that are recent immigrants are more likely to be happy with the kinds of things Dawkins and Harris are saying." Haider continued:

> Plenty of ex-Muslims have no problem with the so-called New Atheists, and believe precisely that kind of in-your-face approach is what is necessary. This is a point of contention within the community – and there are defenders on both sides. I would say very few believe that Sam Harris and Richard Dawkins are actually bigoted – the disagreement is often about the effectiveness of their tactics.
>
> The argument goes: when someone is so steeped into the religion, only a shocking statement will get them to re-evaluate their beliefs. When I was a Muslim, I was constantly told that the Islam is the most progressive religion when it comes to women's rights – something I actually believed and never bothered to verify myself (why would my imam lie to me?). It was an encounter with a loud, abrasive atheist that actually got me to look into my beliefs and, as it turns out, he knew my religious texts better than I did. Did he offend me? Yes! Did he hurt my "religious feelings"? Yes. But I wouldn't have left if it wasn't for his aggression.[27]

Freedom of expression necessarily includes, in the words of the European Court of Human Rights, a right to "offend, shock and disturb". This does not mean people should feel free to say shocking and offensive things at the slightest opportunity, but there are occasions when they are entitled to do so. Without a right to offend, legitimate debate can be suppressed simply because some claim to have been offended by it – and there have been plenty of examples in previous chapters of this book.

Alongside that, though, is a need for people with differing ideas and beliefs to co-exist in an atmosphere of pluralism, tolerance, non-discrimination and respect for each other's rights. Although these conflicting demands may never be fully reconciled, the aim should be to strike as fair a balance as possible between them.

In 2008, a study by the Venice Commission (under the auspices of the Council of Europe) put forward some suggestions as to where that balance should lie.[28] "It must be possible," the commission said, "to criticise religious ideas, even if such criticism may be perceived by some as hurting their religious feelings." It added that "an insult to a principle or a dogma, or to a representative of a religion, does not necessarily amount to an insult to an individual who believes in that religion". Furthermore, insults to religious feelings should not be criminalised unless they contained incitement to hatred "as an essential component".

The commission acknowledged that the dividing line between insulting speech and incitement to hatred is "often difficult to identify". Relevant factors include the intention of the accused speaker or author, the effects of his or her action, the context in which the statement is made, the intended audience and whether the statement was made by someone acting in an official capacity.

The report also cautioned against over-reliance on the law as a means for combating hate speech, since it might raise expectations which could not be met and provide offenders with a propaganda victory by turning them into martyrs:

> As is the case with other problems of society, it is not exclusively or even primarily for the courts to find the right balance between freedom of religion and freedom of expression, but rather for society at large, through rational discussions between all parts of society, including believers and non-believers.

On the question of race and religion, the commission accepted – up to a point – that there is a difference between racist insults and insults directed against followers of a religion. While noting that "this difference has prompted some to conclude that a wider scope of criticism is acceptable in respect of a religion than in respect of a race", the commission said it should not become an excuse to unduly stretch the boundaries between "genuine 'philosophical' discussion about religious ideas and gratuitous religious insults".

The word "gratuitous" appears several times in the commission's report, and it can be quite a useful test for unacceptable speech. Another test is to ask whether the ideas being expressed "contribute to any form of public debate capable of furthering progress in human affairs".[29] Not all ideas deserve to be circulated, the commission said:

> Since the exercise of freedom of expression carries duties and responsibilities, it is legitimate to expect from every member of a democratic society to avoid as far as possible expressions that express scorn or are gratuitously offensive to others and infringe their rights.
>
> Sensible self-censorship could help to strike a balance between freedom of expression and ethical behaviour. Refraining from uttering

certain statements can be perfectly acceptable when it is done in order not to hurt gratuitously the feelings of other persons, whereas it is obviously unacceptable when it is done out of fear of violent reactions.

Freedom of expression must not "indiscriminately retreat" when facing violent reactions, the commission said. "The threshold of sensitivity of certain individuals may be too low in certain specific circumstances, ... and this should not become of itself a reason to prevent any form of discussion."

Arab non-believers include both activists and quietists. Unlike the New Atheists, some go out of their way to avoid causing offence. Badra, from Lebanon, said:

> When I feel that I cannot exercise my rights fully, I may choose not to confront, because the price would be high and I do not like to be dragged into useless or unworthy battles. I always choose to leave. Not necessarily immediately, but at a certain point. By making use of this option, I think that I managed to have the life that I wanted, without hurting, or hurting as little as possible.

How far non-believers can go in asserting themselves depends on their personal circumstances, and living as an atheist in Saudi Arabia requires more compromises than in most places, as Omar Hadi explained:

> The extremists will be offended by anything, but I don't want to attack the community. I don't fast, but I don't eat during Ramadan in front of my mother because that will offend her and I love my mother. She suspects, but she never asks me and I never go out of my way to show her anything. In the same way that I respect my mother and don't want to offend her, I don't want to offend society.
>
> Obviously there are some religious figures that are very popular ... I think they are hypocrites and in it for the money and power, but at the same time I understand that they are highly respected by the majority of the population and I don't want to offend anybody, so you just mind your own business and move on.
>
> I also understand that this goes against the concept of freedom of speech and the right to offend. I understand that, but that's the reality we live in.

WHERE to draw the line in criticism of Islam and its practices is obviously an important question for ex-Muslims but for those who live in the Middle East there is an even more basic question: how to win acceptance for their right to disbelieve. This is not so much a religious issue as a political and cultural one; it shifts the focus of the struggle towards challenging governments and social prejudices rather than theology. There are two distinct but related needs: one is freedom of belief and the other is a secular state – both of which would benefit Muslims, non-Muslims and ex-Muslims alike.

Challenging other people's religious views does not necessarily promote freedom of belief. Certainly, non-believers need to make their presence felt – otherwise their rights could simply be ignored – but the New Atheist approach is more about trying to discredit religion than encouraging tolerance, and in an Arab context this is usually counterproductive.

Tolerance for minorities (of all kinds) is a principle that governments and societies in the region are still reluctant to accept and diversity is seen as a sign of weakness rather than potential strength. The development of electoral politics in some of the Arab countries has also brought a simplistic kind of majoritarianism which does not yet recognise the importance of protecting minority rights.

Working to change this will help non-believers to achieve their freedom, but they cannot do it on their own. They will need alliances with others who seek political and social change, and they may have to convince potential but sceptical allies that freedom of belief is in the interests of all – believers included.

One of the obstacles to public acceptance is the idea that atheism leads to social breakdown and widespread immorality. This needs to be confronted, and there is plenty of evidence with which to do it. Examples from elsewhere in the world show that a non-religious society can be a flourishing and healthy society. Nor does freedom of religion necessarily mean a decline in religious belief; the example of the United States shows it is capable, under certain conditions, of flourishing without the kind of relentless support and enforcement provided by Arab governments – and in the long run religion may actually suffer if it is propped up by governments.

In order to free themselves from religion, non-believers need a secular state. But advances in secularism do not necessarily bring advances in religious freedom. The authoritarian kind of secularism is no better than authoritarian kinds of religion, so secularism has to be developed within a framework of tolerance.

Secularism, as a concept, is widely misunderstood in the Arab countries and is often wrongly equated with atheism. As long as that idea persists there is little prospect of secularising the state. To make any progress in that direction, people will have to be convinced that secularism is not a backdoor route to atheism but a route to freedom – by preventing anyone from imposing their beliefs or non-beliefs on anyone else. There may even be occasions when this requires non-believers to side with believers rather than secularists of the full-blooded anti-religion variety. Tempting as it might be for non-believers to welcome the Swiss ban on minarets, for example, it is important to consider how that impinges on believers' freedom. Similarly, supporting French restrictions on the wearing of hijab while opposing compulsory dress codes for Saudi women does not, *prima facie,* look like a consistent position in terms of personal freedom.

The privileged position of religion in the Arab countries today is very similar to what it once was in Europe – as are the arguments mustered to defend it. Plato discussing punishment of those who "speak or act insolently" towards the gods of ancient Greece more than two thousand years ago sounds remarkably like some twenty-first century Saudi cleric.

Europe, though, has gradually become more secular and non-belief is now commonplace. The journey from Thomas More's acknowledgement in the sixteen century that punishing non-believers is pointless (since "no one can choose to believe by a mere act of will") to acceptance of a *right* to disbelieve did not occur in isolation. The concept of religious liberty developed in parallel with political ideas about limited government, sovereignty of the people and the autonomy of individuals as well as a changing philosophical climate:

> Official attacks on religious disbelief [in Europe] could not be sustained within the broader philosophical atmosphere created by the Enlightenment. The empiricism, intellectual scepticism, and scientific upheaval engendered by the Enlightenment, along with its larger social and economic context, made it increasingly difficult to sustain the strong legal protection of religious authority.[30]

Europe's step-by-step recognition that suppressing disbelief is not a sustainable position raises, at the very least, a possibility that Arab countries will eventually follow suit. The opening-up of public discourse during the last few years, the flow of ideas and the challenging of the status quo has some parallels with the European Enlightenment and may well have similar effects.

Politically, one of the major obstacles is that Arab regimes still view religion as a useful tool in the exercise of power. Governments are better placed to impose their will if they can claim to be acting according the wishes of the Almighty, and Europe was ruled for centuries by kings who claimed a "divine right" to their thrones. This continues today in parts of the Middle East and even the more secular Arab governments like to display religious credentials. It may not last much longer, however. Government claims of religious legitimacy have traditionally been a substitute for electoral legitimacy but that is now less acceptable to the public and might in future become a liability: Arabs have begun to recognise that pious government does not equate with competent government.

It is a mixed picture, of course. Saudi Arabia – the most extreme case – stands resolute against religious liberty and, short of a revolution, it is difficult to see that changing any time soon. But elsewhere cracks are showing. Arab governments do worry about their image internationally (some more than others) and feel obliged to pay some lip service to people's rights even if they are reluctant to uphold them in practice. Tunisia's post-revolution constitution says "the state shall protect religion, guarantee freedom of belief and conscience and religious practices". Egypt's 2014 constitution says "freedom of belief is absolute" and Iraq's post-Saddam constitution says "each individual shall have the freedom of thought, conscience, and belief". These are principles that they have formally accepted, if only for the purposes of window-dressing. The need now is to start turning them into reality.

NOTES

1. Enemies Not Allies: the Far Right. One Law For All, 2011. http://www.onelawforall.org.uk/wp-content/uploads/Enemies-not-Allies-web-version1.pdf
2. "A statement regarding Nick Griffin's use of the term 'Fenian' from his MEP Constituency Office." 18 October 2012. http://www.nickgriffinmep.eu/content/statement-regarding-nick-griffins-use-term-fenian-his-mep-constituency-office
3. "Easter Message from BNP Chairman hits mark!" Stormfront, July 2006. http://www.stormfront.org/forum/t696276/
4. Spencer, Robert: "2 Men, in New York and Florida, Charged in Qaeda

Conspiracy." Jihad Watch, 30 May 2005.
http://www.jihadwatch.org/2005/05/2-men-in-new-york-and-florida-charged-in-qaeda-conspiracy.html
5. Siding With the Oppressor: The Pro-Islamist Left. One Law For All, 2013. http://www.onelawforall.org.uk/wp-content/uploads/SidingWithOpressor_Web.pdf
6. Author's interview, May 2014.
7. "No Bigotry and No Apologism." http://www.exmna.org/about-us/
8. For more information about the history of the term "Islamophobia", see: Richardson, Robin: "Islamophobia or anti-Muslim racism – or what? – concepts and terms revisited." 2012 http://www.insted.co.uk/anti-muslim-racism.pdf
9. Islamophobia: a challenge for us all. Runnymede Trust, 1997. http://www.runnymedetrust.org/publications/17/32.html
10. Berlinski, Claire: "Moderate Muslim watch: How the term 'Islamophobia' got shoved down your throat." Ricochet, 24 November 2010. http://ricochet.com/archives/moderate-muslim-watch-how-the-term-islamophobia-got-shoved-down-your-throat/
11. Richardson, Robin: op cit
12. "Racism and Islamophobia." FAIR website, undated. http://www.fairuk.org/docs/Islamophobia%20&%20Racism.pdf
13. "BNP leader said Islam was 'wicked'." Daily Mail, 3 November 2006. http://www.dailymail.co.uk/news/article-414343/BNP-leader-said-Islam-wicked.html
14. Wainwright, Martin: "Islam is vicious, wicked faith, claims Griffin." The Guardian, 26 January 2006. http://www.theguardian.com/uk/2006/jan/26/otherparties.thefarright
15. "Islamophobia? Muslimophobia? Anti-Muslim Bigotry? A discussion between Ex-Muslims on appropriate neologisms." Hiba Krisht was using the name "Marwa" at the time of the blog post. http://aveilandadarkplace.com/2014/05/21/islamophobia-muslimophobia-anti-muslim-bigotry-a-discussion-between-ex-muslims-on-appropriate-neologisms/
16. "Islamophobia? Muslimophobia? Anti-Muslim Bigotry? A discussion between Ex-Muslims on appropriate neologisms." http://aveilandadarkplace.com/2014/05/21/islamophobia-muslimophobia-anti-muslim-bigotry-a-discussion-between-ex-muslims-on-appropriate-neologisms/
17. https://twitter.com/RichardDawkins/status/365473573768400896
18 . Whitaker, Brian: "The right answer or the wrong question?" The Guardian, 27 March 2004. http://www.theguardian.com/uk/2004/mar/27/religion.world
19. https://twitter.com/mjrobbins/status/327004128171679745

20. http://old.richarddawkins.net/articles/596422-jedi-ism-britain-s-fourth-largest-religion- is-still-going-strong/comments?page=1#comment_596425
21. http://old.richarddawkins.net/articles/4563-human-rights-ruling-against-classroom- crucifixes-angers-italy/comments?page=1#comment_411188
22. http://old.richarddawkins.net/videos/476560-pat-condell-no-mosque-at-ground- zero/comments?page=2
23. http://old.richarddawkins.net/articles/641974-islam-and-islamophobia-a-little- manifesto/comments?page=1#comment_845164
24. Lean, Nathan: "Dawkins, Harris, Hitchens: New Atheists flirt with Islamophobia." Salon 30 March 2013. http://www.salon.com/2013/03/30/dawkins_harris_hitchens_new_atheists_flirt_with_islamophobia/
25. Harris, Sam: "Head-in-the-Sand Liberals." Los Angeles Times, 18 September, 2006. http://www.samharris.org/site/full_text/the-end-of-liberalism/
26. Blackford, Russell: "Islam and 'Islamophobia' – a little manifesto." The Hellfire Club blog, 30 June, 2011. http://metamagician3000.blogspot.co.uk/2011/06/islam-and-islamophobia-little-manifesto.html
27. Author's interview and email exchange, July 2014.
28. European Commission for Democracy through Law (Venice Commission): "Report on the relationship between freedom of expression and freedom of religion" CDL-AD(2008)026. http://www.venice.coe.int/webforms/documents/default.aspx?pdffile=CDL-AD(2008)026-e
29. European Court of Human Rights, Gündüz v Turkey, 2003.
30. Gey, Steven: "Atheism and the Freedom of Religion." Chapter in The Cambridge Companion to Atheism. New York: Cambridge University Press, 2007.

Printed in Great Britain
by Amazon.co.uk, Ltd.,
Marston Gate.